TRUST

A TRUE STORY OF WOMEN & GANGS

TRUST

PIP DESMOND

RANDOM HOUSE
NEW ZEALAND

For Evelyn, and all the women of Aroha Trust

'The sound of a J4 [van] coming up the street
always brings to mind picarious [*sic*] journeys, babies, dogs,
joints, cops, but mainly women. Us —
And when I think of AROHA TRUST, I think of
love, unity, strength, battle, frustration, hopelessness,
decipt [*sic*], confusion, misery, joy,
laughter, hate, struggle.
All in extreme.'

— Jane, aged 17, from her diary

A RANDOM HOUSE BOOK published by Random House New Zealand
18 Poland Road, Glenfield, Auckland, New Zealand

For more information about our titles go to www.randomhouse.co.nz

A catalogue record for this book is available from the National Library of New Zealand

Random House New Zealand is part of the Random House Group
New York London Sydney Auckland Delhi Johannesburg

First published 2009

ISBN 978 1 86979 243 5

Text design: Laura Forlong
Cover design: Seven
Cover photograph: Members of Aroha Trust, United Women's Convention, Hamilton, 1979 (detail) by Marti Freidlander
Printed in China by Everbest Printing Co Ltd

CONTENTS

PROLOGUE

Labour Weekend, 1998

It's dark when we leave Mike Hancock's unveiling in Ōtaki, and by the time I see the woman in the short skirt and stilettos with her thumb out on the highway, I've driven past.

'She might be stranded,' Jane says, winding down the front passenger window and putting her head out to get a better look.

Nayda swivels round in the back seat. 'Either that or she's bloody stupid.'

'Well, we can't just leave her there,' says Gini.

'Okay, I'm going back.' I pull over and wait for a break in the traffic. But before I can reverse up the road, a battered black Holden swerves in front of the woman, a door opens, and she vanishes into the back seat. As the car roars past, I catch a glimpse of her sandwiched between two guys, beer bottles pressed to their lips.

'Follow them! It's the Mongrel Mob!' Nayda says. She'd know: her partner's the head of the Whanganui chapter.

I put my foot down, only slightly reassured to know I'm in the company of some of the best street fighters of their day. Just south of Paekākāriki, as I'm starting to lose them, the Holden veers left into a picnic area and stops. I glide in behind, not too close, lights on full to show we mean business. No one says a word.

Suddenly, the back door of the other car opens and the woman clambers out. We do the same, though I pull my teenage daughter Megan to the back for safety.

'Thanks, fellas,' the woman shouts over her shoulder as she totters unsteadily towards us.

We huddle round her.

'Are you okay?' Jane says.

'Sure! Great party! I always hitch-hike home.'

'Well, you shouldn't,' Gini says. 'Anything could happen to you. And next time we won't be there to save you.'

'Pfff!' says the woman. 'I can look after myself.' And she stumbles off into the night.

'Yeah right,' says Nayda. She turns to Megan. 'Don't you ever do that!'

Megan shakes her head and shivers. 'No way!'

Back on the road, the adrenalin's pumping. We didn't have to do anything, but we would have.

'Put this one in the book, Pip!' Everyone talks at once, remembering other shared adventures, not all with happy endings. Megan sits spellbound in the middle, lapping up stories about a mother she's never known. From time to time, Gini shouts, 'Hallelujah! Praise the Lord!' For once, I agree. It does feel like a sign, a fitting end to the first Aroha Trust reunion.

Woman power! Just like the old days.

ONE

JUDGEMENT DAY

Labour Weekend, 2007

'Sieg Heil! Sieg Heil!' taunts Nayda as she does a sensual, snaky dance around Jane's cramped kitchen. Head tipped back triumphantly, eyes half-shut, she weaves her small, sturdy body in and out of the other women, the pinky and thumb of both hands raised and quivering in the Mob salute. Part show, part menace, it'd go down a treat at the Whanganui pad where she's the pres' missus, but here, at the second Aroha Trust reunion, it simply triggers Gini's old Nomad loyalties.

The two sides of Gini battle it out. 'I'm going to smash her,' the gang girl Gini tells Annie. Then the God-fearing Gini steps in. 'I don't need to do that, do I?'

'No, you don't,' says Annie firmly.

Nayda circles Amelia, once her best friend. Her hip nudges Amelia's once, twice, three times as she breathes into her ear. 'Am I too close?'

Amelia's thinner than the last time I saw her and all day her fingers have fluttered shyly around her face like butterflies. But she doesn't live in Black Power Lane in Kaitaia for nothing. 'Why? Do you want to be?' she says, narrowing her eyes.

Nayda laughs and spins away, cranking the music up another notch as she shimmies past. It's midnight and the wine that was meant to last all weekend's nearly gone, but that's all right cos the beer's holding. The stereo's pumping hits from the 1970s that reinforce the time warp. Everyone's talking and laughing and crying, and the more pissed they get, the more the wounds of the past ooze.

Nayda bails me up. 'We all have our own pain,' she says while she's still making sense. 'But you're the storyteller. You hold all our pain, our mamae — and that's very hard for you.'

I'm grateful to her. It's been a tough day and tomorrow's not looking any easier. Being the soberest person in the room doesn't help. But I'm on the outer anyway — the women want to talk to each other, not the honky who's let the genie out of the bottle.

The energy's getting blacker by the minute. Raised voices. Rough laughter. Tales that make me want to weep. I put on a bright, false smile and feel my separateness like a brand on my forehead. I also feel responsible. Many of these women haven't had a drink forever. But if they decide to get off their faces and defend gang straitjackets we disregarded when we were young, there's no way my 48 kg are going to stop them.

Amelia and Tasi, Gini's younger sister, aren't into the booze, at least for tonight. Sick of the nonsense, they head for the sleep-out across the lawn. A bit later, I escape to the bedroom I'm sharing with Annie, just off the kitchen.

I lie in the dark, listening to 'Young Hearts Run Free' thumping through the floorboards, and try to make sense of what's happening. It was the t-shirts that clinched it, I reckon. They were in the kete that Jane handed each of us at the end of the day: blue; screenprinted with a slasher and shovel in the middle of a gourd, their long handles crossed; two hands clasped together at the top; the words 'Aroha Trust' curved around the bottom. A replica of the ones we wore so proudly when we lived and worked together back in the day. A one-way ticket to the past. Put them on and, hey presto, 30 years of hard-earned wisdom guaranteed to disappear in the blink of an eye.

There were other things in the kete too: chocolates; a painted kōhatu, a cool, smooth rock with the word 'aroha' scrawled across it; a copy of 'the book'. Ah, the book! That's the real catalyst for the circus on the other side of the door.

It's been nine years since I asked the women at the first Aroha Trust reunion if I could write a book about their lives and about the trust, the work co-op we set up for girls in the gang scene in Wellington in 1977. When they said yes, I travelled round the country visiting as many of them as I could track down, recording their lives and memories on tape. I promised I'd show them what I'd written, knowing that it's one thing to talk in private, another to see the words on the page. Now it's judgement day. Eight of the 11 who are in the book have come to Jane's bach at Kāwhia, an hour from Hamilton, to read the draft. Without their blessing, there's no going on.

A few muffled bumps erupt from the kitchen, but it sounds too cheerful to have reached the all-out brawl stage yet. Whatever's happening out there isn't really about patches, I know that. Most of the women have moved on; the rest don't usually flaunt their allegiances like they've being doing all night. It's as if a storm has whipped up the silt from the bottom of the ocean and everyone's frantically dog-paddling to keep their heads above water. Cornered by the past, staring down old demons, they're protecting themselves in the time-honoured way: lash out first, ask questions later.

The day had started quietly enough, gathered in Jane's lounge, groping our way towards our old ease. Some of the women had kept in touch; others hadn't seen one another for three decades. Catching up took most of the morning: welcomes, hugs, waiata, lots of tissues. Jane beamed old photos onto the wall. Charmaine sang a haunting song she'd composed: 'Blessed is the child with amazing grace/And blessed is the child with no one's shame on her face'. We left empty chairs for Bubbles, rumoured to be on her way, and Evelyn, no longer with us.

Finally, it was time to talk about the book. I read a couple of extracts to get us in the mood, then asked if they wanted another one.

'Just start at the beginning,' said Georgie as she folded her arms over the leprechaun baring his bum on her t-shirt, a memento of her recent trip to Ireland to watch her talented young son play rugby.

I squirmed. 'The beginning?'

Others joined in. 'Yeah, the beginning.'

Right. I'd imagined lots of ways the weekend might unfold but never that I'd be asked to read the book aloud to the women contained within its pages. In the safety of my own home, I'd described them and what they got up to in their youth, made judgements and confessions, moulded my memories into a shape that might bear little relation to their own. Now they expected me to reveal everything in front of the whole group, looking them straight in the eye.

They sat patiently waiting.

Trapped, I turned to the first page. We stopped to eat and when the smokers needed a fag. At each break, Charmaine chopped armfuls of flax from Jane's hillside garden and wove it expertly into lilies for her upcoming stall at the Ellerslie International Flower Show. Brought up at her nanny's side for a few crucial years, she's steeped in tikanga, a birthright everyone else in the room would die for.

There were a few bursts of laughter, the odd correction, but mostly my reading was received in silence. At the end of each chapter, I looked up, willing someone to say something. Anything. Each time, after a long pause, I asked, 'Shall I keep going?' It was Nayda's solemn nod that my eyes always seemed to alight on, reminding me of her mother, the first woman I ever saw wearing a moko.

Five hours, 12 chapters in, we adjourned, agreeing to continue the next morning. That's when Jane handed out the t-shirts.

In spite of the carry-on through the thin walls, I must have dozed off for a couple of hours because the next thing I know, the door opens and two figures appear.

'You've got a bedmate,' Annie says, pushing Gini towards me. I scramble out of the way as Gini's ample frame hits the mattress.

'Night, Pip,' she says cheerfully and within seconds her snores are rolling off the walls.

'You better get up,' Annie says. 'There's still three very drunk people out there and I'm knackered.'

I pull on jeans and a warm jersey and enter the fray. The stereo's still belting out music but the kitchen's got that trashed, abandoned, morning-after look. I clear away empties, hide the dregs and coax cups of tea into the diehards. They're at the aimless, incoherent stage, though their stamina's astounding and it's hours before the last of them crash.

A stunned peace descends on the house. No blood has been shed, thank God. I make coffee and take it out onto the deck where Jane's tino rangatiratanga flag flaps gently in the breeze coming off the mudflats. A shag dive-bombs into the silvery water that stretches to distant hills shrouded in cloud. My mind is empty, strangely calm in the eye of the storm.

Before long, Amelia and Tasi appear. My relief at setting eyes on some survivors fades when they tell me they're off to check out Tasi's unoccupied whānau land. They wake Gini because they need her car and persuade her to go with them, even though she's still pissed as a chook. As they vanish over the hill, I feel like I'm waving goodbye to the book. I have no idea when or if they'll be back, and in what state. Annie and Jane are up and functioning, but everyone else is comatose. Bubbles hasn't turned up, Charmaine has to leave by the end of the day, and so far no one's told me what they think.

'Trust the process,' my brother counselled before I came away. But what if the process looks more like a train wreck, bodies scattered everywhere?

The day passes in slow motion. Gini sends a text every time she throws up on the winding road. She signs off with 'kia kaha' and 'praz da lord', her born-again fervour undiluted by the alcohol. Later she phones, vague about their plans. It sounds as if they're in the pub.

When Charmaine staggers out of bed at dusk, I nab her. She's got reservations about the book, she says. I thought as much: she's been prickly since she arrived. I don't argue. It's not for me to insist she expose her life to strangers. I ask her to stay another night so we can discuss her concerns as a group. Not that there is a group. The Three Musketeers are still off on their adventures, and Nayda and Georgie haven't surfaced.

Annie's put a leg of lamb and two chickens in the oven as if it's business as usual. Just as she's serving up, the runaways swing into the driveway. They're in remarkably good shape, buzzing as they show us photos of the land that Tasi wants to move her family onto. Since I recorded the women's stories eight years ago, their pride in being Māori has gone from a slow burn to a forest fire. Their talk is all of whānau, whakapapa, mana wāhine. Annie's the only other Pākehā here, but her ex and her kids are Māori and she's at home in that world. I feel off-balance, as if there's a secret code I don't have access to.

By 8.30pm, everyone's sitting in the lounge in their jarmies: washed-out, subdued, focused. Caffeine's the strongest substance on offer. Party? What party?

I say we can't go any further till we decide if there's even going to be a book. We agree to go round the room, uninterrupted, and say 'yes' or 'no'.

Charmaine mounts the case for the opposition. 'I've sorted a lot of stuff in my life, but underneath there's still a river of tears,' she says, as eloquent in English as she is in te reo. And later, 'I've always been told, "Never cast your pearls before the swine." Do I really want to see my story in Whitcoulls or Paper Plus?'

The other women look thoughtful.

Finally, Charmaine hands me a lifeline. She can see some point in the book if it gave hope to someone in despair. If everyone else wants to go ahead, she'll be in.

Annie's next. She says she'll go along with the group too. My spirits slump. Aroha Trust was her brainchild. I need her to stand up for the book. Someone's got to, or there won't be one.

Then it's Amelia's turn. Of all the women, she seems the most fragile and I wish she wasn't being put on the spot so early. But when she speaks, her voice is clear and strong. 'I want the book to be published,' she says. 'It's all true. And I want to use my own name.'

TWO

HEADING IN THE RIGHT DIRECTION

April 1977

I parked Mum's car in Brougham Street and approached the house apprehensively. A burly young woman with metal in her nose and a bird tattooed on her left cheek flung open the door in answer to my knock. An orange Black Power t-shirt strained across her breasts and stomach, exposing a maze of tats up and down her arms, and a floppy hat was jammed hard over her ears.

'Whaddya want?' she said, looking scornfully at my flowery op-shop dress and black tights, my hair tied in two loose pigtails.

'Is Annie here?'

Her pale eyes glittered like ice. 'Who are you?'

'I'm Pip. Annie's expect—'

The door shut in my face as I heard her yell down the hallway, 'Annie! Pippi Longstocking's here to see you.'

I'd never met Annie before, but her name kept coming up in Dunedin, where I was working in a youth centre and running a house for homeless kids. She'd managed a drop-in centre in the Octagon before my time. Now she ran an inner-city community house in Wellington with her boyfriend Mike and was training to be a nurse at the hospital. Back in my home town on holiday, I'd tracked her down, desperate to talk to someone who understood.

The door opened again. A skinny Pākehā girl about the same age as me, beckoned me inside. 'Hi, I'm Annie,' she said. 'I see you've already met Bubbles.' A smile twitched at the edge of her mouth. 'This is her daughter, Rana.' She reached down and patted the head of a toddler clinging to her leg.

Bubbles? There was nothing remotely frivolous about the woman who'd just scared me half to death on the doorstep. And a mother?

As Annie cooked lamb's fry and mashed potato for the dozen alkies and street people who inhabited the house, we sussed each other out. Our lives had been very different. She was the baby in a two-child family; I, the third in a tribe of six. She'd left South Otago High School in Balclutha with School Certificate, eager to take on the world. I'd been head prefect and dux of St Mary's College in Wellington and went straight to university, emerging with a BA in English. Her parents were freezing workers, committed union people whose left-wing ideals gave her an affinity with the underdog. My mother had spent her life raising kids and my father was a prominent Catholic pathologist who brought us up on the parable of the Good Samaritan and only voted Labour when Norm Kirk promised state aid to Catholic schools.

Over tea, Mike explained how he, his identical twin brother Peter and another guy, Denis O'Reilly, had helped the Wellington Black Power set up a work cooperative called Te Kaha Trust, that later changed its name to Te Waka e Manaaki. At first they'd had to hustle for private contracts, mainly labouring and concreting, but then the National government changed the rules for relief work, allowing them to be employed as a group on community projects for government agencies.

'Me and Bubbles want to set up a work co-op for the girls too,' Annie said. 'They sit round Cuba Mall all day, ripping off welfare cheques and rolling Jap sailors when they're broke. They haven't got a fuckin' clue where they're sleeping from one night to the next. And the boys treat them like shit. Nothing's going to change till they can earn their own money and make their own choices.' She reached for another piece of white bread from a stack in the middle of the table, and began mopping up her gravy. 'Come and help us!' she pleaded, hardly knowing me. 'If the boys can do it, we can.'

I laughed, touched by her instant faith in me and drawn by her energy and vision. But it was far too soon to consider coming back to Wellington. I'd only been gone six months.

That night, Annie and Mike took me to Walton House, a short-lived, optimistic experiment to house the Black Power and the Mongrel Mob under the same roof. I'd seen Denis O'Reilly on TV sticking up for the gangs and rattling the powers that be, his message all the more powerful because he'd been a Catholic seminarian, now turned community worker and gang member. But I'd never expected to sit in a room with him and a bunch of young men wearing tattered jackets with a clenched fist embroidered on their backs. The fist punched out of a bed of red flames and was flanked by two eagle's wings rearing up for flight or attack. The words BLACK POWER, WELLINGTON in white capitals encircled it. The patches screamed 'outsider' at me. But when it came time to leave, a line of big brown hands gripped my small white one in the gang's special handshake. As if I did that sort of thing every day. As if I belonged.

In fact, growing up, I'd had very little to do with Māori. My background was solidly middle-class and Pākehā, my roots predominantly Irish Catholic. I grew up singing hymns, classical music, Irish rebel songs and folk tunes strummed by Dad on his guitar. Every night he'd gather our family of eight together to say a decade of the rosary. On Sunday mornings, priests, often with thick brogues, came for breakfast after Mass.

I don't remember Māori families at church or among my parents' friends. At primary school, we learnt no Māori language, culture or history, although we could all sing 'Pōkarekare ana, I found a squashed banana . . .' and I loved sitting cross-legged on the floor inventing 'Māori' stick games using rolled-up copies of the Catholic *Tablet*.

High school was not much different. At university, I began to understand why. I became part of an informal group dubbed, tongue in cheek, the New Catholic Left. We stopped going to church and started taking the pill, read *Pedagogy of the Oppressed* and *The Second Sex*, argued whether women's lib should come before or after the revolution, and went on student trips to China. Our focus was on class rather than race, but we could see the links. We believed not only that we should change the world, but that it was possible.

University expanded my horizons in more ways than one. Pat — another member of the NCL — was a lanky, six-foot-two Pākehā boy who made me laugh and was my friend before he was my lover. He had warm, blue-grey eyes, a cheeky smile and thick dark curls that framed his face and merged with a bushy beard.

Pat was the first person in his extended family to go to university, a privilege and burden he felt keenly. I was 19, fresh out of home, intoxicated with the freedom of mixed flatting and student life. He was a year older, cocky, rugby-mad and used to fending for himself. He mocked my middle-class manners, introduced me to his dope-smoking friends and dived headfirst into my heart.

All year, we wheeled around the bays on his motorbike, heckled politicians in the union hall, played 'Layla' and 'Moondance' late at night, and talked and touched until the sun came up. Even Stage 3 Economic History became fun, slipping each other notes and whispering until the professor stopped mid-sentence, and suggested we do our courting outside his class.

When we passed our final exams, the world beckoned us irresistibly — and in different directions. We were too young to be tied down, too headstrong to compromise. In our circles, organising the masses in a car plant was considered the noblest path after graduation. But Pat didn't need to work in a factory to rub shoulders with the proletariat: every holidays since he was 15, he'd stripped sheep guts with his dad, brother, uncles and cousins at the Gear Meat Works in Petone. He planned to spend a year travelling around South America. He didn't ask me to join him, nor did I want to go. Like many of our generation, we put our faith in the risky words on the Rod McKuen poster, 'If you love something, set it free. If it comes back, it's yours. If it doesn't, it never was.'

I wanted to make a difference in my own way. Shake off my protected upbringing. Face my fears. And have a good time while I was doing it. I moved to Dunedin, my birthplace, where my brother had a spare room in his flat, to test my ivory-tower principles in a youth centre for wayward kids. It was exciting at first, but meeting Annie made me realise how lonely and unsupported I felt.

We kept in touch. Countless long-distance phone calls later, her persistence paid off. I packed my bags, put my red Honda 50 on the train and headed back to join her. I still wanted to change the world, just not by myself. As for the gang scene, she promised me I'd be fine, and I believed her. She seemed to be.

The Wellington I returned to was very different than the one I'd left, not because it had changed, but because I had. I'd been brought up in the northern suburbs with their spacious, bush-clad sections and big houses inhabited mainly by white people. Now I headed across the city to Annie and Mike's new flat in Newtown, a multicultural melting pot with a bad reputation, where the houses rubbed shoulders, people spilled onto the streets, and cluttered shops sold taro, green bananas and exotic spices whose smells I didn't recognise.

There were nine of us in the flat, including Bubbles and her daughter, Bubbles' young sidekick, Nayda, both their boyfriends, and another Pākehā guy who worked with the gangs.

Bubbles was the undisputed Black Power mama. She'd been running with the boys since she was 17, fighting and drinking with the best of them. She and a few other girls were allowed to wear the gang t-shirt, though never the patch, and were affectionately known as the Mick Patrol; she even had MP tattooed on her left wrist. By the time I met her, she was 21 and motherhood had slowed her down a bit. During the week, she kept house and looked after Rana, though weekends were still for partying. In a rare turnaround, her boyfriend wasn't in the gang and often got left behind.

Nayda's boyfriend was Bugs, a friendly young Black Power boy who later fathered her oldest child. Today, he camps out in all weathers on Wellington's city streets. When I walk past him, I search for clues in his matted dreadlocks, praying mantis limbs and naked body but the truth is, back then, I couldn't have predicted he'd become Blanket Man.

One weekend soon after I arrived, a southerly blew in. The other girls were all away. I hunkered down with the boys and played Five Hundred. The world narrowed to the chipped, cream lounge walls, the threadbare carpet, the glow from the one-bar heater. Reluctantly, I dragged myself away to make scones and pumpkin soup. For the first time, I relaxed in the strange new scene I'd stumbled into. We couldn't go anywhere. No one knocked at the door. I wished the storm would last forever.

Mike's twin brother Peter was there too. Collectively they were known as 'the Wombles', I don't know why. Long and lanky, their faces scarred by adolescent acne, they looked nothing like the small furry creatures who cleaned up Wimbledon Common. But in some ways, the nickname was inspired. They spent years helping people tossed aside by society, working with the Black Power neither as gang members nor as paid social workers but out of a sense of social justice.

When I came to Wellington, everyone assumed that Peter and I would get together. It had a nice symmetry, the four Pākehā: Annie, me and the twins. He seemed interested in an offhand way that I put down to shyness, while I was impressed by his certainty, dedication and the ease with which he moved in Black Power circles. Apart from anything else, I'd be safer and more accepted as his missus.

Late on the second night of the storm, when everyone had gone to bed, there was a knock on my door. Peter's head appeared in the shadows.

'You awake?' he asked softly.

'Yeah.' I sat up, pulling the blankets round me.

'Can I come in?'

I nodded.

He perched on the edge of the bed and rubbed his calloused hands back and forth along his jeans, shiny with dirt. 'I'm not much good at this,' he mumbled.

'Me neither,' I said, hugging my knees.

Warily, we began to offer up titbits from our pasts, two strangers searching for signs that the way ahead was safe. His father was a businessman who disapproved of his sons' political activism. His mother was sick and somehow absent. There was an older sister he spoke highly of. When I met her later, I was surprised to find a professional woman, unashamedly middle-class: I always felt I had to apologise for my own bourgeois background around the Wombles.

'How are ya finding things round here?' he asked.

'Different! I still feel like the new kid. And the patches freak me out a bit, especially when the boys are all together. It'll be good when we get our own work co-op going and I've got a job to do.'

'If!' he said. 'Annie's been talking about organising the girls for months, you know. Long before you got here.'

'Yeah, well, it's not that fuckin' easy,' I said indignantly. 'First we've got to convince them they're better off working than cruising round town all day. Then we've got to find someone who'll hire us.'

'We've got shitloads of work,' he said smugly.

'Yeah, but you've all done labouring before. No one takes girls seriously when it comes to doing outdoor stuff. But I can't see our lot working in an office, can you?'

His voice softened. 'You're a bit naive, but it's good you're here. Annie's got great ideas, but she needs someone like you to get them off the ground.'

I decided to take it as a compliment.

'Wanna tea?' Annie asked.

'Ta,' I said. 'I need something to wash down Mike's mince. I can't believe he didn't brown it first. It looked like pink gravel.'

Bubbles ran her tongue over her lips and grinned at me. 'Tasted like it too.'

I smiled back. She'd been surprisingly good to me since I moved in. I wouldn't have blamed her for treating me as a rival. She adored Annie, who'd helped her get Rana back from Social Welfare, and I was taking up a lot of Annie's time.

'Bubbles and me reckon there's enough girls to start work,' Annie said, handing me a pottery mug with a peace sign on the side. 'There's Nayda and her friend Gini, the one that was round the other day. Not long out of the girls home.'

I thought back. 'Frizzy hair? Didn't say boo?'

'That's her. And Agnes, the gorgeous-looking one who hangs out with the Mongrel Mob. And Amelia. She was at the pub with us the other night: afro, big smile, bit of a flirt. With you, that makes five.'

'Cool!' I said, suddenly feeling terrified. It was all very well to set up a work co-op, but Bubbles had a child to look after and Annie was finishing her nursing training. Day-to-day, it'd be up to me to organise things and I'd only been in town for five minutes. I hardly knew the girls — or the scene.

Bubbles went over to the record player and lowered the needle. Renée Geyer filled the room: 'Am I heading in the right direction for your loving and affection?' I felt a pang of longing for Pat, home from his travels having survived one night in a Texan jail and another in an Argentinean one, now working on a building site in town. We'd met up a few times and the spark was still there, but there was no chance of getting back together. When he'd gone overseas, I was on my way to Dunedin to work in a youth centre. By the time he returned, I was moving in with the Black Power. For me, it was just the way things had unfolded. But Pat thought I'd rejected my old life, and him with it. He had no time for the gang scene and he was right about one thing — there was no place in it for us as a couple.

'We need work,' Annie went on. 'Think I'll throw a sickie tomorrow. We'll go and hassle the Labour Department again, eh. I've had a gutsful of them fobbing us off.'

Annie and I operated differently. Her big-picture Aries offset my conscientious Virgo. Later that would drive us crazy but at first we made a good pair. On her real or invented days off from the hospital, we nipped around town on my Honda trying to drum up work. She barged into government departments, demanding attention; I followed politely, making soothing noises. She and Bubbles convinced the young women that our dreams of work and independence could come true; I opened bank accounts and applied for funding.

We registered our group formally as Aroha Trust. Love seemed to sum up our intentions, although no one had enough te reo to realise that 'aroha' should have 'te' in front of it. Then we drew up five aims that Germaine Greer would have applauded: 'To establish a self-supporting, non-profit work trust for women; to support working women to find job satisfaction through a cooperative work trust organised by women; to provide opportunities for young mothers to participate in the trust; to organise and encourage work and educational opportunities for the women involved in the trust; and to further the awareness of women in the trust in wider issues, especially those relating to women.'

We knew what we wanted: girls around the gangs doing physical work together, regardless of their affiliations, preferably outside, with no boss standing over us all day. Just like the Black Power. The boys were sceptical, another incentive for us to succeed. Feminism was about to meet gang culture.

Annie talked unionist Sonja Davies and lawyer Shirley Smith into being trustees, part of the bridge-building she was so good at. We needed their skills and respectability but made sure we outnumbered them when it came to making decisions.

Bubbles never forgot going to Sonja's office in Trades Hall with Annie to organise the Aroha Trust seal that went on our formal documents. 'It was hardcase, cos I've always remembered Sonja's face,' she said. 'Not long after that she had a book, so I read the book. Without meeting her, she would have had no significance to me whatsoever.'

The time would never be better. Old ideas of race and gender were under siege. New laws had brought in maternity leave and matrimonial property rights. For the first time, there was a welfare benefit for solo mums and easier access to abortion. Girls were being told they could do anything.

Inspired by liberation movements across the world, Māori were also demanding their rights as tangata whenua. Young, educated Ngā Tamatoa activists began calling for self-determination. The Waitangi Tribunal was set up to consider Treaty grievances. A hīkoi the length of the North Island adopted as its slogan 'not one more acre of Māori land', a message soon to be reinforced by the occupation of Bastion Point.

But rapid social change had also created casualties. In the 1950s and 1960s, Māori had been lured in ever-increasing numbers to the cities to meet the demands for unskilled labour. Concentrated in poor communities far from traditional supports, they struggled with poverty, isolation and institutional racism. When things went wrong at home and school, their young people drifted into town and into trouble. Rejected by Pākehā culture and out of touch with their own, they banded together for support.

By the late 1960s gangs began to emerge: Black Power, Mongrel Mob, Headhunters, Stormtroopers. In spite of public unease, they had friends in high places. In 1976, Prime Minister Rob Muldoon partied with the Black Power at their pad. Two years later, Wellington Mayor Michael Fowler stood bail to the tune of $7000 for seven of them after a run-in with the Mongrel Mob.

In an effort to contain the gangs as unemployment began to soar, the government created the Temporary Employment Programme, a relief work scheme that allowed groups to work together on public projects and supervise themselves. Work cooperatives sprang up around the country to take advantage of the new rules. Aroha Trust was one of them. At the time, we didn't understand all the wider social forces, but we did want some of the action.

Annie plonked her bike helmet on the counter at the Labour Department and tapped the bell impatiently.

A middle-aged man put his head out of his office. 'Oh, it's you,' he said from the safety of his door. 'I told you I'll give you a call if anything comes up.'

'Yeah, well we just wanted to let you know we've got five girls registered as unemployed and ready to start work right away,' Annie said.

'As I said, I'll give—'

'I thought you people didn't like dole bludgers.'

The man approached the counter. His voice was clipped. 'I'm sorry, madam, but I can't force anyone to give you a job.'

'What if we find our own job?' Annie said.

He looked at her suspiciously. 'It would have to fit the criteria.'

'It will.' Annie grabbed her helmet and headed for the lift. I threw the man a conciliatory look and followed. Out on the street, I steadied my Honda while she climbed on behind.

'Now what?' I said. The chances of us finding an employer seemed even more remote than the Labour Department doing it.

'Next stop, Newtown Adventure Playground!' she shouted as I accelerated away, the scooter buzzing like a demented bee.

The playground was an overgrown patch of land on the corner of a busy intersection, separated from the traffic by a high wire fence. Outside, brown-skinned kids defended a teetering, packing-case fort and swung like monkeys across a fishing net slung between two poles. Inside the hall, boys thundered across trestle tables and branded one another with tennis balls. A young man with a long blond ponytail and beard bounded over to us, more hyper than his charges. His head bobbed up and down excitedly as Annie explained our problem.

'Well, there's plenty to do here,' he said, pointing out a dirty window. 'That fort's got to go before someone falls to their death. And the whole place needs a good clean-up inside and out. When can you start?'

Annie grinned. The playground was run by the city council and would qualify for relief work subsidies. Aroha Trust was under way.

Two weeks later, on a drizzly August afternoon just after my twenty-second birthday, I left the city council chambers with four young women in their late teens, proudly clutching our first pay packets, each containing seven crisp $10 notes.

Gini tucked the small white envelope into her Swanndri pocket and patted it a few times. 'Let's go to the pub for lunch,' she suggested as she climbed into the passenger seat of our antiquated, olive-green, Morris bread van, bought off the Blacks for a hundred bucks. She didn't usually say much, to me anyway, but I'd seen how the others took notice of her.

'Why not?' I said, pulling out of the carpark. We'd earned a beer.

There were cheers from the back where Nayda, Amelia and Agnes perched on narrow pews around the walls, resting their boots on dusty rakes and shovels.

At the Royal Oak, we ordered hot chips and a couple of jugs, then a couple more.

An hour later, I looked at my watch. 'Shit, look at the time! Drink up!'

Silence.

I drained my glass and got to my feet. 'C'mon! We're late.'

No one moved.

'Gini? Amelia? Nayda?' I appealed to each of them separately.

They stared into their drinks.

I played my trump card. 'Agnes?' Surely reliable Agnes wouldn't let me down.

She inched closer to the others.

'Hey guys, we could lose our jobs.' I was begging now.

Ranks closed. Shoulders shrugged. Four heads slowly shook from side to side. There was nothing left to do but walk out by myself, cheeks burning, trying to pinpoint if the mutiny had been planned or spontaneous.

Back at the playground, the ponytailed youth worker didn't ask questions. When the council manager popped in to see how we were getting on, I muttered something about food poisoning. That night, Annie was sympathetic but didn't offer to help me patch things up: rescuing was never part of her brief. Hardest of all was facing the Wombles.

'Ya did what?' they smirked. 'Went to the pub during work hours?

What were ya thinking?'

'Rub it in, why don't ya?' I felt sick enough without them going on. Peter was right, I was naive. Aroha Trust's days might be over almost before they'd begun, and it would be my fault.

THREE

NEW RECRUITS

Here's how Gini remembered joining Aroha Trust: 'I had a good mate Nayda, and I was still a street kid at that time, and I'd actually gone to school with her and then we met up. It must have been winter because I remember thinking, I'm sick of sleeping where it's wet and cold and ugly. I need at least a roof over my head that is a stable roof, not one that I have to run out of quickly and exit when somebody's coming. And she took me home one day, and it was with all these other people in this house. There were these two Pākehā women — you and Annie.' She gave me an apologetic grin. 'And I still had this thought in my mind that I don't like Pākehās because they killed my mother. They were there, but they weren't there. I could cut off from wherever they were or whoever they were. I could focus on the rest of my life — Māori people.

'And I think they were forming this trust, talking about it, and asked if I wanted a job. And I thought, oh no, that's more commitment, that's more stable, that's more accountability, I couldn't handle that. But then it was like, if my friend could do it and thought it was good, then maybe

I should give it a go. And if boots and things got provided, that was a real help because you didn't have to fork out and buy them. When you steal things, it's touch and go whether they fit nice or they're a bit big or a bit tight. And I thought at least you get measured up for them and they actually fit you, so they belong to you. And this sense of belonging. I thought, oh it's all right, but seven days a week's a bit much. One or two days, yeah, maybe.

'I think that's how I got into Aroha Trust.'

On a grey Sunday evening, when the city seemed drained of colour and life, I drove over to Gini's flat. We'd survived the revolt at the Royal Oak. The next morning the girls had slunk back to work, quiet and hung-over. I was too sheepish to make much of a fuss and the council didn't query their absences. But now on paydays, we had lunch at Natural Juices, a café that served hippie food and no alcohol.

No one answered the door at Gini's, so I let myself in. We'd wangled a place for another worker and I knew her younger sister Tasi wanted a job. Fumbling in the gloom, I ran my hand along the wall and flicked a light switch. Nothing happened. I assumed I was in the lounge though there were few clues: just a pile of ragged blankets in one corner, a pāua-shell ashtray overflowing with butts, white candle wax dripping down the windowsill. I walked slowly through the house, trying other switches that didn't work. Every room was as derelict as the first. The smell of rotting floorboards and blocked drains hit me when I poked my head into the kitchen, and I fled down the hall. Outside, I took gulps of cold air and tried to shake the desolation that had descended on me.

'I called round to see you last night,' I said when I picked Gini up in the van the next morning.

'We were out,' she said vaguely. 'D'ya think it's going to rain?'

'If you're lucky,' I said, looking at the darkening sky to the south. 'I wanted to tell Tasi she can start work. As long as she's registered for the dole.'

'Cool! I'll tell her tonight. She was just going to bed when I got up.'

Gini massaged her forehead with her thumb and forefinger. 'I hope it pisses down. I'm stuffed.'

I turned around and headed back to get Agnes. After we'd tidied up the Newtown Adventure Playground, we'd stayed on to help with the school holiday programme. Then the council found us more work clearing the grounds at a community childcare centre near the hospital.

'I was going to leave you fullas a note, but I couldn't get your lights to work,' I said.

'Got any fags, Pip?' Gini said. She pulled a face as I handed her a packet of B&H Gold. 'Yuk! You should smoke menthols.'

'Lolly smokes! Anyway, they'll taste the same if you've just brushed your teeth.' Then I paused, considering the challenges of dental hygiene in that house. Or getting up for work, for that matter.

She lit two cigarettes and handed me one. I hauled the nicotine into my lungs and tried again. 'So what's with the lights?'

She shrugged. 'We always turn them off at the main when we go out. Saves power.'

It made sense. God knows how many of them lived in that dump and she was the only legal earner as far as I knew. If she was scabbing smokes on Monday morning, they'd all be broke till payday.

Months later, lying on Gini's bed late one night chewing the fat, I brought up the house again.

This time she laughed. 'You didn't believe that bullshit, did ya, Pip? We were squatting there, about 20 of us. It was a fuckin' hole, only had one bedroom. The power'd been cut off, that's why the lights didn't work.'

Even then, I didn't probe further. Like why living in a hovel in the middle of winter with no electricity, threatened by hunger, older predators and the police, was still better than living at home. Or if there was a home to go back to, parents who cared, a safety net when things got out of hand.

In those days, no one talked about their pasts. Young people arrived as if from nowhere, and were accepted — myself included — no questions asked. We worked, lived and partied together, shared clothes and confidences, good times and bad, without ever saying where we'd come from or why we were there. This unspoken pact suited me as well: I was as keen to hide my background with all its privilege as others were to hide theirs with all its pain.

Two decades later, when I visited the women of Aroha Trust to record their stories, things had changed. Now I did want to know what had catapulted them onto the streets and into the dubious arms of the gangs when they were little more than children. I also wanted to know if they'd moved on, and how.

In Whangārei, Gini picked me up from the airport. Her conservative, black knee-length dress and floral waistcoat were in sharp contrast to her heavily tattooed hands and arms, while her frizzy mop of hair had been tamed into a neat cut. A big smile lit up her friendly face, drawing me into its warmth. We hugged for a long time, then went to get my luggage.

I'd booked into a hotel a block away from the humble, three-bedroom house where Gini and her Pākehā husband were raising their six children (three hers, three his). The house was full: her 18-year-old son lived in a flat at the bottom of the section, and some of the other children spilled over to her in-laws, who lived next door and owned both properties.

Throwing my suitcase onto the spare bed in the hotel room, she patted its cover. 'Choice! This one's for me.' Then she walked over to the window and looked down at the swimming pool. 'Hey, kids!' she called to the 10- and 12-year-old she had in tow. 'Let's bring our togs tomorrow.'

I gulped, wondering how the management would react if the whole family moved in.

At their house, Gini's husband was cooking tea, squinting behind thick glasses. She'd just begun a fulltime social work degree while he looked after the children and ran a small native plant nursery from home. He was friendly, but I suspected he wasn't thrilled about me walking in and stirring up the past, taking up the little free time they had together.

The door opened and I was transported back in time. The tall fine-looking young man who walked in from his supermarket checkout job was Gini's oldest son, the image of his father JB, her boyfriend from the Aroha Trust days.

'I'm really proud of him,' she said when he'd left for boxing practice. 'He's not a street kid. He's not wasting money at spacies, or stealing. He's holding down a good job and getting paid and saving and going for his driver's licence. He hasn't got any tattoos. He's really handsome. And he's a good worker. He's got that discipline to stick at it. Yeah, he's a good boy.'

After tea, Gini's husband followed me into the lounge where a tropical paradise, complete with blue skies, yellow sand and palm trees, had been painted directly onto one wall. A born-again Christian like her, he began quoting from the scriptures, insisting Jesus was our saviour and prayer the path to salvation.

To distract him, I asked if I could take a family photo. Gini made the children change back into their school uniforms and lined them up against a backdrop of psalms and religious hangings. But the shutter jammed and I watched, impressed, as they put on their pyjamas and went off to bed without a peep.

Before I left town, I bought a disposable camera and we made a special trip to the depot where Gini was a volunteer firefighter. She spent 10 minutes putting on the full regalia, then posed with one hand on her hip and the other on the hub of the fire-engine wheel, her round face beaming under the bright yellow helmet.

'I've really enjoyed being a mother and doing this social service tohu[1] and being in the fire brigade and the church and the school,' she said. 'It feels as if my life is so full. I never would have thought it would have come out how it has. And I'm so grateful for it.'

---

1   qualification

Ko Ngātokimatawhāorua te waka
Ko Nukutawhiti te tangata
Ko Pūhanga Tohorā te maunga
Ko Hokianga te moana
Ko Punakitere te awa
Ko Ngā Puhi te iwi
Ko Ngāti Ueoneone rāua ko Ngāti Tautahi ngā hapū
Ko Okorihi te marae
Ko Pakinga te puke te urupā

When Gini arrived at my hotel the next morning, I beckoned her over to the photo album spread open on the coffee table. It contained a motley collection of photos from the Aroha Trust days, along with recent ones taken on my visits to the women. I pointed to a blurred, scowling girl with a thick mop of hair crouched beside a weed sprayer in a school field. She was wearing jeans tucked into steel-capped boots, a studded belt, a denim shirt with short frayed sleeves.

Gini's mouth fell open. 'I would have denied that was even me. It looks like a guy. There's just a real hard look on my face.' She studied the image again. 'I can see a gentleness there, a naive innocent child behind that outward hardness. And I remember my hair. It was so long and wild and untamed. When I think about it, I didn't really know who I was. When I was brought up, I got told what to wear, I wasn't allowed to choose anything from day to day. So I didn't know what I liked, let alone what suited me. My hair is naturally black. Those days I used to dye it orange, which is the furthest colour I could get from black. I used to think it was cool because everybody had orangey-coloured hair. Or I thought they did.'

I asked Gini how it felt to see that young girl.

'Like I've been robbed of my childhood. I would have been 20 years old and now I'm 41, it's like I'm a different person. I know who I am, I'm confident in what I'm doing, and I know where I'm going. At that time I was so lost; I was just so alone. Floundering from day to day, not even knowing what I liked to wear, let alone look like. It's a real eye-opener.' She let out a long breath. 'Whoa.'

Between us lay my small tape recorder, poised to capture her life in her own words. She asked to begin with a prayer. A quick family history followed. Gini's maternal grandmother (Ngā Puhi and Tainui) had four children to different fathers. Gini had heard stories: 'That she was ātaahua — beautiful — to have all these different men. That she was a kind lady and everyone stayed at her whare. The family was quite religious back in the country up in Kaikohe. They had church in the valley every Sunday morning, and the bell would ring and people would come from all around. Now that I have faith, I think, maybe it's come from their prayers.'

Church played a big part in Gini's childhood too. The third of eight children, she grew up in Tītahi Bay. Her mother belonged to the Rātana faith. 'They wore this orange uniform with a half-moon hat. She took us all along there and it was all in Māori so we didn't understand a word of it but there was always a nice big munch at the end.' Her father, who'd migrated to New Zealand from Niue as a young man, did the same. 'Dressed us all up and took us to his Presbyterian church which was all in Niuean. Didn't understand a word of that either but I remember afterwards they had a nice big feed as well.'

Going to church was the only time the family was happy together, Gini said. 'Underneath it wasn't like that at all. It was very strict and very regimental and very disciplined.'

Gini's father was an angry man. 'He had a lot of hurt in his life, before he even got married, probably to do with leaving the Islands. After the honeymoon period wore off and all the children started coming along, I think reality hit, and he had to go out and work every day, and he had a lot of things that he hadn't dealt to. He was a bit of a drinker and that would encourage him more to be violent. He took a lot of it out on my mother.'

Family meals were eaten in fear. 'We had a long table with benches along the side and my parents sat at either end and there was not a word spoken. It was just silent as. Nobody dare speak cos my father would just backhand them off the stool. It was horrible. So I got brought up thinking that's what happens at meal times. You don't talk. Now that I've got a totally new relationship, that's all we do, is talk at the table. Being brought up the opposite, it's like you've been deceived and robbed all those years of a natural event.'

A big fan of Muhammad Ali, Gini's father passed on his boxing skills to his sons and daughters. 'He'd make a ring of stools, turn the timer on the stove for five minutes and tell two of us to fight, holding the hands of his favourite to punch the other one harder.'

Still, these were the good years. Her father worked hard as a linesman for the Power Board, and brought chippies and lollies home for the children. On Sundays, he marinated raw fish and cooked curried chicken and rice, still her sister Tasi's favourite food, even if he gave most of it away to his friends and relations.

Gini's mother kept the family together. 'She was a good mother. I have good memories of her playing with us and teaching me to cook and clean and sew.' She also acted as a buffer, sending the children out of the room during arguments with her husband. 'I don't remember him hitting us much, I think it was because he hit her.'

When Gini was 13, she lost that buffer. A drunk Pākehā milkman knocked her mother down in a hit-and-run accident as she crossed the road with her young son to refill her husband's beer flagons at the pub.

Gini's father was shattered when the local minister arrived at the house with the news, she said. 'You can see somebody shrink and it was like that, like a glass breaking. But later on, my thoughts towards him were so mean and evil that I thought, he's probably just so shocked that she didn't get his beer more than anything.'

Gini's mother lay in a coma in Wellington Hospital for three days, but the children were never taken to see her. When she died, her husband refused to let her whānau take her body home to Kaikohe; he'd always discouraged contact with her family. Instead, she was laid out at Takapuwāhia Marae, and farewelled at his Presbyterian church rather than with her Rātana faith.

Gini remembered kissing her mother's forehead. 'She was cold as, like she was frozen. It gave me the shivers.' From then on, she avoided the body, and the people talking and singing around the coffin at the marae. 'We were just children, running round outside playing. It wasn't until after we'd been to the cemetery and days later that it dawned on me, my mother's not coming back.'

By then it was too late for tears. 'Everybody had cried days back at the marae and how come I'd left it till now? To hide your emotions and to hold back all that crying, it does something to you, even if you can't say what it is. It's like holding a piece in your body that can't get out.'

I asked if her father had been able to comfort her.

'I think he tried to gather us all around and hug us all at once. But it was the total opposite of his character to ever touch us in such a way to show affection. We were so used to the discipline, the strictness, the regiment, so when he was doing it, it was foreign, like, what are we doing here?'

The horror that followed her mother's death wiped out many of Gini's childhood memories. 'I do remember there being toys when she was alive, and playing. And I remember at Christmas time we used to hide presents around the house and it was like a treasure hunt, and it was really exciting. But I don't remember having birthdays. I don't remember having very many Christmases. I don't remember any after she died. All these are just vague from when she was alive. My life changed dramatically after she died. It was like somebody put a brick wall there and I couldn't see past it, and from then it was hard and' — she searched for the right word — 'yuk. All the way.'

Gini's father brought his mother over from Niue to help with the children, but her English was poor and she spent most of the time in her room. 'She was used to sleeping on the hard floor and using those brooms with all the sticks bundled together, and hitting for any little thing, and pinching, and things we were not used to. I think her intentions were right, but it was a very tough family. There seemed to be nothing done out of love, it was all done out of fear.'

The family had a big vegetable garden and plenty of lawn. 'But we had no toys or books or anything like that. We shared one bike between us, this little two-wheeler. We wrecked it so fast because we couldn't get enough of it. We had to entertain ourselves with hopscotch and we weren't allowed to play really because there was always work to do, cleaning or tidying, anything couldn't be done spotless enough.'

By this time, Gini's older brother was in borstal and her older half-sister in a psychiatric hospital. Gini, third in line, took on the role of caring for her younger siblings, getting them to school, cleaning, washing, cooking and shopping. 'I sort of became the mother,' she said. 'I got put into that position and I didn't like it at all. My father used me — mentally, physically, emotionally and even sexually.'

Every week, he gave her $10 or $15 pocket money, 'and in those days that was a lot of money'. He also gave her money for the groceries, together with a shopping list made out in his beautiful handwriting, and the price of each item beside it.

'I think that's when I started stealing. Because he was raping me. I felt like he owned me.'

I winced at the transaction she described so matter-of-factly.

'I got to be a really good thief. I could walk around the shop and buy about $2 worth of stuff and have about $100 worth of groceries in my bag ready to carry home with my brother. I did this weekly for months, even years. I got used to having a lot of money and wasting it. I think that's why I can't save now because easy come, easy go. Also I didn't realise what suicide was then, but I didn't want to be here tomorrow. I wasn't planning to have a nice, bright, shiny future. I was just living for the day.'

One day, she got caught shoplifting. 'And oooh, I was sooo scared. Because I knew he was going to whack me till I was blue.'

'Oh,' I said. 'You were afraid of your father, not the police?'

She looked at me incredulously. 'Oh yes, my father. Not the police!'

She couldn't recall the exact beating. 'I was used to getting hidings. And hidings were really hidings. I was bruised every part of my body, except my face. I was blue, literally. I was almost immune to these hidings. I was walking around half-dead. And then to have to go to school with all these bruises hidden under my uniform and trying to sit in class and concentrate. I couldn't study.' She said it again, as if I might need convincing. 'I couldn't.'

Before her mother's death, Gini had been helpful and enjoyed school. Afterwards, she became a bully. 'Fighting a lot, even with boys. I got rough and nasty.'

Surely someone noticed the change, I said.

'No, not that I remember. Now I think, where was Social Welfare? Why didn't anyone come around and do home help? How come we didn't get people—?' Her voice trailed away. 'I think it was because my father was a proud man. He would look after his family. He would go out and work. To humble himself to accept help from any other agency would be like he's not a good enough father.'

Once she told a friend about the incest. 'She was shocked, but we were just 13-year-olds and didn't know what to do with it. And those days people believed the parents more than the children. So I kept it a dark secret, even from my family, my brothers and sisters, so I was carrying a real heavy load.'

Gini was too scared to tell anyone else in case they didn't believe her and her father found out. She started running away. 'One time I was in my pyjamas and he was out in the shed cutting kindling and I said to him, "I'll go and check the mail." This was about seven o'clock at night. I opened the front door and slowly crept out and went down to the letterbox. My bundle of clothes I was going to change into were under my window outside and I picked them up and I started walking because I knew that if I ran, my sandals would go *flip-flop, flip-flop*. My heart was beating really fast because I thought, I'm out of here. By this time, Tasi had already run away. My brother had left and it was just me and the little, little ones. About half a k down the road — I was running hard out — I could hear these footsteps behind me and he caught me. I couldn't even scream because it was in the dark of the night. I think now if I had just yelled and screamed, people would have rung the police or something. But I was in shock. I remember him coming up behind me and grabbing me and taking me home, giving me a hiding. And to think, why couldn't he see I wasn't coming home because of what he was doing?'

Finally, three years after the abuse began, Gini had had enough. 'I put all his scaring behind and thought, I'm going to tell because I'm sure it's not right.' She confided in the woman next door, but swore her to secrecy. Next time she ran away and got caught, she told the police. 'I got the impression they didn't believe me and were going to take me back there anyway, but the neighbour confirmed my story.'

Gini testified against her father in court, though not in his presence. He was deported to Niue, she said, the family was split up, and she and Tasi were sent to Miramar Girls Home. 'It was a relief because there was no way the police would ever take me back to that house.' But the experience left a terrible legacy. 'Every white person, because of the driver, was to blame for killing my mother. Every Islander because of their nationality was to me labelled an abusive father. I hated them all.'

Tasi, nearly three years younger than Gini, was vaguer about the events that broke up her family. 'I didn't know the way he was treating Gini,' she said of her father. 'I just told this officer that he was giving me a hiding all the time. We were in the courtroom one day and I found out we were going to be state wards and that was that, more or less.'

Tasi's story unfolded in a motel room in Whanganui on a quiet Saturday morning in February 2000 after I'd plucked her away from her partner and seven children and we'd stocked my fridge with supplies to get us through the day. Covered from neck to ankle in black, in a long skirt and top, her thick dark hair falling loose almost to her waist, the Aroha Trust tomboy looked like a figure out of the Old Testament. Like Gini, she was a born-again Christian, but even more fervent: her sect forbade women to wear trousers, cut their hair, drink or smoke. Only her tattooed hands and wrists, and three ink dots beside her left eye, hinted at the life she'd once led.

As soon as I turned on the tape, Tasi wanted to talk about her mother. Her dark eyes brimmed with tears. 'She had such a hard life with my dad. Bringing up all us children. I don't know how she managed actually, but she done it. He was really stressing her out a lot. But she never showed it once, you know. Taught us. She was really good to us. Really loved us a lot.'

To help pay the bills, her mother went cleaning at night. Her father had a second job too, as a bouncer at the pub. 'We had plenty of money,' she said bitterly. 'My father used to give it all to his friends at the pub, that's how much money we had.'

Of all her mother's gifts, Tasi regarded prayer as the greatest. 'She taught me to pray and, ever since then, I prayed right through my life. Even when I was going through hard times, I still remembered how to pray. I really, really thank her for that. That got me through.'

I began to understand the two sisters' religious fervour. It was more than just a way to make sense of their father's brutality, more even than a framework on which to rebuild their shattered young lives. It represented their undying love for their mother. No wonder whatever the problem, God was the answer.

Tasi remembered a song by the Stylistics playing on the radio while her mother's body was laid out at the marae. 'It was called "Betcha by Golly Wow!"' She smiled at the silly title. 'I don't know what that means, but every time I heard that song, I always cried. When I was at school and when I was at the girls home.'

At the funeral, Tasi realised 'it's just us against the world now. Māori people didn't know what was going on at home; they didn't know that our father was so abusive. And the Island people, they more took his side. I thought, we're just going to stick together. And that's exactly what happened.'

Gini looked after them, she said. 'She became our mother. She still is today. Which is quite good, because a lot of us always fall back on her.'

But Gini couldn't protect her siblings from their father. 'He'd come home at night and be real drunk and give us a hiding just about every night for two years,' Tasi said. 'Two years!'

Twice he attacked her hair. The first time, she spent the day roaming around the creek at the back of their street. 'I couldn't go to school with a bald head. Actually, I found me a hat when I was down the creek, and I wore that hat right through intermediate, which was terrible cos the boys used to pull it off my head.'

When her father discovered she'd tattooed dots on her hands, he beat Tasi almost unconscious and cut her hair again, this time down the middle, like a Mohawk. 'I thought, right, I'd better get out of this house cos he's going to kill me.'

Tasi moved in with her Niuean uncle and cousins, along with her older brother, fresh from borstal, who was beginning to kick around with the Black Power. She was 12 years old.

What did they do all day?

'We just drank coffee. We had it really easy. No one was working, just my uncle. He brought all the food. And then there was my brother. He'd go and do burglaries and get food like that. It was good. They were really good to me.'

She wasn't concerned about truanting. 'I was only worried about banging into my father. But I stayed in the house most of the day anyway. Just cleaning up.'

Remarkably, she still valued his upbringing. 'As I grew older, I was real thankful that he was strict. He taught me how to respect other people and be strict on my own children. That was good. But when my mum died, he was very hard.'

Tasi's story differed from Gini's in one important respect. She thought her father went to Niue for a holiday after Gini testified against him, while Gini believed he'd been deported.

With their agreement, I went looking for the truth. Gini's Social Welfare records confirm that police laid a complaint in relation to her allegations of incest, that the case was first heard on 31 July 1975 and — crucially — that her father admitted the charge. But they also suggest Tasi was right.

'[Her] father is a proud man who has done his best to manage his problems but has more or less admitted defeat,' Gini's social worker wrote to the magistrate of the Porirua Children and Young Persons Court when Gini appeared on several offences including running away from home and theft. 'He returned to Niue Island this month as he felt he could no longer cope with life as it had become for him in New Zealand.'

The social worker's report is chilling proof of many of the women's claims that parents were always considered to be in the right. In the first paragraph, she acknowledged Gini's father had committed incest, but never referred to it again. The most she conceded was that 'it seems he has tried too hard and that his discipline of the children has been overdone and his requirements have become rather unbalanced because of his anxieties'.

Nor did the social worker link Gini's behaviour to her home life. Instead, she described her as 'an open, pleasant girl willing to cooperate but with a tendency to be devious and dishonest, like her sister Tasilofa'. And later, '[Gini] has been associating with groups of young people, many of whom have been in criminal activities and she seems to like the life of the underworld'.

While the social worker's attitude now seems inconceivable, young sex abuse victims are still being failed by the New Zealand justice system. Research published in 2008 by forensic psychologist Suzanne Blackwell shows that only a fraction of cases that come before the courts are punished. Lawyers bully young complainants and play on myths to get clients off, such as accusing the child of lying if they didn't report the offences immediately. What's more, jurors fall for these myths, are less likely to believe teenagers than younger children, and increasingly demand DNA evidence or witnesses before they're willing to convict, even if they believe the child.

After two years in Niue, Gini's and Tasi's father returned to New Zealand (further proof he'd left voluntarily) and remarried. Two years later, he was convicted of incest in Auckland, this time involving another family member. His appallingly light sentence — seven months' periodic detention and 15 months' probation — suggests his previous offending was not taken into account. Since then, rape and incest have continued to plague his whānau, spreading through the next generation like ripples in a pond.

FOUR

LEARNING THE RULES

We finished clearing the grounds at the community childcare centre and hired a trailer to get rid of the rubbish. I'd never manoeuvred a trailer before but, hey, life was full of things I was doing for the first time.

'When you reverse, just remember to turn the steering wheel the opposite way you want the trailer to go,' the helpful hire man said. But at the Happy Valley tip, I discovered my brain didn't work in mirror images. The harder I tried, the more I jackknifed our load, first one way, then the other.

Swinging their legs out the back door of the van, Gini and Amelia watched the trailer's crazy, zigzag dance and shouted instructions. 'Turn left! No, right! No, left!'

Beside me, Nayda yanked her knitted hat over her ears and slid further down in the seat. 'Fuck, I'm glad Dad isn't here today.' Her father drove heavy machinery for the council. 'Oh no! Here comes one of his mates. I hope he doesn't recognise me.'

'We're fine,' I said, waving the man away. 'I'm getting the hang of it.'

But I wasn't, and when no one could stand it any longer, we

unhooked the trailer, hauled it through the churned-up clay and heaved the contents over the edge, holding our breath against the stink. Then we hitched it back up and took off, wheels spinning in the mud, yahooing and waving our fists out the window. Another Aroha Trust mission successfully accomplished.

●

An old friend from university invited me to a party. I was struggling to manage more than one world at a time, but Annie persuaded me to take her. She thrived on variety and was intrigued by — if scornful of — my former student life.

We sat in the corner most of the night, arms around each other's shoulders, passing judgement on the other partygoers. Pat arrived but steered clear of us. In spite of their similar backgrounds, he and Annie didn't really get on. I suspected he thought she was a bad influence on me.

'I'm going to head off,' she said eventually. 'Go see your man!'

'He's not my man anymore,' I said.

She raised her eyebrows and handed me a slim blue packet of Cameo cigarettes, the ones she always smoked, one of the few ladylike things about her. 'Here, you'll need these more than me.'

'Thanks,' I said, although I didn't fully appreciate the gesture at the time. Annie wasn't mean, but she was always broke. It was me who gave her cigarettes when she ran out, me who paid for dinner at restaurants she hauled me into because she loved good food and lacked my scruples that the money we spent could have fed a family of five.

Pat was leaning against the mantelpiece, one long leg crossed in front of the other. My heart missed a beat as I went over to him.

'Anyone would think you two were lesbians,' he said, rolling his eyes.

My smile faded. 'She's my friend,' I snapped. 'If we want to hug each other, we will.'

On Saturday afternoons, we watched the Black Power play rugby league for Miramar. The game was hard, fast, aggressive — just the way they liked it. They didn't always win, but other teams always knew they'd played them.

When the season came to a close, Peter asked me to the club's end-of-year do, our first formal date. Everyone said it would be flash: candles on the tables, supper, a band.

We usually relied on the boys to get our dope: $20 for a tinfoil bullet of marijuana, enough for three or four fat joints, or $8 for a smaller buddha stick designed to blow your head off. Sometimes we'd splash out on caps of hash oil, smearing precious drops on tinfoil, lighting it from underneath and inhaling its pungent fumes.

But it was winter and cannabis was scarce. I sent an SOS to my brother in Dunedin. A few days later, a single joint arrived in the corner of an envelope.

'Sorry, I'm saving it for me and Peter,' I told Annie. I hoped it would entice him away from the boys.

An hour into the party, he and I slipped away from the warm hall and huddled in a doorway out of the misty rain. I ran the joint through my lips to moisten it. Peter cupped his hands around mine, making a cave to protect the match from wind gusts. I sucked hard and held in the sweet smoke for a long time, savouring the brush of his fingers and the shared, secret moment as much as the buzz.

Back inside, I joined Nayda and Annie on the dance floor. I never saw Peter dance, nor any of the boys for that matter. They might shuffle on the spot, stamp their feet, punch their fists repeatedly in the air in the Black Power salute, but never really dance.

When I sat down, Bubbles appeared with a camera. It's the only photo I have of me and Peter. I'm wearing my favourite top, a soft, bronze-coloured shirt dotted with pink flowers, with a black velvet collar and cuffs and two long ties at the neck. Our hair falls in glossy, shoulder-length ringlets, like we've both been to the same salon. My eyes are dreamy and my hand half-covers a wistful smile. Peter's looking down, lost in some private space. Just stoned, I suppose.

It was a good night, a rare coming together of gang and non-gang worlds. I don't remember there being any trouble. This was noteworthy, although I was too new to know that then. At some stage on a night out, there'd always be trouble: a brawl, flashing police lights, a high-speed chase, paddy wagons. And if trouble didn't come knocking, someone was sure to track it down. It fired everyone up, focused their frustration on something outside themselves, fed the raging beast of disaffection and despair for another week. Occasionally, an outsider was unlucky or foolish enough to get caught up, but mostly it played out within the gang, or between the gangs, or between the gang and the cops. Nothing was more disappointing than missing out on the action. Plenty of time in the cold-eyed dawn for wound-licking and remorse.

The next time I appeared in the top with the pink flowers to go to the pub, Annie was stretched out on the couch reading. She was staying home to babysit Rana, and study for her nursing exams.

'Are you wearing that again?' she said, her feet jiggling restlessly over the arm.

I tugged at the top, suddenly self-conscious. 'Why? What's wrong with it?'

'I dunno. Too straight, too middle-class, too something. But don't listen to me. Wear it if you want.' She waved her book at me. 'You should read this. *Soul on Ice*. Eldridge Cleaver. It's fuckin' amazing.'

One night Mike arrived home with a small, wiry boy from the country who needed a place to stay. That made 10 of us. He introduced himself as Arthur, although for the first few days he kept forgetting to answer to the name.

Arthur was quiet and hung his head as if something essential had been knocked out of him. But he was helpful and polite, did dishes and played with Rana. He was smart too, keenly interested in the way the world worked. At the pub, the two of us tussled over women's lib, city versus country life, vegetarians and meat eaters. I pulled myself away when Peter wanted to go home early. The week before, while we were out drinking, Nayda had packed a sad when her boyfriend chatted me up and pulled me onto his knee. I was used to socialising with male friends without being accused of trying to steal them or two-timing my own partner. But the rules were different here and I needed to watch myself.

'You and Arthur seem pretty tight,' Annie said the next day.

'Yeah, he's really cool.'

'You sound surprised.' She gave me a knowing look. 'Why don't you go with him?'

I was too shocked to answer. Surely she didn't think I'd consider dating a boy who was obviously on the run. Or that I'd just ditch Peter, even if I sometimes wondered if he'd notice.

That afternoon, our bread van broke down. I trudged home on foot and Arthur offered to walk back with me to see if he could fix it. Rana was toddling around the house while Bubbles had a nap.

'Let's take her with us,' he said. I wouldn't have thought of doing that.

As he fiddled with the engine, I sat on the kerb, my arms folded to keep out the wind. Rana crouched beside me poking pebbles into a crack in the footpath.

'Are you going with Peter?' Arthur asked, his face obscured beneath the bonnet.

'Kind of,' I said, wondering why I felt so reluctant to admit it.

It was my job to collect the rent at the flat. I kept it in a green vinyl purse. One night, visitors arrived: a rough-looking man and woman with a couple of young kids. As I went to get milk for their tea, I noticed the purse was not on top of the fridge where I thought I'd left it. I searched my bedroom, then pulled Mike aside.

'Are you sure it's gone?' he said.

I nodded miserably. 'I was counting it on the kitchen table. It's due tomorrow.'

'And you've looked everywhere?'

I nodded again, then slid my eyes towards the visitors, who were beginning to pack up.

He sighed. 'Leave it to me. But you better be fuckin' right.'

He stopped them as they were walking down the hall. I cringed behind the kitchen door, watching through the gap.

'You can search us if you want,' I heard the man say, followed by a rattle of coins as he emptied his pockets onto the hall table.

'Sorry, bro,' Mike said. 'I need to see your missus' purse too.'

'It's okay,' said the man in a flat voice.

The woman handed over her shoulder bag, jiggling a sleepy child on her hip while Mike fumbled through its compartments. There was no sign of the money and they left in a flurry of awkward goodbyes. Mike walked past me without a word and closed his bedroom door. I went to bed too. As I slowly got undressed, wondering where another $60 rent was going to come from, my eyes were drawn to a line of paperbacks along my windowsill. I lunged at them, swept them to the floor and curled my fingers around the fat, slippery rent purse. Then I sank to my knees, too ashamed even to cry.

The city council gave us a few tips and set us loose painting the Orange Hall in Newtown. I put my head around the toilet door. Junior, a new girl, waved her brush at me, looking panic-stricken. There was a smudge of black paint on her nose and another across her brow. A friend of Tasi, she was a beautiful young woman with high cheekbones and almond eyes. At 17, she already had a baby that her mother was looking after.

'I hate this fuckin' job,' she wailed. 'They're only making us do it cos we're girls.' She tucked a strand of dark hair behind her ear. 'And the paint's giving me a headache.'

I laughed. 'No, that's the hangover. Where did yous end up last night?'

'Me and Tas sneaked into the Abel Tasman. The pigs came round hassling the boys. We hid in the loos, but they got us anyway.'

'And?'

'Took us down the cop shop. We didn't get home till two.'

'Bummer,' I said. Suggesting she stay out of the pub till she was 20 would have been as useful as telling her to get a proper job.

Behind her, little rivers of black paint were running down the windowsill onto the orange walls. I tried to ignore them. She was right about the work. The hall was badly lit, every surface covered with decades of grime. We struggled to apply the thick oil paint evenly with old brushes. As for the colour scheme, whoever at the council had decided to take the name of the building literally deserved what they got. Maybe if we made a complete hash of it, they'd provide rollers and proper training.

At the far end of the cold hall, Gini and Agnes swayed gently to Rod Stewart blaring from a transistor at their feet. Even in baggy overalls, with a red spotted scarf tied round her head, Agnes looked like a model. But her madonna-like beauty was deceptive: outside work, she partied with the Mongrel Mob and could drink like a man.

There was no sign of Nayda and Amelia so I climbed the steep wooden stairs to the street. There they were, sitting on the footpath in the sun, their backs resting against the wall of the building.

'Snapped!' I said, almost in awe of their ability to skive off so soon after smoko.

Amelia flashed me a smile and jumped up, eager to please now that I'd appeared. Nayda took a defiant drag on her cigarette and flicked the butt into the gutter before following slowly.

'Hey, my sister wants to meet you,' Amelia called over her shoulder as they clattered back down the stairs. 'When you're waiting for me outside in the van in the mornings, she goes, "Who's that sitting on the horn? If it was me, I'd go without you."'

'I like the sound of your sister,' I said.

Every day, I spent the first hour driving round town hounding reluctant girls out of bed. It was the only way to make sure they got to work. For the first half of the week they'd usually be where I'd dropped them off the night before, but after payday, it was anyone's guess. Drunk or stoned or both, they could have crashed at a mate's place, had a fight with their boyfriend, been kicked out of their flat, got picked up by the cops or be otherwise occupied. One of our girls was nicknamed Suzy Wong because she could never be found if a Jap ship was in port.

Amelia lived with her big sister in a 10-storey block of council flats near the zoo. After work, we climbed flights of concrete stairs reeking of stale beer and urine, and entered a cluttered flat full of small children and great smells. I could see the glistening skin of a whole chicken bubbling in a big aluminium pot on the stove. Amelia's sister, a single mum in her mid-twenties, put steaming bowls of soup in front of us and hunks of sweet rēwena bread, also home-made. I wanted to hug her. These days, it was usually me doing the mothering.

AMELIA'S STORY

Ko Ngātokimatawhāorua te waka
Ko Maungataniwha te maunga
Ko Te Tōwai te awa
Ko Ngā Puhi ki Whangaroa te iwi
Ko Kauwau te hapū
Ko Karangahape te marae

Amelia certainly needed looking after, though I didn't know how badly until I recorded her story in Kaitaia on a muggy February day more than 20 years later. Elusive as ever, she arrived at my motel an hour after we'd agreed, just as I was giving up hope that she was going to show. Rolled-up jeans and a black t-shirt highlighted her well-preserved curves, and the lovely smile I remembered lit up her round face. She'd got carried away looking through old photos and letters, she said, stirred up by my visit the night before to her modern three-bedroom house, one of six built in a cul-de-sac by the Black Power; her brother was president of the local chapter and her ex-partner a member.

Amelia was brought up in Taradale, the sixth of 15 children. Both her parents came from small towns in the Far North and could speak Māori fluently. Her father was a bushman, 'a strong man in every way', who was often gone for work, leaving her mother to manage the large family.

'She kept our home all together, she was the centre pole,' Amelia said. 'We never had much of anything. She always used to say to us, "As long as you've got each other, that's all you need." She was a good mum.'

When the children got sick, her mother used home remedies. 'Like when we got scabies. That was the first and last time in our lives we ever got scabies. It went right through the whole house and it was too expensive to go to the doctor for all of us, so Mum would make this stuff up herself which was sulphur — yellow sulphur in powder form — and honey. We would get that chucked down our throat. Yuk! But it fixed us up.'

Everyone had their jobs, girls inside, boys out. Theirs was the cleanest house in the street, Amelia said. 'Next to godliness where my mother was concerned was cleanliness.'

When it came to food, nothing was wasted. 'A hundred and one ways to do with mutton, from the flap to the bones.' By the time she was nine, Amelia could cook. 'If you could make a Māori bread with a dough on a newspaper and it didn't stick and didn't show the print, you had it sussed.' She laughed. 'That's what my mum said. And that's me. I make the mean bread — still.'

At school, Amelia was 'very athletic but not very brainy'. Sometimes, she'd take lunch wrapped in newspaper. Other times, her mother brought a big box of food for the whole family. Amelia was embarrassed in front of the other kids. 'They'd say, "Oh, gosh, they've got to eat like that, they're so poor." We used to have the best lunches though. Big pieces of fried bread, big as your face, to yourself. Mum would bring all the fillings, and the meat all sliced and wrapped. Make her own cakes. Roasting-dish cakes.'

When Amelia's father was home, he was head of the house. 'When we had dinner, we always sat in our same places and never looked at anyone else's food to see who had more. You ate your food and no talk. And you didn't get off the table till you were excused,' she said, echoing Gini's mealtime experience and hinting at a violence she never named. His size and reputation scared off their friends and he forbade the children to play with their Pākehā neighbours. 'He'd say, "Something might get stolen, you'll get the blame. That's Pākehās for you".'

When Amelia was 12, her mother walked out. It wasn't the first time she'd left, but this time she didn't come back. Amelia was the only one to see her go. 'Just playing happily at home one day in the end room which looks out on to our driveway. We had a real long driveway, stony, you could hear people coming in and out. And I remember hearing the gate tinkling and I saw Mum with her suitcase. I went out and said, "Where are you going?" And she said, "Go back inside".' Amelia's voice was quiet, desolate. 'Yeah. And that was that.'

Amelia's mother spent most of the rest of her life in a psychiatric hospital. 'Some things used to be too much for her. I didn't really understand at that time. All I knew was that she was leaving us, and how could she? Now that I'm older, I understand. Cos my dad used to drink a lot, be a real party man, popular with the women. And Mum just had enough.'

Without its centre pole, the family crumbled. The oldest child still at home, Amelia had to look after her siblings, including her six-month-old baby brother. 'I grew up pretty fast. There was no time for me not to want to do anything. I wanted to go to school, but I couldn't. I didn't want to do some of the housework, the nappies and the washing, but I had to.'

By the time an older sister came home to help, Amelia had started college and was 'a real rebel, smoking and doing all the things you weren't meant to do'. Her sister couldn't control her and she was taken into care. 'I was glad to go. It was a sad house cos Mum had gone. That really ripped my heart out when she did that.' She corrected herself, in case I thought she was accusing her mother of deliberately abandoning the family: 'Not when she did that, but when she left.'

But Amelia couldn't settle anywhere, running away first from a family home and then from two sets of foster parents. One teacher at college took an interest in her. 'She used to look at me in the way that I was someone, cos I always used to feel like no one. She always used to say, "You've got a beautiful smile and are always happy." I've gone through my whole life people telling me that. One time she said, "It's going to win you friends twice-fold, having the personality that you've got. Just got to put it to better use." Cos I used to try and be real tough, but not really, a crumbling mess inside. All surface.'

I asked how the teacher had helped.

'Just talking. I had so much bitterness in me, it was consuming me and turning me into not a nice person.'

In the fourth form, Amelia beat up another pupil. 'I didn't feel too great afterwards cos there were about four of us onto one, and she was a Pākehā girl. She called me a nigger, that was all.' Not long after, she was expelled when she knocked out a teacher who tried to stop her fighting. It was then that her big sister brought her to Wellington. Another sister got her a job in the hospital laundry, passing her off as much older than her 14 years. Two of her brothers belonged to the Black Power and, before long, Amelia's social life revolved around the gang.

It still does.

FIVE

WORKING GIRLS

Aroha Trust was becoming popular. We had more girls wanting work than the city council would employ. Somehow we set up another team with the Wellington Education Board, I don't remember how. The same rules applied. The agency provided the work, we supplied the workers and day-to-day supervision, and the Labour Department subsidised our wages.

Gini and I moved over to the new team, leaving Agnes (the only other person with a driver's licence) to chauffeur the city council girls. From then on, we juggled members of the two teams according to the trust's needs and the girls' preferences. Our employers just had to put up with the constant to-ing and fro-ing.

At the Education Board, we reported to the deputy general manager, a big, blond man with faded good looks and a body going to seed. He gave us an old cream van, tools and an open door to his office. We gardened, cut scrub, fertilised playing fields, sprayed weeds at local primary schools — tasks that were too big for regular caretakers. The work was mundane and physically demanding, but there was freedom travelling from school to school up as far as the Kapiti Coast, and satisfaction doing work usually done by men.

'When you realised the skill — you did it with your bare hands without a machine, a lawn mower or weedeater — I felt quite proud of myself,' said Gini, her memory jogged by a photo of herself holding a clump of long grass in one hand and a sickle in the other.

'I remember this day actually,' she said. 'It was a hot day — and there I am in these hot overalls and this hat on my head and with just a whole attitude on my face.' She chuckled. 'I really enjoyed that sort of work. It was outside. It was in the fresh air. There wasn't someone standing over you to make sure you were doing it perfectly, wonderfully, how they expected. I even remember thinking that there must be a bit of Island blood in me coming out — they have those big knives and they cut their grass very short — but not daring to tell anybody because I'd already cut off from that Island association and that European association. Thinking, I'm pretty handy with this sickle, I can get this grass pretty short, and then my whole world falling apart because I cut my finger. I actually got a few stitches. I've still got the scar today.' She chuckled again, holding it up for me to see.

Amelia liked the work too. 'Me and Nayda were always together, joined at the hips. We used to go down the rugby fields side by side, walking, turning these packs with fertiliser. They were strapped on our front. I'd strap up Nayda and she'd strap up me. We used to wear masks and hats cos by the time we got to the other end of the field and back, we were all dusty from the wind blowing the stuff in our hair and it used to hurt our face. Even though you had a mask around your mouth, it would still get in your eyes. You were shaded up — you looked like hoods actually — astronauts. It was good, though. Doing work hung-over to the max, cranking up these packs with fertiliser.'

When everyone got fed up trudging around on foot, I'd relent and drive the van up and down the fields while the others sat in the back with the doors open and a sack of fertiliser between them, flinging handfuls of the beige pellets left and right.

'A little voice would be saying to me, "You should be doing a good job,"' Gini said. 'But it would get wiped out by, "Oh c'mon, this is the easy way, let's do it and get out of here." I do remember a few of the schools complaining that we were doing this, or leaving piles of the stuff where it should have been spread evenly — dumped here, dumped there — and not even caring less about it, even though our job was on the line.'

Some schools appreciated our efforts. Junior remembered Te Aro School putting on afternoon tea. 'They were really rapt with us for the work we'd done,' she said. 'We had cut down all the banks and done all that for them. We got to meet the Deaf children in their classroom. It was such a privilege for us.'

I asked her if the girls usually worked hard.

She laughed. 'You're talking to the wrong person. Because we were so young, we'd get bored really fast and we'd slack around, but if we were trying to outbeat each other, we'd get right into it. Most of us loved scrub-cutting. We liked to get in and rip everything apart.'

Junior and I were sitting in the lounge of her rented house in Westport, having dispatched her three children to school. The older girl and boy were her ex-husband's, a Black Power member she'd met at church. The youngest, a chatty six-year-old, was a friend's son. Recording Junior's story had been in doubt till the last minute. When I rang her mother, her only phone contact, a few days before my agreed visit, she hadn't seen Junior or the kids for a week and had no idea when they'd be back. I flew down anyway, hoping she hadn't gone into hiding, and was relieved to see a woman in a brightly coloured jersey, baggy stretch pants and Ugg boots waving from the doorstep when I pulled up outside her house.

At 38, the high cheekbones and wide, gentle smile were all that remained of her youthful beauty, while her gravelly voice spoke of cigarettes and hard times. Chronic asthma, too, as I discovered when I drove the family up to Denniston in my rental car for a look, and she climbed wheezily to the top of the hill before lighting another cancer stick. We stared down the steep valley where coal had been shuttled to the coast, marvelling that people had given birth, brought up families, lived their whole lives in unlined huts on that isolated, windswept plateau. It was a degree of hardship that I could scarcely imagine.

Back in town, I bought takeaways for tea. The children's requests were painfully modest — one piece of fish, a hotdog — even though I urged them to have whatever they wanted. I sensed they weren't used to treats, or visitors like me. That night the girl, who seemed older than her 13 years, gave up her bed for me and I slept surrounded by posters of teenage heart-throbs.

Junior told me she'd rescued all her charges from abusive families, perhaps trying to make amends for not being around for her own son when he was growing up. 'That's when my life changed, when I saw that they needed someone,' she said proudly. 'And everybody told me I couldn't do it.'

She was right to be proud. For as long as I'd known her, she'd had trouble looking after herself, let alone anyone else. Like Gini and Tasi, she eventually turned to Jesus, but only after years in and out of jail. The evangelical church she'd joined in Rotorua had let her down. 'The men always supported one another,' she said, referring to sexual abuse and pornography. 'The women were there to serve. That was our leaders' motto.' What's more, half the church members came out of the gangs, reminding me once again that no matter how good the women's intentions, their pasts hounded them like a stalker.

When things got too bad, Junior left her husband and everything she owned, including her dog, and moved south to be near her mother who she hadn't seen for 20 years. That was a year before my visit. In her lounge, a tapestry of the Sacred Heart of Jesus in vibrant reds and purples hung on one wall. Expensive Māori arts and crafts were laid out on the tiled hearth and mantelpiece: patterned kete, bone jewellery, glossy kauri carvings given to her by Charmaine and others when she left Rotorua so she could open a craft shop. But it hadn't happened yet.

'What are your dreams for the future?' I asked.

'To have a big house full of kids that haven't got homes. And have a good man that will support my dream. Cos none of us have had a home. I've got no home. These kids got no homes. All my life that's all I wanted. Was a home.'

When Junior was conceived, her fate hung on a bet in a Temuka pub. If the baby was a boy, his birth parents would keep him; if it was a girl, they'd give her to her mother's cousin. When she was born, Junior was duly handed over.

Junior's adoptive mother worked at the local pottery factory. She was a proud woman, 'more Pākehāfied than Māori', who looked down on her daughter's birth family. 'We were brought up not to really associate with Māori. Even though the pā was only over the bridge, I was always taught that they were dirty. And my brothers and sisters were dirty little Māoris. Or they weren't good enough for our side of the bridge.'

Her adoptive father was a freezing worker, good with his hands. He was always making things. 'Three bass steel guitars. Carvings and not even carvings. Anything he done, he done it well. He made tables. Just really beautiful things. Pāua-shell things.' Junior's eyes softened when she spoke of him. 'He was awesome. He was the one who really wanted to adopt me and I was his pet.'

But he was often sick. 'He used to be like a tohunga.[1] He could see into the future, see things that other people couldn't see. He'd talk to his ancestors and chant a lot. He used to have fits. But he was never ever violent. He was the gentlest man out.'

When he was well, her father worked hard. 'But then he used to go off with his walking stick and start talking in Māori and going round the house and praying. So they'd say, he's gone a bit loopy. They didn't understand then, because we lost a lot of our reo[2] down south. They just thought, he's mad and stuck him in Sunnyside and filled him up with drugs.'

For seven years, Junior's father saved to build his wife 'the flashest house that any of the family had seen'. He added special touches for his daughter. 'He built a sliding window from their room into my room so I wouldn't be scared at night. Then he put

1   priest
2   language

stars on my wallpaper cos I used to sing "Twinkle Twinkle Little Star" with him. And he got the boys racing cars and Mum what she wanted. And then he died. At 34, 35. Young.' Her words skidded to a stop.

'How did he die?' I asked.

'Overdose,' she said quietly, fingering a large piece of greenstone that hung tight around her neck. Her breathing rattled in the silence. 'Pills. From the doctor's.'

More silence, then the words came tumbling out in bursts of exhaled air, sometimes slurred or muffled or in the wrong order, but conjuring up strong images. 'He knew he was going to do it. He knew that it was going to happen. I was home, I was sick with scarlet fever, something like that, some fever. So no one was allowed to come in. Except Dad. Dad come up. Then that day Mum was crying. And Dad came in all dressed up to go to the freezing works. Told me to sing this song, "Please Release Me", cos he liked that song. Elvis Presley. And that was the last time I saw him alive. Walked out the door. Mum was still crying. Then a taxi — in those days taxis would come up and give you bad news. And it turned up.'

It was the week before Christmas, the family's first in their new house. 'And he had already got Mum to get our presents and they put them in the hall cupboard.'

Junior was 10 years old. When her father's body was brought home, a small piece of white paper was still stuck to his cheek to cover a shaving nick. 'I remember taking it off and thinking, well, why isn't he getting up? I couldn't understand why I couldn't cry either. Everyone else was crying. Just didn't realise he was dead, I think.'

It was years before Junior found out that he'd committed suicide and understood why her grandfather hadn't taken him home to Ngāruawāhia. 'It's a tapu thing. They should die, proudly die, something like that. So he never went back.'

After the death of her father, Junior's story became depressingly familiar. I was struck by how many of the women lost a key carer between the ages of 10 and 13, on the verge of their teens. In every case, their lives — which had been hard before — became unbearable.

Junior's mother began to drink heavily. Her new partner beat her and they both beat Junior. When she started playing up at school, a teacher came round to see what was going on. After he left, they beat her again. Junior held out her left hand. The three middle fingers were bent and misshapen.

'Iron bar from the heater. For getting into trouble. It was my fault cos I went to go like this' — she put her hand up as if to protect her head — 'and they hit it and it broke my fingers. I had to go to hospital the next day. They didn't take me. Had to catch the bus into Timaru and go and get them fixed up. I had to say that I fell over.'

Surely someone questioned her story, I said.

'No. In those days you didn't. If you got a hiding, you got a hiding. End of story. You deserved it.' She gave a harsh, wheezy laugh.

Her stepfather's abuse 'was not just physical', and Junior took off so often, the local kids called her 'the runner', hiding her in broken-down shacks on the pā, bringing her food. When her cousins told their parents what was happening, an uncle went round to the house. 'Then it was time to move — and move fast.'

For the next two years, the family travelled up and down the country, mostly staying with relations. Junior was trapped in a grim cycle of abuse, running away, living on the streets and getting caught. Hidings distinguished one city from another like landmarks.

In Auckland, her stepfather beat her worse than usual. 'He used to hate my hair out. He used to tie it up in a rubberband so it really, really hurt and I let it out to go to school and he had watched down the road, dragged me back in, buckled me. So I had all these cuts from my back down to my legs and I was all bruised and cut up.'

Her friends took her to their aunty who went to the police station. Junior was sent to Bollard Girls Home but returned to her mother two weeks later. Her stepfather was never charged.

'They put on a really good performance for the social worker. I was called a liar even though I had the scars all over me. My mum and them were really good at, you know' — she put on a prim voice — "Junior's a bit slow for her age. Naive. And we're trying our best that we can for her." So it was time to go home and it was time to move again.'

In Wellington, they stayed in Newtown with her mother's alcoholic brothers. One day Junior went to the phone box to call her friends because once again she wasn't allowed out. 'There's this little Indian shop on the corner. And the only telephone. And across the road was the bus stop. My stepfather had followed me there and he smacked my head into the telephone and I split my head and then I took off. I ran to the zoo and ended up at Wellington Railway Station, and ended up joining up with the Mongrel Mob.' Her gang days had begun.

I'd been wondering how reliable the pictures in her mind were, so damning, yet so long ago. Now I had my answer. She'd just described my neighbourhood in impressive detail. I walked past that phone box on my way to work. I caught the bus at that stop by the zoo, bought milk and the Sunday paper from that dairy across the road. It was still owned by Indians.

What I found hard to comprehend was why Junior had moved back to Westport to be near her childhood tormentors. She wasn't the only one. As adults, almost all the women returned to the towns and cities where they grew up or where their whānau, or partner's whānau, lived. The pull of family suggested a deep need for connection and belonging that transcended even the most horrific abuse. In Junior's case, what she was escaping from may also have been worse than anything the past could throw at her.

I asked her how she got on with her parents now.

'I know that Mum, when she gets drunk, feels really guilty at what happened,' she said.

And her stepfather?

That raspy laugh again. 'Oh, we cope with each other. I just think, well you're too bloody old now. When I realised that it wasn't my shit — it was their shit and I shouldn't be carrying it — that's when I let everything go. Sometimes I get pissed off because I see the old stuff coming back with him. You know, the grumpiness and the yelling, and I don't trust him sometimes. And a lot of abuse of the old lady. But apart from that, I just keep away, and he tries to do these things for me, and I try and be nice to him, and it's only for my mother's sake I'm here.'

It was with trepidation that I met Junior's parents. Her mother was a tall, gaunt, quietly spoken woman with an air of sadness. In her seventies, she still worked as a cleaner. In her spare time, she biked everywhere, doing good works for elderly people in the town. Junior laughed. 'They're a bit younger than her.'

Perhaps it'd be easier to hate her stepfather, I thought, watching the muscly man in black shorts and singlet pushing a hand mower across the lawn. I could see why even the Black Power had been scared of him in his heyday. But he offered to fix Junior's washing machine while I was there, and brought round a video about Denniston for me to borrow when he heard my husband's grandmother had been born there. Kindnesses that unnerved me.

As I was leaving, Junior let slip that she'd decided to send the two boys back to Rotorua. 'I don't want them to grow up like I was, going back 20 years later and not knowing their family when they've got families that want to know, and they should know them. But then again, it's my own selfishness. What am I gonna do without them?'

'How do you know they'll be safe?' I asked, alarmed by what she'd told me about their circumstances.

She talked fast. 'They're much older and they've been back and forwards. They know I'm always here. They know that I'll always love them. And now the families have mellowed out a lot; they've straightened up over the years.' Then she said it all over again, as if trying to persuade us both that she could protect them, even from a distance.

SIX

MĀORI MATTERS

Annie and Bubbles were plotting ways to get 14-year-old Charmaine out of Weymouth Girls Home for the weekend. We were off to the first national hui of work cooperatives at Mōkai Marae near Taupō, and they wanted her to come too. I'd never met Charmaine, but she'd lived around the Black Power since she was 12. 'It was a whānau thing, rather than a gang thing,' she explained. 'Because I was the baby, an instinctive protection racket was put around me. Bubbles played a big part too as the Black Power mama. At the boys' discos, she'd tie me to her belt with a scarf to keep me safe.'

Annie had baulked when the young girl first turned up at her house. 'She kept nutting off, saying, "You've got to go home", Charmaine recalled. 'And I'd say, "I haven't got a home." My mother just lived up the road then, so I took Annie to meet her. I hadn't seen her for a couple of years. I said, "Hi, Mum, this is Annie." And my mother said, "I don't give a fuck if she's Queen fuckin' Victoria. Fuck off!" I said to Annie, "See! Let's go. I'm outta here. Later!"'

When Charmaine was caught and sent to the girls home, Annie and

Bubbles kept in touch with her. Now Annie rang and sweet-talked the Weymouth superintendent. 'There'll be heaps of Charmaine's friends at the hui,' I heard her say. 'She needs to see everyone again. When she gets out for good, we'll be the ones giving her a job and a place to stay. Well? No one else is offering, are they?' She listened for a while, then gave us a cautious thumbs-up. 'Getting her there's not a problem,' she went on. 'The Ponsonby Labour Co-op will pick her up in their bus and bring her back afterwards.'

'Lo and behold, they agreed to it,' Charmaine said. 'Cos they had nowhere else to send me. They kept saying prior to Aroha Trust that I was a prime candidate for Arohata [borstal] and I suited the profile really fine. So anyway this bus rocked in, picked me up and I jumped on that bus fast.' She laughed, pretending to issue instructions to the driver before anyone could change their mind. 'Close the door! Boot it! Get out of here! Go-o-o!'

All the way to Mōkai, the busload practised singing 'Tūtira Mai Ngā Iwi' for the pōwhiri. Charmaine's pure voice soared with excitement. Something good had happened for once. She was free for the weekend. She was off to see her mates.

I was looking forward to the hui too. I'd spent three months trying to hold onto my ideals in the face of the day-to-day muddle that was Aroha Trust. Now it was payback time: a few days off work, a trip away, a chance to enjoy our success and feel part of something bigger. I also hoped it would be good for me and Peter. Our relationship seemed to be going nowhere. He was always working or dealing with a crisis or heading off with the boys. I didn't want to live in his pocket, but I did want to go for a walk or to the movies or sit around sometimes, just the two of us. When I brought it up, he made me feel self-indulgent. None of the girls spent much time alone with their boyfriends. I needed to get used to the way things were round here.

It was late afternoon when our busload, about eight Aroha Trust girls and twice as many Black Power members, arrived at Mōkai. We milled around outside the main gate waiting to be welcomed onto the marae. The Ponsonby bus pulled up and a pretty young girl with auburn hair rushed down the steps and threw herself into Annie's arms. Then she bent down and picked up Rana and smothered her in kisses.

'Charmaine, this is Pip,' Annie said, drawing me into their circle.

Charmaine scowled. 'Is she one of us?'

Annie laughed. 'Yeah. Remember? I told you about her on the phone.'

'Hmmph,' said Charmaine, turning her back on me. She handed Rana to Nayda, hooked one arm through Bubbles' and the other through Annie's, and dragged them off to get her bags.

The hui was Bruce Stewart's idea. Bruce was an older man, an ex-con who ran another Wellington work trust, primarily for the Mongrel Mob, from Tapu Te Ranga, the urban marae he was building up. Bruce was always trying to unite the gangs. He'd been a key figure at Walton House, the combined pad where I'd thrilled to my first Black Power handshake.

But the house had imploded and now it was war as usual. Which was mad. The boys all came from the same backgrounds. They were brothers and cousins and whānau, alienated from society in the same ways, filled with the same frustration and anger that they wasted on wasting each other. They'd be no trouble at Mōkai, though: a truce would be called for a few days.

After a long wait, we were marshalled into two groups, men and women. I stuck close to the other girls and did what I was told. I wasn't used to being on marae. Tapu Te Ranga seemed too new, too lacking in history to count. For a while, we went there on Sunday nights to learn tikanga Māori. But we couldn't handle Bruce's paternalistic style. His women were usually in the kitchen, and the old ways he tried to teach us seemed at odds with our feminist principles. The traditional Māori warrior image might give the boys pride and mana, but the last thing we girls needed was anything that encouraged more macho strutting.

A kuia dressed in black called us onto the marae, 'Hāere mai, hāere mai, hāe-e-ere mai.' We shuffled slowly forward and were seated. Then the speeches began, all in Māori, all by men. We'd been up since dawn and the drone of the unfamiliar, lilting language where every word ends in a vowel tugged me towards sleep, only to be revived by the effortless harmonies of the waiata. Charmaine stood to sing with the Ponsonby group, her face radiant, all trace of the sulky girl gone.

Afterwards, we formed two long lines for the hongi. I watched anxiously for cues. Should I kiss cheeks or press noses, one press or two, eyes open or shut, mumble 'kia ora' or just nod? Finally, we ate at long trestle tables and laid our belongings on mattresses in the hushed meeting house. With a heavy heart, I watched Peter unroll his sleeping bag across the other side of the room. There was no space for me to join him.

Bruce, wearing his trademark blue overalls, stood up the front and scratched his straggly, salt-and-pepper beard. Bodies stretched and settled. Someone whispered, 'Remember not to sit on your pillow.'

Bruce began talking in his slow, jumbled drawl. 'We're not here just to kōrero, leave behind a big heap of words,' he said, challenging us to spend the afternoons working to repay our hosts, Ngāti Tūwharetoa and Ngāti Raukawa. 'Dignity and pride start when your sweat is dripping into the ground together and you are having fun together. Mahi is more than your work, it's your whole way of life.'

As night fell, other people rose to speak. The words were inspiring but the voices all male. Even if women had been allowed to speak inside the meeting house, none of us would have dared. We were young, shy and heavily outnumbered. Aroha Trust was the only women's work cooperative in the country, although the Christchurch co-op, Taua Mahi, had one team of women workers. It was good to catch up with those girls at the hui. Before we'd set up our trust, I'd gone down to get some tips from them. Out in the bush, scrub-cutting, they'd been decisive and hardcase, but back at the depot, around the guys, I saw their confidence drain away.

I'd also driven up to Auckland with Mike Womble and a quiet Black Power boy to check out the Ponsonby Labour Co-op. There, the few women working alongside the men seemed even more invisible. I'd come back convinced that we were right to go it alone rather than join forces with the Wellington Black Power. Not that they'd ever issued an invitation.

On that trip, we'd stayed in Ōtara. I'd never been there before.

'Let's go for a walk and have a nosey in the morning,' I said to the quiet Black Power boy sprawled on the couch.

'I'm not leavin' this house except by car,' he said.

'What's wrong with your legs?' I teased.

'It's too fuckin' dangerous out there.'

'What d'ya mean? I thought you were meant to be the mighty Black Power.'

'Not round here I'm not. Not on my own.'

'Then take your patch off. No one will know who you are.'

He gave me a scornful look. 'You can't just wear your patch when it suits, you know. You gotta wear it all the time.'

'That sounds more like a prison,' I said.

He shrugged and went back to watching TV.

Next morning at the hui, I sat on the edge of the veranda in front of the meeting house, enjoying the first surprising warmth of spring. Peter stood in a huddle on the lawn with the other trust leaders, all guys, mostly a bit older than me. I liked and admired each of them, but as a group I found them intimidating. They seemed so sure of themselves, so clear about what they were doing and why. I suspected they didn't take Aroha Trust seriously. I wasn't sure I took us seriously myself.

Annie walked over and plonked Rana in my lap.

'Can you mind baby?' she said. 'Charmaine's threatening to go on the run. Bubbles and I need to talk sense into her.'

I awkwardly hugged the little girl who looked on the verge of tears, and hoped Annie wouldn't be too long. Rana was cute and well-behaved, but children really weren't my thing.

After lunch, we split up into work teams. Determined not to end up peeling spuds, Bubbles and I volunteered to help paint the meeting house. I have a photo of us, two small figures in t-shirts and rolled-up jeans, perched on the edge of its sloping roof, our feet braced against the tiles. In the foreground is a carved Māori warrior gripping a long weapon. Our smiles show that we had no idea what was about to happen.

Within minutes, a kuia strode outside and started shouting and waving her fist at us. Bewildered, I scrambled down. Bubbles — who rarely took orders from anyone — followed meekly. It took some time to work out what we'd done wrong. Women weren't allowed on the roof. It was disrespectful. It had sexual connotations. Something to do with the building being male. Menstruation came into it too: our very presence was unclean.

I felt foolish and secretly pissed off. Everyone had watched us get up there; someone had taken photos. If it was so out of bounds, why hadn't we been told earlier? And why was it women who had to stay on the ground? To me it seemed like another convenient excuse to keep us in our place, to stop us reaching for the sky.

Looking back, Bubbles and I weren't the only ones who didn't know the proper marae protocol. Nor did most of the other people at the hui. The work trust leaders were mainly Pākehā, sympathetic to the aspirations of tangata whenua, but unfamiliar with their culture and tikanga. The trust members were mostly Māori disconnected from their roots.

As Charmaine said, 'Aroha Trust gave us the vehicle to be educated as women. We were all looking for an answer that would make the world a better place. But no Māori subjects were spoken about. There were a lot of hui being held with government and gangs, a lot of hui being held with the women. Crikey! Left-wing politics! I knew all about bloody what's his face, Karl Marx, before I even knew who the prime minister of my own country was. I remember the dude came to do the Corso binge and how to fight for the rights of the South African people. So here we were campaigning about workers' rights, campaigning about the disempowerment of black people in the world, but we still hadn't come home to Māori rights.'

That homecoming began in the years after Aroha Trust in the form of kōhanga reo and kura kaupapa, Treaty settlements, forestry and fishery deals, the designation of Māori as an official language, Māori radio and television. Google 'Mōkai Marae' now and you'll see that its iwi list horticulture, geothermal power, sustainable farming and broadband internet among their business ventures. The website has a photo of the meeting house that Bubbles and I clambered over, beautifully restored.

I bet well-meaning, ignorant young volunteers like us would never get near its roof today.

When it came time to say goodbye, Charmaine clung to Bubbles.

Annie gently pulled her off. 'You gotta go, Charmaine. If you fuck up now, you'll blow your chances of coming to live with us. We'll save you a job, I promise.'

Weeping quietly, Charmaine allowed herself to be led away. As the Ponsonby bus drove through the gates, she stood looking out the back window, a small, forlorn figure being returned to captivity.

'It was the hardest thing for me to do,' she said, remembering. 'But I hopped back on that bus because I knew I had something to look forward to.'

On the Wellington bus, I chose a seat by myself, propped my pillow against the cool glass and closed my eyes, hoping Peter would come and sit beside me. I fell asleep to the hum of rubber on asphalt and the sound of Tasi strumming her guitar. When I woke, it was dark outside and I was still sitting alone.

Two months later, Weymouth released Charmaine into Annie's care. At 15, she became the youngest member of Aroha Trust. Thinking back, Annie shook her head in disbelief. 'It was totally crazy they gave us a young woman and we were only young women ourselves. Knowing who we lived with and who we knew. It must have been crazy.'

CHARMAINE'S STORY

Pukenuiaraho te maunga
Waiotahe te awa
Ohiwa te moana
Ūpokorehe te hapū
Te Rangi Matoru me Mataatua oku waka
Te Hapuoneone te iwi

'I was saved by the letter E,' Charmaine joked. 'My mum didn't want to give me a Māori name because there was a lot of racism around. She was working with a French woman at Hygea Laundromat in Newtown who said to her, "Call her Charmaine. It means the lucky one. But make sure it's got an E. Without an E, it means streetwalker."' She gave a loud cackle, rat-a-tat-tat, like a machine gun.

We were sitting in the lounge of her Rotorua house on a warm February morning in 2000. On one wall was a poster of Te Tiriti o Waitangi, on another the Declaration of Independence of New Zealand signed five years earlier, recognising the sovereignty of the northern tribes.

The house was full of flax. Charmaine was an accomplished weaver, with a Bachelor of Rāranga from Waiariki Polytech. Not a day went by, she said, when she didn't have a piece of harakeke in her hands.

We'd been talking non-stop since I'd arrived the night before — or rather, Charmaine had. My main concern was to stop her telling all her stories before I could tape them, although the stock seemed limitless.

Two of her four children lived with their respective fathers, the other two with her. In the morning, Charmaine was too nervous to eat; she'd had several sleepless nights, she said. Not at the prospect of seeing me again after 20 years, but because she knew the power of bringing up the past.

When I turned on the tape recorder, Charmaine spent a long time talking about her childhood while I struggled to keep up with the large cast of characters.

Charmaine's father was a Norwegian who already had a wife and baby. Her mother, from Te Whānau ā Apanui, was too ashamed to tell her parents she was pregnant again: they were already looking after her first child. Instead, she promised the baby to a Tūhoe relation who couldn't have children of her own.

'It wasn't a light decision and it wasn't made in the flash of the pan,' Charmaine said. Her Tūhoe grandmother came to stay with her birth mother for two weeks to make sure she knew what she was doing and to strengthen the baby's whakapapa because she was going from one iwi to another. 'In Māori terms, that's a big transition to have a baby released outside the tribal system.'

To legalise the adoption, Charmaine's whāngai mother married a Pākehā. 'She knew in the eyes of the system, if she'd had a Māori man, there's no way they would have given her the baby.' Later I went looking for proof of this claim, and was shocked to discover that Māori were legally forbidden to adopt Pākehā babies until 1955. Although Charmaine was born seven years later, of mixed race, laws are easier to change than attitudes, and she may well have been right.

After nine months, the marriage failed and Charmaine was sent to live with her whāngai mother's eldest sister in Rotorua. Meanwhile, her birth grandmother had died 'of a broken heart' when she learned her first granddaughter had been given away.

Word went out that Te Whānau ā Apanui wanted the baby back, but Tūhoe concealed her, Charmaine said. 'They took me into the hills, they took me everywhere. They hid me, they hid me, as the baby they hid me, so that they couldn't find me.' Charmaine's voice was dramatic and insistent. Almost everything she said, she said at least twice, often three or four times, sometimes in both English and Māori, a wall of words that threatened to overwhelm me.

Charmaine's arrival put enormous pressure on her aunty who had an alcoholic husband and 'was really rigid in her ways'. Charmaine became the scapegoat. 'Whenever something went wrong, I got the blame, I got the bashing. And I can remember reading a report from Social Welfare when they pulled in to see me, and it said, "This is the most pathetic and sad-looking baby I've ever seen."'

One hiding stood out in Charmaine's mind. 'I can remember my aunty saying, "Why aren't you like the rest of us?" and beating the shit out of me with a shoe until from my chest upwards was covered in black and I was under the hedge whimpering. My cousin saw me and she screamed, "Look what you've done to this fuckin' kid." So she ran out on the road knowing that there was another aunty going past in the car and waved the car and put me in the car with the aunty. That's the worst horrific bruising she can ever remember seeing on any one child.'

'Did the aunty in the car do anything to stop the beatings?' I asked.

'No, we hide everything.' Charmaine's voice seethed with exasperation.

'Did anyone take you to hospital?' In too many of the women's stories, adults stood by while children were abused.

'No.'

'No other adult came to your assistance?'

'No.' Charmaine paused. Then she said, 'My nanny. My nanny took me and healed me.' This was the woman who'd spent two weeks talking to Charmaine's birth mother before the baby was handed over. 'She used to give me all this rongoā to drink. Bush medicine. We didn't go to Pākehā doctors. Everything about my life growing up until my grandmother died was all Māori.'

Years later, Charmaine asked her aunty why she'd stayed with her alcoholic husband. 'She said, "I married him for better, for worse." That is a statement that isn't said lightly. Meaning — in terms of her being raised in the traditions of the old people and being a vessel of that knowledge — they had to honour their word. Pen and paper is important to the Pākehā, but in the Māori world, you said something, you did it. The power of the word was paramount.'

I felt myself bristle. Charmaine judged almost everything in terms of Māori and Pākehā. I, too, come from a tradition that believes in keeping your word and the sanctity of marriage, I wanted to say. And where's the honour in being loyal to a drunken man until you get so stressed out you beat an innocent child black and blue?

When Charmaine was four, her grandmother became so concerned that she summoned Charmaine's whāngai mother to take the little girl back to Wellington. 'But I interfered with drink time, I interfered with a lot of things. A child does.' Finally, with all other options exhausted, her grandmother brought her into her own home where she already cared for two other grandchildren and her intellectually disabled adult daughter.

For Charmaine, these were the lucky years. 'I loved it with my nan. I was always around kuia. They all had moko. I was in that world with the old people. That was a lovely world to be in.'

I wondered how a woman in her sixties had coped with all her charges. Charmaine must have been a troubled child. At her aunty's, she'd spent hours alone on a rocking horse. 'I'd rock and rock and rock until I couldn't keep my eyes open, then fall off and go to sleep. And I would always cry. I was a real cry baby.'

But discipline was not an issue, she said. 'My nan never said a mean word. My nan raised us with tikanga. My nan never ever had to hit a child. She would just give you a look and you knew very well, and put your head down. She was not a screaming meemee.'

Charmaine's first toy was a duck woven by her grandmother. 'We call it rakiraki[1] quack quack. And we'd be naughty, well rakiraki smack smack. But it was in jest, eh. My nanny never ever once had to say, "I love you." You just knew that.'

A gentleness crept into her voice. 'My nan was a very hard worker. My nan raised the four of us. At the same time, her floors were so polished and so bright, you could eat off them. She was a very proud woman. Very hard-working. She had a kai garden that would feed us. My nan was also really creative. She was a weaver, so I spent a lot of time with her, all the time preparing. She'd

---

1   duck

always tell us stories. And come a certain time of the year, we'd all sleep on the whāriki[1] outside under the stars. My nan was really protective of us. Nobody but nobody touched her mokopuna.[2] No school. No whānau. No one. She was staunch on that. She oozed with charisma, with a kind of power, an energy force around her. In terms of her tribal standing, she was very respected.'

Charmaine's grandmother taught her to pray and encouraged her spiritual experiences, including visions. 'She would nurture the strength of my taha wairua[3] where I never doubted for a moment what I saw. She was my doctor, my nurse, my psychotherapist, my dream interpreter; she was everything. And she told me, always speak with your heart and you'll never go wrong. When you are right, stand your ground and don't give a piece of dirt to nobody. When you are wrong, be humble. I've always lived by that.'

I nodded knowingly, remembering how stubborn and sharp-tongued Charmaine could be, but also her sense of justice and courage in naming the truth.

At primary school, Charmaine quickly learnt to bridge her two worlds, Māori and Pākehā. 'I used to have to go home and teach whatever I learnt at school. My nan could write, but she struggled with it. By the time I was about eight, my writing and my nanny's writing were the same, so I could forge her signature to say I'd done homework and I hadn't.'

At the same time, Charmaine could do waiata and poi, and took rēwena bread and other Māori food to school. 'Me and my nan would put the safety pins on me and off I'd go with my bag of tītiko — periwinkles I think is the Pākehā name for them. All the kids would tease me, "Oh, you're eating snails." There was a Māori teacher married to a Pākehā woman. He'd come over and trade lunches cos he'd get hungry for kai Māori. He'd give me a

---

1   woven mat
2   grandchildren
3   spirituality

cheese bread for a bag of tītikos. What a rip-off!'

She threw her head back and cackled again, sending her long hair rippling down her back. It was the same hair, plaited by her grandmother, that Charmaine stuck up a horse's nose on her way home from school one day. A photo appeared on the front page of the local paper with the caption, 'How to make a horse laugh.' Her nanny kept it till she died.

Charmaine was 10. 'I can remember they'd taken me up to the hospital to see her. And I looked at her and I could wrap my thumb and my finger around her wrist. Like this.' She made an 'O' with her thumb and middle finger. 'That told me just how little she was. I said, "Nanny, you come home, they're not giving you a kai." And she cried. And she died within days of that.'

Tears streamed down Charmaine's face. 'My world shattered. She was my mountain, she was my world, she was everything that I could ever dream of in terms of innate knowledge of things Māori. She gave me a whole lot of spiritual food that has never let me down to try and protect me from what was yet to come.'

Charmaine was speaking more and more in Māori. I couldn't understand all the words, but I knew they embodied her grandmother's love and her own identity. 'Everywhere I went in taha Māori, I never had to say what my name was. They all knew te whānau ā Tauwhiri.[1] Not like the Pākehā world,' she said scornfully. 'You've got to get up and give your name, say who you are and that still doesn't add to jack shit. In our world it means everything.'

Charmaine was sent back to her mother, now living in Rotorua. There her luck ran out again. 'Life turned to shit. There were wild parties. I'd have to sleep on the roof cos she had all these nutters running through trying to chase me, wanting to do all sorts of crazy numbers. Violence. It was horrific. I started going wild from there. I had to steal my food, steal my money, buy my own

---

1   Charmaine's grandmother's family

clothes, buy my own books, cos she was always in the pub.'

Once Charmaine got caught stealing chocolate. A policeman took her home. 'No one was there of course. It was all dark and empty. I said, "You'll have to give me a leg up so I can climb in the window, I've locked myself out." I open the door and he goes, "Where's your mother?" I said, "She's in the pub. You take me to DeBretts and I'll show you which one she is." And he wouldn't. He said, "I'll be back in the morning." He quite happily left me there alone.'

After the pub, her mother would bring the party back to the house. 'My mum could be so undignified. She'd try and get me to kiss all these people that were drunk, to say hello, then she'd make excuses cos I'd get really grumpy and aggro. She'd say, "She's just shy".' Charmaine put on a surly teenage voice. 'No, I'm fuckin' not. I hate it.'

When her mother got breast cancer, Charmaine was sent to yet another aunty in Wellington, her sixth home in a decade. 'I turned up, Māori girl, and I had all the rongoā Nan had given me before she died, from the tohunga. She tipped it all out. She didn't want nothing to do with taha Māori, even though she's fluent in te reo Māori. "Oh, I don't want anything to do with those bungle jungle ways." That was the last piece of my nan, apart from my hair. My hair was really long, down behind my knees, when I got to Wellington. My nan always preened my hair. She loved it.'

Charmaine lived in Newtown and went to South Wellington Intermediate. 'That was really hard,' she said. 'I went from a marae-based life into this place down in the city.' She pushed a school photo in front of me. 'See!' Among the rows of white faces was only one other Māori girl.

'No one took into account my grieving,' she said. 'I was grieving for my grandmother, but no one ever asked me what that was like for me. I was just expected to adapt to all these changes.'

One day Charmaine phoned a boy in her class about a school

project. Her aunt was enraged. 'She beat the shit out of me for about three hours non-stop calling me all the sluts under the sun. And I didn't even know what a slut was.'

When her uncle tried to defend her, the hidings got worse. 'She would see that as him having an attraction to me, and so she had to make me really ugly. So my hair got cut off. She attacked it with a butcher knife cos people used to say what beautiful hair.'

Tasi, Junior and now Charmaine. On the brink of adolescence, their long hair incensed their caregivers to the point of violence. For Charmaine — like the others — it was one outrage too many. She ran away: life on the streets was preferable.

The tape ended, and Charmaine went out to have a cigarette. I tried to make sense of her story. Her grandmother seemed so strong and capable, steeped in tradition and tikanga Māori. But her mother and aunties seemed overwhelmed by bad choices, dysfunctional relationships, alcoholism and violence. How had things deteriorated so badly so fast?

'My mother's generation got caught in what I call the wave of confusion,' Charmaine said when she came back. 'Big-time confusion. They took the brunt of being Māori, they took the brunt of speaking Māori and being bashed at school. They knew to be Māori wasn't going to help their children. Te reo Māori wasn't acknowledged as the reo of this land. They had come from a whole history of confiscated lands. They'd come from a whole history of everything traditional being absolutely mutilated through acts of what I call cultural genocide.'

To cope, they married white people, gave their children Pākehā names, spoke in English to them. Charmaine's mother even changed her Māori name to Jean by deed poll. 'These were all the acts that started to seep within the walls of our homes. They were pushing for us to learn things Pākehā. Even though it would cut their souls.'

That night, Charmaine and I adjourned to a Rotorua bar. The

talkathon continued: apart from a few hours' sleep, we'd been going for 30 hours. I reached for a glass of wine. Charmaine ordered coffee; she hadn't had a drink for nine years, not since going through the Taha Māori alcohol programme at Hanmer Springs.

'It gave me back my life,' she said. 'For the first time someone actually asked me my story. No one had ever asked that question before.'

Her need to talk began to make sense.

Social Welfare paid for Charmaine's children to go to the Prince of Wales health camp while she was at Hanmer, and for all the treatment she needed. 'They paid,' she said with venom. 'That was the first sign of validation that I wasn't going mad, it really happened.'

Charmaine had two spells at Hanmer, the first for three months, the second for six weeks. 'It feels like open-heart surgery. I inherited an amazing whakapapa through Tūhoe; I inherited alcoholism and pain as well. I was angry at the system, angry at how alcohol had flooded through the whole Māori nation and had destroyed the lives of a whole lot of children. No one could talk about the pain; the only way was to get drunk. It was about powerlessness. I had ended up the same.'

At Hanmer, Charmaine began to find answers. 'I understood the isms of alcohol and the behaviours and the patterns. I was able to forgive my mother. I understood that I was consistently used as the scapegoat for anyone and everyone; I'd become the burden of that pain. I no longer accept that role. Secrets keep people sick and so we don't have secrets today. It was really, really empowering. I was able to grieve and grieve safely without anyone stopping the process of that grieving.'

It was there for the first time that Charmaine also heard men talk about their pain. 'That blew me away. I saw they had been subjected to the same acts of violence that could be perpetuated on children; their story was no different than mine.'

As we wandered home through the dark streets, I wished

there was someone in her life to love her now. We lay in our separate beds, still shouting to each other across the hall. I tried to outlast her. To go to sleep would mean that I, too, had stopped listening.

By lunchtime the next day, I was getting agitated. We'd been driving round for an hour looking for a guitar. Charmaine's mates weren't home or they'd been meaning to fix the strings on theirs for ages, or they'd lent it to someone who hadn't given it back. Now I felt exhausted, with a three-hour drive to Ngāruawāhia ahead of me to see Jane. But first, Charmaine wanted to sing.

Success at last: a ponytailed, beneficiary-advocate friend had the elusive instrument. Back at her house, Charmaine strummed a few chords as she introduced a song she'd written years before. 'This one's called "Blessed is the Child". It's about the qualities that create a healthy child. It's not money. It's not all these nice clothes. It's about being emotionally available.' Her voice, its purity undiminished by years of smoking, ached with longing and conviction as she sang the haunting melody:

Blessed is the child with amazing grace
And blessed is the child with no one's shame on her face
The eyes will tell the window to the soul
Blessed is the child who's allowed to grow.

Blessed is the child in a loving home
And blessed is the child who knows no anger in her soul
Time will tell and time will surely show
Blessed is the child who's allowed to grow.

Blessed is the child who can feel her way
And blessed is the child who knows how to say
I'm in pain, please don't go away
Hold me in your arms, please don't push me away.

As I left, Charmaine pressed a pair of tiny kete earrings into my hand. I knew they took as long to weave as a full-sized basket. My last glimpse was the 'For Sale' sign on her front fence. The landlord was selling up. Charmaine and her children had to find somewhere else to live.

SEVEN

LOCKED-UP LONELINESS

Annie pulled a bottle of milk out of the fridge and sniffed it, then crouched down and checked her toast under the grill. Her creased white uniform poked out from beneath a baggy grey jersey. How she'd managed to pass her final nursing exams living in our overcrowded flat with a steady stream of gang members coming through, I'd never know. Now she had to do six months' practical work at the hospital to qualify.

'That guy from the Engineers' Union rang last night,' she said. 'The one who rents out their houses.'

My early-morning fug lifted. We'd been looking for our own place for ages: a house where the girls would be the tenants and Aroha Trust would make the rules. Men would be allowed to visit, even stay the odd night, but on our terms for a change.

'I gave him a bit of a sob story,' Annie went on. 'Told him there's girls living on the fuckin' streets, and squatting, and doing God knows what for a bed. Well, I didn't say "fuck" but—'

'Well done! What did he say?'

'He was really sweet. Sounded quite worried about us.'

She piled two teaspoons of sugar into her tea and stirred vigorously. Outside it was still dark. Annie was on morning shift, but as usual she was running late. Warming my hands in front of the bar heater, I watched her move around the kitchen, loose-limbed, her small breasts far more suitable than mine for those bra-burning days.

I envied her brisk confidence. It was there when she stood at the bench, elbows splayed, spreading butter across her toast with quick, strong strokes, giving it her full attention. And it would be there when she strode out the door and down the street — as if she was six foot tall and bulletproof, not a skinny little white girl. It wasn't arrogance so much as a deep sense of her right to be there. She didn't seem to notice or care what others thought; she never tried to fill silences or smile if she wasn't in the mood.

But she drew people to her. 'Annie was my healing to things Pākehā,' Gini said later, the ultimate compliment. She brought out qualities they didn't know they had. She made them believe in themselves — and they loved her for it. So did I.

'What else did he say?' I asked.

She grinned at me triumphantly. 'They've got a place at the top of Abel Smith Street. It's being done up. We can move in when it's finished.'

'Shit-hot!' I shouted, forgetting the rest of the household was still asleep. 'What it's like?'

'Four bedrooms, that's all I know. We can go and have a look tomorrow.' She laced up one white shoe, then the other and threw her plate in the sink. 'We need to make plans. I'll come and sleep in your bed tonight, eh.' She narrowed her eyes at me. 'Unless you get a better offer.'

'I wish.'

'Like that, is it? Never mind, pal. You'll work it out.' She swigged the last of her tea and was gone.

Annie often came and slept with me at night. I was never sure if she really wanted my company, or she and Mike had had a fight, or she just felt like a change of scene, but I was always glad to see her. We'd yak for hours about everything — except our love lives. I didn't tell her about my problems with Peter and I knew little about what went on between her and Mike. She was an intensely private person. But I too kept my feelings to myself. What happened in my heart was no one's business but my own.

That night we lay in the dark talking about our new house. Both of us would move in and have our own bedrooms, we agreed, the only concession to our seniority. If others were happy to share, at least four other girls could come as well.

'It'll be cool,' Annie said. 'We can have our meetings there and hang out together after work. No one'll get kicked out if they have a fight with their man. And you won't have to run around town picking everyone up in the mornings.' She turned onto her side and propped her cheek on her elbow. 'I want to come and work with you fullas now.'

'Not long to go,' I said, although another six months running the trust on my own seemed like an eternity.

'I'm sick of sick people. And as for fuckin' shift work—'

'You're not going to chuck it in, are ya?' Desperate as I was for her to join me, I couldn't imagine anyone not completing something as big as a three-year nursing diploma, especially when they were so close to the finish line.

There was a long silence. 'I can always come back to it later,' she said at last.

'Shit! You are serious.' I fumbled on the floor for my smokes, feeling excited and vaguely guilty at the same time. Everything was falling into place. Annie coming to work for the trust. Our own house. There was only one problem. 'What will you and Mike do when we move?'

'He's going to go back to Brougham Street. Mike Hancock's due home from India in a couple of weeks and there's room for him there as well. Did I tell you we got a letter from him yesterday? He signed it Mike Footcunt.'

I chuckled. I was looking forward to meeting this other Mike who'd lived with Annie and the Wombles before going off on his OE. I lit two cigarettes, passed her one and lay on my back trying to blow smoke rings at the ceiling, an art I never mastered. It was my turn to be quiet. Annie and Mike had been the one sure thing in the scene since I'd arrived. Without them as a couple, the world seemed a harsher, more unreliable place.

'What?' said Annie.

'It's just that you and Mike have been together for as long as I've known you.'

'Well, he can't come and live in an all-woman house, can he? Cheer up, Pipi! I could do with a bit of space.'

Halfway along Epuni Street, I turned left up a long, overgrown, unlit path. A dog barked and I froze. Peter's Doberman, Che, barrelled round the corner, wagging his tail. I patted him half-heartedly, hoping he wouldn't jump up on me: I was about as good with animals as I was with children. The other girls loved him. Sometimes, they'd bring him to work. If they were broke, they'd tie a note for Peter round his neck first: 'To my owner: Can you please give me some lunch money?'

I could hear Peter calling Che. When I came round the corner, he was standing at the door of the tumble-down, two-storey wooden house he shared with a bunch of young ones, the place so full they'd often be sleeping wall-to-wall in the lounge. He stopped mid-whistle, looking surprised and, I hoped, guilty when he saw me.

'What's up?' he said.

'We need to talk.' After the hui at Mōkai, I'd written him a letter. He hadn't replied. I was sick of dreaming up excuses for him. I'd come to call it quits.

If I hoped he might try to make me change my mind, I was disappointed. But we talked for a long time, our tongues freed by our new honesty. I was angry with him for being too gutless to call it off, and angrier with myself for taking so long to see the truth. It was the idea of him I'd fallen for, not the person. I'd learned that you can't think your way into love, you can't cram it into a convenient shape to fit your needs or prop up some image of who you'd like to be or who you'd like to be with. The head had to follow the heart, not the other way round.

It was after midnight when I went to leave.

'You can't walk home by yourself at this hour,' he said.

I raised my eyebrows — it was a bit late for him to be concerned about my well-being now — but I didn't need much convincing to stay. I was glad we'd stopped pretending, but I was sad too. Tomorrow was soon enough to be single.

On the day of the shift to our new home, we loaded our belongings into the Red Baron — the nickname the girls had given the red J4 Austin van with a broad white stripe round its body that I bought off an old student friend for 50 bucks — and drove to Abel Smith Street on the southern edge of the city. The Black Power sergeant-at-arms, his fierceness softened by a kind face and frizz of black hair topped with a colourful bandana, set himself up in a sagging armchair on the veranda. In the months that followed, we'd often find him there when we got home from work, a self-appointed security guard.

Gini, Annie, Tasi, Junior and I moved in that first day with Gerry, a serious 17-year-old who had a two-year-old daughter. The only rule was that you had to be a member of Aroha Trust. That meant you were earning and could pay board, and you accepted our collective principles, at least in theory.

Gini's bedroom fronted onto the quiet, leafy street. It was big, with a bay window and a fireplace. 'I reckon I got the nicest room in the whole house,' she remembers. 'I had it all to myself. I felt quite privileged, to tell you the truth. I'd never been in a nice house as such, where you could do whatever you want in that room. Keep it clean, keep it messy, that was your room. And I remember feeling safe and secure there most of the time.'

Junior loved it too. 'Me and Tasi. We didn't have anywhere else to go. It gave us the best time of our lives actually. Scrub-cutting, getting off the streets, having fun and having our own bed to come back to.'

I took the bedroom past the kitchen. One wall was papered in a swirling black and gold pattern. I painted the other walls black to match. Not out of allegiance to the Black Power, I don't think, but because it seemed sophisticated. And because I was overdue to paint a bedroom. When I'd first gone to Dunedin, I'd moved into a dingy little room in my brother's flat. One night at tea, I announced my plans to brighten it up with a coat of paint.

'That's a bit bourgeois, isn't it?' he'd scoffed. 'I thought socialists weren't meant to care about their surroundings. What about the poor people who can't afford paint?'

I was deflated. He was right. Doing up the room was a self-indulgent whim. I never mentioned it again.

Annie bagged the attic room at the top of a small staircase, halfway along the hall. Within months, a quiet 16-year-old would cower in the far corner reliving the horror of being raped there by a senior Black Power member while the rest of us slept. A shivering ball of pain, she babbled incoherently, swigging whisky straight from a 40-ounce bottle. All night we kept vigil. But if anyone tried to reach out and touch her, she screamed 'GET AWAY FROM ME', her eyes gleaming with terror. Our job was simply to bear witness. I marvelled at the other girls' ability to absorb her suffering without flinching. I felt like a novice in the presence of masters.

Eventually, she passed out from alcohol and exhaustion. The next evening, she appeared downstairs, wan and crushed and reticent.

Looking back, I can understand why she didn't want to talk. We didn't have the skills to deal with her distress; she was just protecting herself. There was no way she would go to the cops either. No one went to the cops. What happened in the scene stayed in the scene. And if anyone had doubts about misguided loyalty, fear of retribution kept their mouth shut.

It concerns me now that we didn't make sure that young girl got help. A few years ago, she died of an alcohol-related condition.

Perhaps we waited for her to reach out. Perhaps we didn't know who to turn to. Perhaps we tried to get her to talk to someone and she refused. I don't remember. What I do recall is how isolated we were. We relied on our own resources, rarely seeking or being offered assistance.

I checked Annie's memories of the relationship between outside agencies and Aroha Trust.

'I don't think they would have been interested and I don't think we wanted them in our lives,' she said.

We trusted no one. Social workers, probation officers, cops, shrinks — they were all the enemy. I bought into this attitude as much as anyone. The way we were treated by people in authority fuelled my antagonism as much as the other girls'. But I had another reason too: I was scared of being seduced by the establishment.

The first time the cops raided the youth centre house I ran in South Dunedin, a policeman about the same age as my father took me aside. He told me that I was out of my depth, I should look after myself, there was nothing I could do to help the young hooligans living there. Overwhelmed by his concern, and afraid that he might be right, I burst into tears. Looking over his shoulder as he patted me kindly on the back, I saw the bewildered faces of my young charges. It was the last time I let my guard down in front of the police.

When I came back to Wellington, I severed my ties with mainstream society even more. I continued to visit my parents and see Pat from time to time, but for the most part I lived in the city's underworld. Still, the establishment was part of me. I'd been one of its success stories. I saw life through its eyes. I was scared that, if I let it in, I would not be strong enough to resist its logic. It might pick me off, make me betray the young women I'd chosen to stand beside. It was easier to reject all its representatives out of hand.

When Charmaine was released from Weymouth, she flew straight to Wellington and moved into Abel Smith Street too. 'It was really neat,' she remembered. 'About three carloads of everyone turned up at the airport to welcome me back, and away I rocked with the trust. And we started scrub-cutting. I was glad to have employment. For the first time in my life, it meant I didn't have to steal to survive.'

At the time, I had no idea why Charmaine had been in the girls home. Years later, when I recorded her story, she filled me in. After her aunty butchered her hair, she'd run away and joined the street kids.

'One night I was going up town. I remember it was a really cold winter night, Wellington night, and there was this Pākehā girl and she was quite confident in herself and quite cocky and quite everything else. She called me a black bitch and the words of my aunty's just rang in my head and my head exploded. I attacked the shit out of her. I wasted her. I kept wasting her and wasting her. It was like she had become the pillar of all my pain. Just those words at that time, and I was on the streets, nowhere to go, no home and all the violence. Not understanding, no one to talk to.'

The girl ended up in hospital. 'From then on, the police were hunting me like a wild pig. They found me about six months later and the girl's uncle was a cop so I got a good bash, and then I got sent to court for assault. From there I was starting to see the ugly side of the system. The judge rubbished the shit out of me and I got my first nine months in the girls home.'

The term 'girls home' gave the wrong impression, she said. 'You spent so much time in lock-up, it was jail. Those little cells were hidden from the public eye, so on the front you see this nice little house and all those people running round looking really, really nice and underneath it all was a dungeon.'

Charmaine said she was kept in that dungeon for the first six weeks, and much of the next two years. I asked her what it was like.

'Cold. It taught me about hate. I just got to sleep a lot on concrete floors.'

The cells had bars on the windows, a steel bed, toilet, table and mirror. Nothing else. 'You stayed there and put on this smock and these degrading underpants. They took the mattress away at half-past six in the morning. So I'd curl up back into a ball and rock myself to sleep. I slept most of my time in the cells.'

When Charmaine finally made it up to the main house, the other girls gave her a hiding. 'That's just part of the initiation.' Although she was still a virgin, she was sent to the VD clinic. 'You all get lined up and this guy shoves your feet into these stirrups and shoves all these steel things inside of you. Just really horrible. Fuck, it blew my world out of the water.'

All the women gave similar accounts of being taken into care. Whether or not they'd committed a crime, they'd be searched, deloused, checked by a doctor, have chemicals rubbed into their hair, and kept in isolation. Why? For their own protection. Until they calmed down. To punish them. To show them who was boss.

When Gini found herself in the cells at Miramar Girls Home, she felt like she'd exchanged one cage for another. 'Not like the prison at home with the abuse, but locked-up loneliness.'

Tasi agreed. 'I just wanted to hurt somebody. I thought, how dare they? I haven't done nothing wrong.'

Gini remembered lying on the bed after she was sent back to the cells for fighting. 'There was only a bed in this little room, and all the rest was brick wall and a little window you could see the daylight out of. That was the first time I ever remember feeling alone, all on my own, with nobody or nothing. Having no worldly possessions, nobody that cares about you, nobody even knows you're there, your family or anything. So I thought about this God. I thought, are you out there somewhere? Where are you? There were magazines in this cell, but I didn't want to do anything because I felt helpless, I felt like a lost sheep, waiting for the guard to come past and give me some food or waiting to hear the ring of the bells, a sign of life, or somebody out there.'

At first I was sceptical about the amount of time the women said they spent in the cells — secure unit, security, lock-up, clinic, solitary — all different names for the same thing. But their stories were remarkably consistent. Slowly, I realised that while I was growing up in Godzone, young people in the care of the state were routinely isolated for days, weeks and sometimes months, with no stimulation, no visitors, no time limits and no rights of appeal.

Even so, for Gini it was better than what she'd left behind. The Māori women wardens reminded her of her mother. Compared with her father's discipline, the rules and punishments were tame. Most important, she had her own bed. 'I knew that nobody was going to come and wake me up in the night and have sex. Ughh.'

Sometimes she deliberately set out to be sent to the cells, 'because a friend was down there or I needed time out or just because going down there added to your reputation of being the toughy or the kingpin of the house.'

Nearly 17, Gini was older than most of the other girls, and certainly harder. 'If they had things I wanted or liked — like a ring or watch or jewellery or pieces of clothing — I'd just take it. And if they still wouldn't give it, we'd end up fighting. I was so sure of myself that I could fight. Because of all the physical abuse from my father, I felt like I could handle any form of pain. I mean, what's a few punches in the nose when you've had it with the axe handle all around your body?'

She kept pushing the boundaries. 'Getting down the solitary was one thing, but what else could they do?' Sometimes the girls had food fights when they were let into a larger cell for meals. 'Chucking the food everywhere — just going for it. What the heck? Who cares? They can clean it up. This is their cell. There's no way we're going to lift a hand to clean the mess. No trouble to make a mess, rip things, ruin the place, carve names.'

The larger cell had a blackboard and chalk. 'Sometimes I'd fill it up with words that had special meaning to me,' Gini said. 'Nicknames for all my mates and places I'd been to. That's where I changed my name from Jennifer to Jenny to Gini.'

I asked if she was ever offered counselling.

Yes, she said. At the beginning. 'But I wasn't ready for it. I'd closed off that area of my life. I'd made it through and I didn't want to go back there and remember anything. I built a barrier and hardened my heart. Nobody tried after that. It was like, you've made your decision, you can live with it.'

Whenever she could, Gini ran away, catching the bus to town with a bunch of other girls, always watching their backs, usually only lasting a few days. There were lots of reasons to take off. 'To see my brother. To see what it was like in the big city. For the mere fun of the adrenalin buzz. And to see what the consequences were when I got caught.'

'And what were they?'

Aroha Trust emblem: Carver Greg Whakataka helped us come up with a design for our t-shirts. The gourd edged with a koru pattern symbolised new life and hope; the slasher and shovel, their long handles crossed, represented our work and socialist ideals; the two clasped hands at the top stood for unity and sisterhood.

People power: Jane drew a large wall poster for Aroha Trust's first birthday party incorporating elements of our emblem, the Wellington Black Power patch and 'Power to the People'.

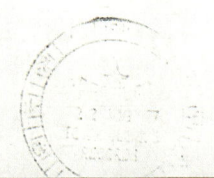

TC 60/1378

IN REPLY PLEASE QUOTE

FOR ENQUIRIES PLEASE TELEPHONE

MR. CLARKE   jb
724-599   EXT. 856

WELLINGTON CITY CORPORATION TOWN PLANNING DEPARTMENT

P.O. BOX 2199. WELLINGTON C.I. NEW ZEALAND.

22 August 1977

Memorandum for –

TOWN CLERK

re: SPECIAL WORK FOR REGISTERED UNEMPLOYED
MEN AND WOMEN

The Labour Department has made contact with my
Department and offered labour for special work
for local authorities on a 100% subsidised
basis.

I am advised by the Labour Department that a
group of five women, known as the Aroha Trust,
could be utilised at the Newtown Adventure
Playground for approximately two-weeks on
clearing rubble and creating a play area,
collecting materials, building structures and
general maintenance of the playground on a
fully subsidised basis.

This work has been approved by the Labour
Department and subject to your approval
arrangements may be made for the commencement
of this work immediately.

K.N. Clark,

CITY PLANNER

FILE

Landing our first job: In August 1977 the Wellington city planner wrote to the town clerk saying five Aroha Trust girls could be employed at the Newtown Adventure Playground under the government's special work scheme. We were under way!

The Aroha Trust girls: Clockwise from top left: Pip, 22; Junior, 18; Georgie, 21; Annie, 22.

Thumbs up: Charmaine, 15, and Tasi, 16, at our all-women house in Abel Smith Street, 1978. Charmaine had just got out of the girls home and Tasi had been living on the streets.

Gini, 19, and Nayda, 18, clown around outside our Newtown flat, 1977. The bush-shirts and jeans we wore weren't just practical for the physical work we did, they were an essential part of our protection.

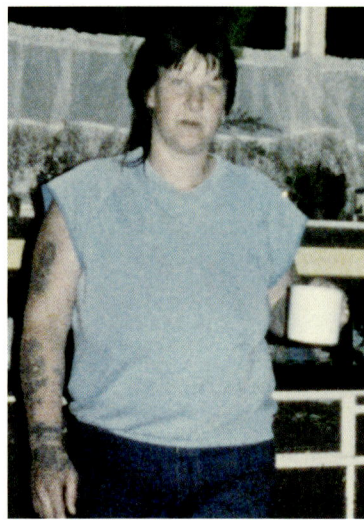

Charmaine, aged about 5 years, with her nanny: 'She was my mountain, she was my world, she was everything that I could ever dream of in terms of innate knowledge of things Māori.'

Black Power mama: Bubbles in her late twenties.

Gini, Amelia and Nayda enjoy a feed of crayfish just down from the Lion Tavern in Thorndon, one of our regular pubs. Little did they know that a quarter of a century later their life stories would be preserved on the site opposite, where the new National Library was being built.

Out on the town: The public bar of the Royal Oak Tavern was a favourite drinking hole, not least because of its excellent jukebox. Aroha Trust girls, from left: Amelia, Agnes, Gerry, Penny. Love the clothes!

A rose between two thorns: Junior flanked by two members of the Nomads gang.

Pip, Jane, Nayda, Tasi and Rangi at 'The Cave', a Wellington nightclub: I don't think we wanted our photo taken, or, judging from the empty glasses, perhaps we couldn't afford more drinks. Usually, we'd buy overpriced jugs of Coke and surreptitiously add rum or bourbon that we'd smuggled in.

file 60/1343

awb

2nd May 1978

Memorandum for: HIS WORSHIP THE MAYOR
                 TOWN CLERK

Re: TEMPORARY EMPLOYMENT PROGRAMME

This report is to apprise you of the present situation
regarding the Corporation's participation in the programme.
The Parks Department is maintaining its activity in
employing people to work its parks throughout the city.
The number employed is normally about 40, and the employees
form part of regular work gangs under normal supervision.
Works Department is currently undertaking a programme to
employ 30 people under a similar scheme.

The administration of the scheme is under the control of
the Industrial Officer. Applications for approval of
projects for 100% subsidy by the Department of Labour are
made by his office, but job applicants apply directly to
the employing officer in the department concerned. Application
is automatically made for the sum of $20 per week per man
to cover overhead and other expenses.

In addition to this scheme the Corporation is also involved
in providing work for the various Work Rehabilitation Trusts
which are active in the city. Of these, the foremost is
the Tapu-te-ranga Trust, of which the Mayor is Chairman.
The Corporation has also engaged the Te Waka Manaki Trust
and the Te Aroha Trust, and is pleased with the results of
the relationship. A number of jobs which the Corporation
is able to consider under the Temporary Employment Programme
are particularly suitable for the contract type of
relationship which the Trusts offer. At the same time, the
Trusts are developing into an important agency in the City
because they seek and provide for young maori people an
alternative to theft, alcohol and violence which is the
preoccupation of many who come to the city from other areas.

Our relationship with the Trusts is robust. I have made it
clear that the Corporation is only interested in providing
work opportunities to those groups who invest their earnings
in a permanent alternative to crime and violence. This means
that a Work Trust must have proper objectives and a basis
for accounting for their earnings.

Progress report: Nine months after taking Aroha Trust on, the assistant town clerk told the mayor the scheme was working well but it was not for 'groups working toward weekend revelry'. I wonder what he thought we did on the weekends.

- 2 -

Groups working toward weekend revelry still have the
opportunity to seek unemployment assistance, but not under
this scheme.

Mr Bruce Stewart of the Tapu-te-ranga Trust is most helpful
in the administration of the scheme. There is an arrangement
for the distribution of work among the Trusts whereby a
Council of Mr Stewart and the leaders of the other Trusts
meet with me to discuss the jobs available, their requirements
and duration. This meeting will also provide a forum for
any complaints either the Corporation or the Trusts have in
regard to the scheme.

The Maori Affairs Department has inquired about the scheme
and I have met Mr Huia Smith of the district office. The
Department is not in a position to do much for this group
of young maoris. It is more geared to handling casework,
provision of housing, and training programmes. I have agreed
to keep Mr Smith in touch with the Corporation activities.

There has been little publicity of the scheme, and until there
is a history of progress on the part of more than one Trust
I believe we should say little but give what support we can
to the groups which are making a real effort to come to terms
with life in the City. In this respect the Tapu-te-ranga
Trust is the focus, being the most stable group. Mr Stewart,
the leader of the group, requires little assistance, but has
good liaison with officers and is aware that assistance in
the administration of the scheme is available as required.

Assistant Town Clerk

Men's work: Under the watchful eye of two builders, we renovated a house in Newtown, a flagship for the Wellington City Council's housing renovation advice service. From top left: Jane, Pip, Lady Jane, Tasi and Jane.

She shrugged, dismissive. 'Put back down in the solitary. Nothing, when I think about it, that would break your spirit if you didn't let it.'

Everyone ran away. It became a vicious cycle. When they were caught, they'd be put in isolation again. Alone and angry, they'd try harder to escape.

Bubbles became a state ward when she was 10. 'Every time I could get out of there, I was gone. I would have been Houdini's best friend. The stupid part of it was even though I was running away from their system all the time, the last few months at home with my mother I was doing the same thing.'

Bubbles said she spent more time in the cells than out of them. Her voice was filled with disgust as she described the potty in the corner. 'I couldn't stand it. I used to try and hang on all night, all day and wait till I got out for a shower in the mornings to use a proper toilet.' She still remembered the energy-sapping boredom. 'I just used to sleep. And sing. Had no pens, no pencils. No nothing in there. Just used to sit around. Do nothing.'

Classed as uncontrollable, she was sent to Kingslea, a long-term girls home in Christchurch at the opposite end of the country from her mother who, with five other children to look after, never visited. Although she kept on trying to escape, it was there Bubbles met an exceptional teacher who helped her pass School Certificate. 'I later found out that he became the coordinator of a health camp for children so he must have been quite a compassionate, good person,' she said.

At 15, she was transferred to Arohata borstal in Wellington, a move that required a special court order for girls younger than 17. She escaped several times, once for almost a year, 'the longest time on record at that stage'. She hid at James K Baxter's commune, Jerusalem, on the Whanganui River and narrowly avoided being arrested when a policeman, Rana Waitai, recognised her at a Rātana celebration but let her go. In gratitude, she named her first child after him.

Eventually, homesickness lured her back to Wellington. 'A police force called the Flying Squad would come through the hotels from Thursday to Saturday night. One of them recognised me and I gave him a bullshit name. He walked back out, and I went, "Oh yes, I've gotten away with this one." And about 12 more come back in and converged on our table and everything else cut loose with it.'

As soon as I asked Amelia about being in care, she began to cry. 'Sorry,' she said. 'It was awful. The welfare homes couldn't hold me. My escape from one of them was like I was in Colditz. They used to have a dog running round the house on a wire, he could go right round. I outfoxed that dog. One night when I knew I was going to do the jump, you know, take the leap, my dinner got swept in my lap and I squashed all the food, put it in my pocket and then did the dishes normally. I called out to the dog to come round on my side and I threw the food so it would go and get it. I ran with my backpack on my back, and I slept on the beachfront in Napier, the Marine Parade. I stayed hidden for a week, sleeping in the sunken gardens, which are still there today, and eating out of rubbish bins and stuff. Cried a lot. Yeah. I was scared. Hungry. Always hungry. But I had a lot of good friends that used to help me and give me food.'

After a week, some Mongrel Mob members took Amelia to their house. Terrified, she ran away again and gave herself up. She was sent to foster parents. 'They were real rich as, and they had a farm and I liked staying there. I felt like a princess because their house was so flash. I had a room to myself and a walk-in wardrobe, I couldn't believe it. Some parts of being in welfare were okay. I always had new clothes.'

But still she took off.

I asked her why.

'I used to like running away and the freedom, I must admit, but to get away from things that were happening at that time. I had an experience in my life that I still can't talk about. Now that I'm older, I would have thought they should have picked that up. There was no counselling in those days.'

Amelia hated the way her welfare placements were never followed up. 'They'd just pop me anywhere and never check me out a week later, or even a few days. You know, really check me out.'

But it might not have made any difference. The husband of her second set of foster parents 'was a dirty prick, especially when his wife used to go out, he was a bit close for comfort. So I did the runner from there. Every time I did take off, I was always checked out by a nurse and a doctor, and they'd say, "You're making these stories up." I spent a lot of days at Social Welfare locked in a little room.'

Junior agreed. 'Society didn't see the abuse. A hiding was a hiding. You never talked about sexual abuse. That was really cut out; it didn't happen. You're here because you're naughty. And the only thing I ever done was run. They always put me down and said I was a liar and it was my own fault and so I kept on running. It was the only way I could escape.'

One night, Charmaine said, she and another girl overpowered a staff member and locked her up in a cell. 'Fuck, that was a nice feeling. Throw the keys away. You sit there, see how you like it.' Her voice rose with indignation. 'We were children. You know, that's what people forget. We were 12 years old, made to live like this. Today, if any parent did that to their child, they'd be imprisoned. And they legally had the right to treat us that way.'

'You were obviously unsettled and violent,' I said, trying to make sense of it.

'No! I was reacting. Nobody asked the right questions. I wasn't being validated as a young Māori woman. I was being treated as an animal, locked up and punished.'

Charmaine's social worker, a white middle-class male, had little interest in her, or empathy, she said.

I asked if there'd been any adults she could trust.

'Fuck, no! It was really, really sad. There were two ladies I got really close to. They got reprimanded if they got close to you, so you learnt you weren't allowed to have emotions. They weren't allowed to do anything good for you. One lady wanted to take me home and she wasn't allowed to.'

No one considered Charmaine's cultural roots. The only time she spoke Māori was when she got wild. 'They'd say, "Charmaine's speaking Rarotongan, we think, or maybe Pidgin or Tahitian." Just had no idea.'

In Miramar, the girls composed an impressive ode to racism to the tune of 'Island in the Sun'. Charmaine sang it for me:

> We are the girls from Miramar
> Handed down by the Pākehā
> Picked us up for I and D
> For being a fuckin' menace to society
> Super, super, set us free
> Send us back to our families
> We promise to you that we'll be good
> Like the little Māori girl of New Zealand should.

'I look at those lyrics today and once again they had perpetuated the belief system that said I was a bad little Māori girl,' she said.

Junior got the same message. 'I had bad blood, I was always told that. So I ended up being the way they wanted me to be. Within myself I was the kindest person, I wouldn't hurt anyone. But I had to survive somehow.'

Mostly, Junior hurt herself. 'Always trying to commit suicide. I didn't really want to die. I just wanted people to listen to me and the only way I could do it was cut my wrists or hang myself.'

The first time Junior was sent to Miramar Girls Home, another girl in her cell tried to rape her. 'She just ripped off my pyjamas, shit like that. So I tried to hang myself.' She was prescribed anti-psychotic drugs and anti-depressants: Tegretol, Meleril, Tryptanol. 'It was guinea-pig time.'

Because Junior was dyslexic and spoke with a lisp, people often thought she was simple. 'I used to flip out. It was frustrating for me to try and explain myself to people cos they couldn't understand me. They'd go, "Okay then, Junior, we'll try you on this medication", instead of just listening. They should have listened.'

Once, she and another girl ran away and got as far as Nelson. 'Ended up at these commune parties and sleeping on beaches and wherever I could sleep. Even if it meant sleeping on your back, so what? You're 12 and a half. I needed a place to stay. Rape me. At least I've got somewhere to stay.'

When she was caught, she was sent to Kingslea, where she spent almost six months in the secure block that was built around a square courtyard. 'It was a really heavy place. We didn't come out for tea or meals, nothing like that. Oh, you're allowed to go out and play on the tramp for an hour.' A woman would give her 20 minutes' schooling a day, but 'I was just too slow and I used to be always drugged up anyway and they'd just take me back to my cell.'

'What was it like spending all that time on your own?' I asked.

'Nutty. Sometimes I'd spin out. I had my fourteenth birthday down there and they made me scrub my cell out with a toothbrush.'

She wasn't the first woman to make such a claim. Amelia told me she had to clean the footpath with a toothbrush as punishment at one of her welfare homes too.

'I ended up just nutting out,' Junior said. 'Really nutting out. Because I'd been there so many times. I'd spent a whole year in security, on and off, on and off.'

'Why were you there so long?'

'Because I used to get so frustrated. I used to just grab things and smash things so that they'll listen. Nobody wants to talk and there was no one you can talk to. There was only officers, I was going to say screws, and the only time you'd see them was when they come in and lock you up. And the radio, if you're lucky, would be on in the hallway. But apart from that, you used to just sit there. There's nothing you can do. You've only got concrete walls. If you're lucky, you can get out and polish the hallway. But I was never that lucky half the times. I remember thinking, I'm going to have a baby so that I wouldn't be lonely anymore. And I was going to treat it better than I was.'

At the same time, Junior was terrified of moving up to the main house. The rape attempt preyed on her mind, and she was scared of the big girls who picked on her. 'I wasn't as staunch as them. I always used to try and give people things so they wouldn't hurt me. So I used to just slit myself up and end up back in security.'

The effects of solitary confinement are now well documented. Even short periods of isolation — two weeks or less — without company or stimulation for most of the day can cause long-term psychological damage. Even strong people can experience lasting personality changes, become socially withdrawn, self-destructive, aggressive and depressed. If they believe they're being punished rather than protected, it's worse.

In the early 1980s — just a few years after the Aroha Trust women went through the system — the Human Rights Commission concluded that some of the Department of Social Welfare's practices in its youth residential homes raised 'serious and substantial questions'. They included everything the women described to me: admitting young people to secure blocks when they first arrived as a matter of course, confining them without legal rules, lack of education facilities in secure blocks, compulsory VD testing, and no recognition of different cultural backgrounds. Twenty years later, five adult male prisoners at Pāremoremo were awarded $2500 for every month spent in similar conditions.

As a result of the Human Rights Commission report, strict new regulations were introduced, including a three-day limit on secure care. Any extension had to be granted by a youth court judge and could not exceed 14 days. Larger residential homes were shut down and children were kept in their families, whānau and communities wherever possible.

But the practice hasn't been wiped out completely. While the government scrambles to provide appropriate secure beds for young offenders, some are kept on remand in tiny police cells with no exercise or other facilities for as long as two weeks at a time. Principal Youth Court Judge Andrew Becroft, a long-time critic of the practice, has described the situation as scandalous. 'Ask any judge who has conducted a coroner's inquest into a police cell suicide as to the profoundly traumatic and unexpected effects solitary confinement in a small cell can have on a 15-year-old youth,' he said in his sector newsletter some years ago.

Better still, ask the women of Aroha Trust.

EIGHT

OUT ON THE STREET

Soon after her seventeenth birthday, Gini was released from Miramar Girls Home to a job at an aluminium factory and a place in a youth hostel. She hated both. 'I half wanted to go back to the girls home because all my friends were there — and I had no ambition to save or to work.'

She hit the streets looking for friendship. 'There was a group of us, we lived down at the railway station in trains, and under bridges and anywhere we could sleep. We had no possessions to our name except the clothes we wore. If we needed a change of clothes, we'd steal them. Just walk past a rack in a shop and take something off and run for it. Get down the road and change into it. I don't know what we did for cleaning ourselves. We just stole and we smoked and drank and thought we were having a good time. We were still too young to be legally allowed into the pubs, so we were the lot that used to hang around at spacie parlours and bludge off people down at the railway station. Ask them for 50 cents and collect a whole heap of money by the end of the day. And sit there when people had finished eating their meals and rush in and finish off their plate and clean it.'

After her father's harsh discipline and the conformity of the girls home, Gini relished the freedom. 'You're not told what to do, you don't have to be accountable to anybody, you can live how you choose. We used to break into the trains and sleep on the beds, and that was real comfortable. And eat the breakfasts that were in the kitchen cabins there. For me it went back to that issue of hating Pākehās. They owned the trains and the railways. I used to think, these guys owe me.'

Survival was the bottom line. 'I was like a little boy, a tough, rough, scruffy boy,' Gini said. 'I wanted to be hard and tough and strong — mostly to handle that way of life. I couldn't run around in a pretty little dress. You know, jeans, anything to run away from police on the spur of the moment. There weren't any girls in our group that dressed like girls; they were all tomboyish.'

Friendship was all-important. 'You had to be able to trust each other. There was loyalty, there was unity in what we did, whether for good, bad or ugly. We shared everything — except each other. We wouldn't let the cops take one without the other. We'd purposely try and do something to get picked up for disorderly behaviour or assault or bad language, just to be with one another down at the cells, and then all let out, and then all go to court, and all go and celebrate after, and all go and sleep in the train. So it became a real family thing.'

Nayda used exactly the same phrase. 'I was looking for that family thing. I found it in Gini and all these young kids the same age as me. The companionship.'

Ko Te Arawa me Horouta ōku waka
Ko Tongariro me Hikurangi ōku maunga
Ko Tongariro me Waiapū ōku awa
Ko Ngāti Tūwharetoa me Ngāti Porou ōku iwi
Ko Ngāti Tūrangitukua me Te Whānau o Uepōhatu ōku
  hapū
Ko Te Ātawhai Nayda Te Rangi taku ingoa

Nayda didn't seem like a typical street kid. She came from a stable, two-parent family, although beneath the surface were elements common to almost all the women: financial hardship, significant responsibility for younger siblings and cultural disconnection.

Nayda grew up in Porirua, the middle child of seven. Both parents spoke Māori fluently and had migrated to the city as young adults for work: her mother from Ruatōria, her father from Tūrangi. He drove a bulldozer at the Happy Valley tip for the council. Her mum didn't drink or smoke, and stayed home while the children were young.

'It was hard, but we lived very basic,' Nayda said. 'My mother used to make Māori bread. I used to do a lot of baking. We used to eat fish heads and pork bones. Offal was free then; you got it from the butcher for nothing. We never starved.' There were also perks from her father's job: shoes still in Hannahs boxes; chocolate and bread damaged in transit; dry-cleaning no one had claimed.

Nayda's father enjoyed a beer. 'But he wasn't a boozer, woman-beater. Never, ever hit my mother. If my father did swear, my mother would be, "Don't you talk like that to our babies!" He'd go, "Oh, sorry, Mum." This is the normal that I know.'

On Sundays, her dad got out his steel guitar. He'd played in a band and Nayda's mum had been a singer. Nayda laughed. 'The only one who's musically inclined is my younger sister.'

Apart from holidays on her grandparents' farm in Tūrangi, and occasional visits back to the marae for a tangi or wedding, Nayda grew up in an English-speaking world. 'I always said to my mum, "Why don't we know how to speak Māori?" She goes, "Oh, you kids. I used to speak to you in Māori and you used to answer me in English." I can remember my grandparents speaking to us in Māori. I regret not listening.'

Nayda wanted to go to Turakina Māori Girls' College like her older sister, but iwi scholarships were limited and she was sent to Porirua College. In the early 1970s, when she was in third form, her mother got a kauae moko[1] with the blessing of the old people, though it was done by a Pākehā tattooist.

'I was really scared for my mother. I had Pākehā friends and everything was very European. I wouldn't say I was ashamed, but I was ignorant. She got a hard time even from a lot of other Māori. I can remember my father's family: "Who does she think she is?" There was her and one other woman and a tāne[2] who had it done at that time.'

Nayda was always called by her middle name. Her first name was Te Ātawhai, meaning caregiver. 'Most appropriate,' she said, especially after her mother began training as a teacher in te reo Māori. The oldest child at home, she took charge of her three younger siblings. 'It was up in the morning, get them to school, come home, get the washing in, cook tea. Everything would be done by the time my parents got home.'

She didn't mind at first. The responsibility helped her overcome her shyness and develop leadership qualities. And she had the weekends to herself. 'I could go off with my friends, as long as come Sunday night, everything was ready for the kids.'

Nayda was still living up to her first name when I stayed in her spotless rented house in a quiet Whanganui cul-de-sac 20 years

---

1   chin tattoo
2   man

later. Like a number of the women, her child-rearing years started when she was a teenager and only stopped as she approached 40. She had five children to three different partners; the youngest was two and a half. But she was beginning to think beyond motherhood. She'd recently completed a catering course at Whanganui Polytech and planned to do business studies.

While we talked, a leg of lamb and potatoes slowly roasted in the oven. In the late afternoon, she made a coleslaw and packed a basket of food to take to Hiruhārama,[1] where her partner lived. He'd been looking after their three youngest children and his own teenagers to give us time together. She insisted on separate houses because of his gang affiliations — he heads the Whanganui Mighty Mongrel Mob. Years of abuse in her previous relationship, also with a Mob member, had taught her to guard her independence.

'Come with me!' she said when I told her I'd never been to James K Baxter's famous settlement.

We rattled along the winding river road in her battered Ford Telstar. Fighting off car sickness, I tried to open the side window, but it was jammed shut. My seat, permanently reclined, was doing nothing for my back either. Nayda handed me a joint and I took a couple of tokes.

'It's skunk, good stuff,' she said, though she didn't indulge while she was driving. I rarely smoked marijuana these days, and by the time we arrived I wasn't making much sense, even to myself.

Nayda's partner, just back from a swim at the river with the kids, was teaching her 12-year-old daughter to drive on the rutted lawn. He was polite and welcoming and I wished my head would clear. The house, which belonged to his family, was bare and clean inside. A Mob jacket and a bulldog's face surrounded by signatures on a large square of red cloth on the wall were the only gang traces, though outside he was building a bar for the boys.

---

1   Jerusalem

After tea, Nayda and I wandered up the hill to the little Catholic church. An old nun pulled apples out of the pig bucket and gave them to us to eat. On the way back, we stopped to talk to the teenagers stretched out in the warm grass, their eyes as glazed as mine felt. Later, on the drive home, Nayda's daughter said one of them had asked who I was — and if I was kind.

While we stood chatting to them, another joint went round and I had a half-hearted puff, feeling like an accomplice in their apathy. In the Aroha Trust days, I'd been a fan of marijuana. Unlike alcohol, it chilled people out; there was always far less mayhem when everyone was stoned than when they were drunk. It wasn't till I had my own teenagers that I appreciated its energy-sapping toll on young minds and bodies.

None of the teenagers at Jerusalem were at school or working. Nayda too left college without qualifications. At 16, tired of the responsibility at home and to escape growing tensions with her parents, she went flatting with her older sister in Wellington and worked briefly in a government department. Loneliness drew her to The Sunset Strip nightclub, where she teamed up with Gini, an old school friend. She ditched her job, fell out with her sister and joined the street kids.

On the streets, Nayda found other young Māori and the camaraderie she longed for. 'I began to live on my wits then. I liked the excitement of stealing and drinking and going to nightclubs. Everybody congregated at the railway station about 11 o'clock before they locked the gates. You'd go there with your bottle of lemon and gin, and you'd sit up and talk and party. I'd go, "C'mon, we'll stay at my sister's flat. She's gone home for the weekend." And then go to Pigeon Park for the day, or the beach. It was a new thing to me. It was freedom, it was excitement.'

For Charmaine, life on the streets was good for different reasons. 'We weren't getting beaten up, no one was bashing the shit out of us. It was hard and cold and scary, but there was some sense of peace and there was a kinship amongst us. Even though none of us spoke about our lives, we all had this unspoken bond.'

I was struck by the nostalgia with which the women looked back on their street-kid days. For many, it was their first, heady taste of life away from the horrors of home or the constraints of institutions. They used words like family, freedom, companionship, loyalty, excitement, fun, peace. These things made up for not knowing where the next meal was coming from or where they would sleep. In many ways, they were still children, innocent and vulnerable. I sensed that both boys and girls were fiercely protective of one another.

What did they do all day, away from the controls of home and school?

'We walked everywhere; that's about all we done,' said Tasi with typical bluntness. 'It was hard sometimes when we had nothing to eat or nowhere to have a good sleep. No bed or anything. I didn't mind being round my friends. It's a bit hard with no food, though. I wasn't into drinking, I was just into eating hamburgers.'

Tasi's interest in food was legendary — and undiminished, I discovered, when I took her and Nayda out for dinner in Whanganui during my visit. At the end of a large meal, she ordered two pieces of cheesecake: one to eat then and one to take home for her husband. Across the table, I didn't dare catch Nayda's eye in case she was as dubious as me about the destination of the second piece.

Hunger was also Mahina's main memory of being a street kid. When I arrived at her impeccable farmhouse to record her story, she pulled a chocolate cake out of the oven and served me a big piece on her grandmother's best china. The next day, I got home-made apple square. I'd been nervous about seeing her again for the first time since the Aroha Trust days. I remembered an awkward, light-fingered girl, who put her hand over her mouth and giggled if she was singled out.

Three years before my visit, her longtime partner Tam had been killed when his motorbike slid on black frost. I hadn't realised he'd been a Black Power member when I knew him — I never saw him wear a patch. To me, he'd been a gentle young guy who lived at Brougham

Street with the two Mikes, a homebody always quick to share a joint.

Mahina was rebuilding her life with a new partner and 11-year-old son, a friendly little soul who made me cups of tea; her other son had left home. With pride, she showed me around the land belonging to her partner's great-great-grandparents. In less than a year, they'd done up the 1910 wooden homestead, built a two-storey A-frame next to it with a granny flat on top and a garage below, and planted shrubs and poplars up a long concrete drive. All this while both worked fulltime in other jobs. When it was finished, the property was going to be magnificent.

MAHINA'S STORY

Of all the women I visited, Mahina was the biggest surprise. She was an imposing figure even in baggy grey shorts and gumboots. A ropy scar around her neck — the legacy of surgical removal of a home-made tattoo — gave her a slightly menacing appearance. She still giggled a lot, and her answers were so abrupt that I often felt like I was interrogating her.

I'd heard that she was the garden supervisor at a large variety store and that one of her projects had featured in a national gardening magazine. She played it down. 'I says it's only a garden, but they liked the way it was done, landscaped and all that. It was actually a cottagey garden. A lot of the structures I built myself: arbours, and my own chairs made out of manuka and old tōtara fence posts.'

But I didn't expect the BA in Horticulture or the thesis she'd started on windmills. 'The reason I picked it is I thought it was going to be easy, but it's quite hard,' she said in her understated way. Nor did she seem the sort to put matching towels and soap in the bathroom, hoard china, old linen and porcelain dolls, and still have the three-wheeler bike with the bucket back that she'd pedalled around the veranda of her grandparents' farmhouse as a child.

When Mahina was seven, her parents took two of her four brothers to Wellington, leaving her and the other two with her grandparents on their sheep and dairy farm. 'I was a bit shattered,' she said. 'I didn't know what was going on; I felt like I wasn't wanted.'

It was three years before she joined them for a holiday and by then it was hard to adapt to their rules. 'You weren't allowed to touch, touch, touch. On the farm, if you wanted to turn the TV on, you could. If you just wanted to get something out of the fridge, you could just help yourself.'

Mahina's grandfather was the local policeman in Motueka, 'a good sort of guy who never judged you'. She was named after her grandmother, now in her nineties, and still phoned her every weekend. 'I look to her more as a mother figure than my own parents,' she said.

Mahina's grandmother would speak to the children once in Māori and then in English. 'Some days I used to understand what she was saying, other days I didn't.' At the same time, 'she used to always put the Māoris down. It was because a lot of Māoris never get anywhere; they didn't want their children to end up like those Māoris. But she always used to say, never forget where you came from.'

After three years at boarding school, Mahina got School Certificate and went to live with her mother, now separated from her husband and working as a midwife at Wellington Hospital. 'We got on all right for a little while. But she got so used to her life being revolved around her and nobody else, she used to hate another person being in the house; she didn't like making a mess.'

When her mother told her to get a job or get out, Mahina drifted down to Pigeon Park and joined the street kids. 'I didn't like it because you had no food. But it was better than being with my mother. You could do anything you wanted to do.'

Squatting in a house in Hopper Street, Mahina and her mates slept till lunchtime. 'Then we used to go and shoplift. It was easy because there were no cameras. We used to go in with jackets on and jumpers, and just fill up your jumper and walk out. Put jeans over another pair, tops under another top and so on.'

Mahina was convicted four times for burglary but each time got away with a fine. Even when she became old enough to get the dole — 'you could survive on that' — the stealing continued. 'We used to knock on people's doors. If nobody was home, we knew that was a house to burgle.'

While Mahina was scrounging cigarettes and lighters, alcohol and petty cash, others were involved in bigger rip-offs.

'We used to follow the post lady and steal all the welfare cheques,' Bubbles said. 'As she was putting them in the mailbox, we were not far behind her taking them out. Then we'd go to the post office and cash them. In those days you walked in, you presented a cheque, the money was given to you on face value. Nothing else was asked of you. We used to taxi all round the post offices in Wellington, Porirua, Tītahi Bay, Lower Hutt, and some days used to end up with about two, two-and-a-half thousand dollars.'

The money went as fast as it arrived. 'Clothes, food, household items. Pissing up. Cruising around in taxis cos we walked everywhere normally. No one had a licence, let alone a car. That was totally foreign. If you needed a car, someone would acquire a car and you'd all hop in to where you were going and leave it there. And if you needed one to come back, you'd acquire another.'

I might have doubted the scope of the welfare cheque scam except that, unprompted, Nayda described it in more detail. The only ID needed to claim a benefit was a cardboard card with your name and signature on it, stamped by Social Welfare, she said. There were no photos or computers; if you went into the office saying you'd lost your card, they gave you another one.

'You could steal the stamp and a whole pile of cards off the receptionist's desk quite easily. You'd walk out with them. Go round all the letterboxes in certain areas, grab all the cheques, and you'd sit up that night and you'd fill out their name and you'd sign a bullshit signature.' Next morning, as Bubbles had said, they'd cash them at different post offices. 'It's not that you were stealing that person's cheque. They'd go in and get a duplicate.' She laughed. 'Why go to work when you can do that?'

Nayda's vivid storytelling, accompanied by flashing eyes and much hand-waving, drew me into the murky world she'd inhabited as a teenager. She mimicked a phone call home.

Her mother, stern: 'What have you been doing?'

Nayda, contrite: 'I got caught pinching.'

Mother: 'Oh, you're bloody lucky they didn't lock you up.'

Nayda: 'Oh well, they did, Mum.'

Mother: 'Good job! You won't go out and do that again, will you? Are you coming home?'

Nayda: 'No!'

Mother: 'Okay then. Goodbye.'

Nayda mimed the phone being hung up in her ear. 'My mother wasn't going to muck around. She wasn't going to bother herself with me when she had the others at home. I'm doing what I wanted to do. I got myself in the shit. Well, she's not going to chase after me and drag me home. That was for me to do.'

I tried to hide my dismay. What was her mother thinking, wiping her hands of her 16-year-old daughter like that? Anything could have happened to her — and sometimes did.

But Nayda blamed herself. Her mother didn't have time to come looking for her, she said. And none of her siblings was ever in trouble — though her sister was so young when she got into a long-term relationship with a Mob member that her parents made him her legal guardian.

'I know I shouldn't have worried them,' Nayda said. I think if I'd been able to stay at home when I left college, things would have been different.'

A few months after she began working for Aroha Trust, Nayda got pregnant, although she didn't know it at the time. When her boyfriend went to Taranaki, she persuaded Gini to hitch-hike with her to find him. It took a black eye to convince her the relationship was going nowhere. 'We arrived home late at night and my mother and father were up waiting for me.' She breathed out heavily. 'They were so glad when I went home; I was seven months pregnant with their first mokopuna.'

NINE

WORLDS OF DIFFERENCE

About the same time as Nayda went home to have her baby, Jane came to Wellington on holiday with a girlfriend, half-intending to stay. They had a fight and the friend took off. Sixteen, alone, with nowhere to go, Jane went home with a man she met in the pub.

'I made up this bullshit story about how my husband had just died and that's why I didn't want to have sex with him, and he beat the shit out of me,' she said. 'I started desperately trying to find you. All I knew was the name Aroha Trust.'

More than two decades later, we sat on the grass at Hamilton Gardens, juggling paper plates of corn chips soggy with sour cream and tomato sauce, waiting for Dave Dobbyn and the Finn brothers to play. Those guys had staying power, I thought admiringly, watching them warm up on stage: they'd been around for longer than I'd known Jane. We'd first met in Dunedin where she was a regular at the youth centre I worked in after I left university. I was new to the city, as lonely as she was, and we quickly became friends in spite of the six-year age gap.

'How long were you stuck with that creep from the pub?' I asked her.

'At least two or three weeks. I was basically a prisoner in his house. When he was out at work, I finally managed to get your phone number at Abel Smith Street through the council. But it was over Christmas, so you were away.'

I thought for a moment. 'I think me and Annie hitch-hiked to Auckland that summer.' We'd stayed with some women who were cranking out pamphlets attacking Muldoon's government for closing down the Auckland abortion clinic on Christmas Eve, making Australia the only option for many. I'd avoided the arguments. I felt deeply ambivalent about the ethics of abortion, though it never stopped me helping any woman who needed one.

Jane's voice pulled me back. 'I was so relieved when I tracked you down. I rang up saying, "Help, help! Come and rescue me!"' She laughed. 'JB and some of the boys came out and made the guy hand over my suitcases. They did a big heavy on him. I remember thinking, wow, this is so cool having someone to stick up for me.'

'The Black Power did come in handy sometimes,' I had to admit.

I'd had mixed feelings when Jane turned up in my life again in Wellington. I was still establishing my own credentials in the gang scene; babysitting her was not what I needed. It wasn't as if she would blend in easily: her golden hair, big breasts and willowy figure made sure of that, even if she did cover up more than she had in Dunedin.

These days, the gold rings adorning both hands were the only visible sign of the blonde bombshell who'd caused such a stir back then, but I knew that fragile young girl would have gladly traded places with the self-assured community worker sitting beside me who seemed to know everyone in the crowd.

The weekend after Jane arrived on my Wellington doorstep, Aroha Trust was booked to clear a section for some friends of my parents. We did small private contracts whenever we could, putting the money into a kitty that covered the cost of our vans, trips and other communal activities. I asked her if she wanted to tag along. I think I hoped it might scare her off.

'It just about killed me,' she said. 'It was scrub-cutting on the side of this bloody hill in Wadestown. It blew me away, it was such hard work, but I was determined I wasn't going to show myself up.'

Afterwards, I took her home to meet Mum and Dad. Home was a sprawling, single-storey white house in Wadestown, up a sweeping driveway lined with macrocarpas. Dad was sitting in his La-Z-boy reading the paper. He looked grey and ill as he leaned forward to give me a hug.

'Dad, this is Jane, a friend from Dunedin,' I said.

Dad clasped her hand between both of his. 'Pleased to meet you, Jane. I've got very happy memories of Dunedin. That's where I went to med school and met Pip's mother.'

'Hello,' she stammered, too shy to look at him.

Dad was proud of my involvement with Aroha Trust; he saw it as missionary work. It was what our family did. My brother taught in Samoa for two years after he left school, and the sisters on either side of me went on Volunteer Service Abroad. As far as Dad was concerned, I was just doing my good deeds closer to home.

He was no stranger to hardship. A severe asthmatic, he was sent to boarding school when he was five in the hope that the strict routine might improve his health. His father died when he was 10 and his mother was dogged by illness for the rest of her life. Dad felt huge responsibility for his three younger siblings, who spent time in orphanages and with other family members. When the family was reunited, they survived on a meagre widow's pension. Dad only got to medical school through a cousin's financial generosity. Then, in his mid-forties, at the height of a successful career as a pathologist, he started having seizures. It was 10 years before a brain tumour was diagnosed, and his long illness rocked our family deeply.

I kissed his forehead and took Jane to meet Mum. She was standing at the oven, spooning dark liquid over a leg of lamb. The smell of garlic and rosemary filled the kitchen. Mum was a great cook, raised on rural hospitality. Her father, an orchardist, was mayor of the small Central Otago town of Roxburgh and ran the local branch of the National Party. Her mother was his second wife, a farm girl much younger than him with a trio of formidable sisters.

Mum was less enthusiastic about my gang life. Her solution was to not talk about it and feed anyone who turned up. I often took Jane and Annie to visit, and sometimes other girls, the Wombles and Mike Hancock. Once I introduced Shorty, a member of the Nomads, to my father. Both could be charming and gregarious when they chose, as they did on that occasion.

I don't think Mum worried about me unduly. She seemed to think that I knew what I was doing, even if she didn't. Besides, she had enough on her plate with a sick husband and two teenage daughters still living at home.

Dinner that night was a rowdy affair around the oval dining table that seated 12. My older sister was planning her wedding.

Mum zeroed in on me. 'What are you going to wear?' she asked.

'Annie's lending me her red suede boots and Chinese silk jacket,' I said. 'Don't worry! I won't disgrace you.'

She looked sceptical.

Jane sat beside me, head bowed, playing with her food and blushing if anyone looked in her direction. We did the dishes and left, smoked some hash oil and met the boys at the Lion Tavern. I know these details because she recorded them in her diary at the time. In an extraordinary act of trust, she gave me a copy when I began writing this book. It was like the black box in an aeroplane. As I trawled my own mind for uncertain memories, I wished I'd had the foresight to keep one myself.

About the dinner with my parents, Jane wrote, 'Fuck, talk about far-out and freaky. I couldn't have hacked that carry-on for too long.' After that, she recorded a typical night out. The pub was 'pretty cool. We stayed there till closing time and after a few hassles and a few more smokes, we arrived at The Cave. Me, Nayda and Pip. That's a pretty freaky place too. All the sailors (wee Nippies) are there to pick up a slut. They invade the place after the pub if they haven't had any luck there. Then the poofs and pros all gather round them and try to make some money. It's sort of a gathering place for the un-straight scene. Wellington's a really open city. Unlike Dunedin, queers and gay guys and girls can come out into the open. People aren't so narrow-minded and straight as they are in great lumps down south.'

After the Hamilton concert, Jane and I wandered through the gardens in the dark. In the middle of a small, curved bridge, I rested my elbows on the stone ledge that still held the warmth of the day. I needed to talk.

Charmaine, whose place I'd just come from, had told me I was the right person to write about Aroha Trust. 'You've always been neutral,' she'd said, somewhat to my surprise. It didn't matter to her that I was Pākehā. 'You know what it was like cos you were there. I wouldn't have felt comfortable talking to someone who hadn't lived that journey.' But, she warned, she wouldn't be part of anything that fed into middle-class preconceptions about gangs. 'Where was the middle class when I needed someone to take me in? The gangs gave me food and shelter. Yes, the men were violent, but they also protected and looked after me. They became my whānau.'

I asked Jane how much say she expected to have in what I wrote.

'It's your book,' she said. 'Write it the way you see it.'

'But what if you don't like it?'

'Stop agonising!' she scolded. 'Everyone's agreed to talk to you. They want something to happen to their stories. You've got to give them back somehow.'

Jane took the next day off work so we could record her story. First we went to watch her 10-year-old son compete in the school swimming sports. To our delight, he won the backstroke and was part of the winning relay team, but we tried not to shout and jump about too much and embarrass him in front of his mates.

It was almost midday by the time we were settled in the lounge of her lovely old house in Ngāruawāhia, originally built by the town doctor. Ornaments and knick-knacks — mostly handmade by Jane — crowded every flat surface. Three fabric sculptures, each about 12 cm long, specially caught my eye. They looked like oversexed Cabbage Patch dolls, lounging seductively in bikinis and sipping champagne.

'They're called rich bitch beach babes,' Jane said. 'They're sticking their fingers in the air at the image of what beauty is. Women can be voluptuous and round and they don't have to be size two to be beautiful. They're a bit inebriated, I have to admit. They're girls having a good time on the beach and sticking their finger at the world.'

Self-portraits, in other words.

JANE'S STORY

Ko Aoraki te mauka
Ko Waitaki te awa
Ko Takitimu te waka
Ko Ōtākou te whenua
Ko Kāi Tahu, Kāti Māmoe, Kāti Hāwea, Waitaha me Rapuwai
ngā iwi
Ko Jane Stevens taku ingoa

Jane grew up in Dunedin in a two-storey brick house on a steep section, built by her parents with a cheap government loan. 'It was a relatively middle-class suburb, part of the pepper-potting housing experiment in vogue at the time,' she said. Upstairs, the large family (her mother had 10 children, of whom six survived) crammed into two bedrooms and a small, open-plan living area with no window to admire the stunning harbour view.

Bit by bit, Jane's father, a bus driver, dug out the clay cellar to add extra bedrooms. 'He just worked and worked and worked and he could never enjoy himself. He always had to keep trying to make things better for us and other people.' Even so, he never liked visitors because he thought the house wasn't good enough.

When Jane was six, her mother had a heart attack giving birth to twin boys. Deprived of oxygen, they were born with brain damage. Her mother also had epilepsy, which made her very sensitive to noise. 'Can you imagine how much sound six kids made? It just drove her demented. For her health, she had to spend as much time away from the house as possible, so she ran a second-hand shop in South Dunedin for years; it was her sanctuary.'

After the twins were born, Jane's father cleaned buses at night and ran the house during the day. 'I don't think he slept much during those years so it was no wonder that family life involved a lot of yelling and throwing things. At the time I thought it was horrific, but now I understand my parents were in an impossible position. We were the pariahs in this quite nice street. Everybody else hated us; they thought we should be in Brockville, where all the state houses were. They were forever ringing up Social Welfare and complaining. About the fights, the noise, the kids running wild. I didn't know it then, but Social Welfare would often threaten to take us away.'

When Jane was eight or nine, things got too much for her father. She didn't want to elaborate except to say it had a huge effect on her. 'I felt that we were so awful that we must have made him feel like that. I think that's why I thought I had to try and make things better for him all the time. And I couldn't, as a kid. You can't, no matter what you want to do.'

Some time later her father's bus crashed and she immediately thought the worst. 'But he'd just collapsed. Exhaustion, I think.'

With her mother sick and her father working, Jane — the only girl in the family — was forced into a mothering role. For years, she shared a tiny bedroom with her younger twin brothers in the cellar, 'a really damp, yicky place with lots of spiders and slaters and stuff'. A talented artist, she 'tried to turn it into something that reflected me. To this day there's a mural outside my door where I painted all these dark and evil-looking creatures all over the wood.'

Jane struggled to remember good times from her childhood. 'I've got quite a block about it,' she said more than once. A carnival at Ōtākou Marae was a rare happy memory. 'They had those bucking bronco things, those wooden horses with the round barrel, and you've got to get on and try and stay on them. That was an amazing day; we just ran wild all day and played.'

Both Jane's parents were Kāi Tahu, but the family spent little time at the marae. Her father, from whom she inherited her colouring, was blond and fair-skinned, like many South Island Māori. 'Dad always desperately wanted us to be accepted. He was of that era where, if you look Pākehā, you should try and assimilate because it's so difficult otherwise.'

On her mother's side, Jane's grandmother claimed to be purely Scottish while her aunty passed off her dark looks as Spanish. 'I was led to believe that there was something dirty about us; there was this side we should be ashamed of.'

On her first day at school, Jane was sent out of the class for biting a boy. 'I hated it because we were treated like shit by other kids cos they saw us as being poor. I got hell cos I had patched-up clothes. The whole family had those horrible brown plastic sandals that got passed down from one to the other if they lasted long enough. There were so many of us. And we weren't even Catholic.'

Jane hated school but she hated home just as much. Recalling her childhood years in her diary when she was about 15, she wrote: 'It seems I had to live either in terror or shame. I remember nights spent sobbing in my room terrified of my father's anger.'

At intermediate, though, one teacher stood out. 'If I was late for school, he'd be welcoming in front of everybody; he'd take my coat off for me, he'd put my chair down for me, and I would feel so stink, it was 10 times worse. But there was an intellectual challenge there; he knew how to get me to respond, to do my best, whereas nobody else had ever bothered. He was interested in me but not in a sexual way, I didn't think, and maybe that wasn't anything special, but it felt like it. I used to run away and sit outside his house when things got bad at home, and pretend I lived there.'

The teacher was Robin Bain. Twenty years later he suffered a violent death, along with four other family members. His son, originally jailed for the crime, is currently in court as the case is retried. Jane was shattered by speculation that Robin was the real killer, about to be exposed for having sex with his teenage daughter.

'He'd been my only good experience at school; he was like the pillar that made the rest of it make sense. After that, I wondered whether he'd picked my vulnerability. I had zero trust in men, even at the age of 12. The revelations about his daughter were the last straw in destroying my confidence. I still want to believe he's innocent and wasn't a pervert, but—'

As a teenager, Jane increasingly resented being poor and having to look after her siblings. 'I was stealing by then and generally being a little bitch. I started really fighting back against some of the things that were happening to me. Some of that was to do with my family. Some of that was to do with sexual abuse. But I didn't understand the effect that has on you. I just went completely off the rails at high school.'

Again, she didn't want to go into detail. 'I think I responded by becoming very violent, using drugs and alcohol. I got kicked out of my first high school for stabbing a boy in class. I used to carry a knife and I don't even remember why. He was a really big guy, he had glasses. So I just grabbed his glasses and stood on them and smashed them. He quite understandably got upset about that, so I pulled out a knife and stabbed him in the stomach in front of the teacher.'

What scared her now was how good she'd felt. 'Really powerful and in control.' She was probably drunk at the time, she said. Although her parents didn't drink, she was hanging round older guys in bikie and V8 gangs, and had easy access to drugs and alcohol.

Jane was assigned a social worker and psychologist, and narrowly avoided being sent to a welfare home. Another high school agreed to take her and the headmistress let her spend most of her time in the art room. But she was on a downward spiral that, looking back, seemed impossible to stop. When she bashed a girl — 'she was a spoilt rich bitch, so I picked on her' — she was given an ultimatum: leave or be taken to court.

It was then Jane started coming to the youth centre where I worked, though we spent far more time playing pool in the draughty hall than poring over the School C correspondence work she'd been assigned.

When the centre director set up a halfway house and I volunteered to run it, Jane convinced her parents and Social Welfare to let her live there. She looked at me and grinned. 'You were the house mother, but I don't know that you were much better than the rest of us when it came down to it.'

'I wasn't a very good mother,' I agreed. I was only 20. I was still learning to look after myself.

'You certainly didn't keep us on the straight and narrow,' she went on, rubbing it in. 'I was probably happier, but I don't know that I was any more under control than I had been. I have memories of the cops overrunning us. Fighting, assault, drinking underage.'

I shuddered. I'd been out of my depth in that house, inexperienced and unsupported as we lurched from one crisis to the next. It was impossible to impose the discipline decreed by the director from the comfort of his own home. Those kids had been defying adult rules and curfews for years; they weren't about to start obeying mine.

And I had no training to deal with their distress. One night I walked past a girl sitting on her bedroom floor running a pocket-knife slowly across her wrist, a thin trail of blood in its wake. I kept on walking; I'd seen her do it too many times before.

Jane was on a similar self-destructive path. 'I'd drink whatever people would give me and I'd take whatever drugs were around like acid, horse tranquillisers, tablets, dope. I never got into heroin though, more because it wasn't around than that I wouldn't have tried it.'

While she was living in the youth centre house, Jane overdosed on pills. Luckily, she told people in time to have her stomach pumped. Later, back with her parents, she overdosed again. 'The really scary thing was I went to bed knowing that I'd killed myself and I didn't tell anyone,' she said. 'But I woke up the next day; I was alive; I didn't manage to do it properly. I couldn't believe it. I was part relieved. I felt like a complete failure and I was so thankful I hadn't told anybody cos that would have been even more embarrassing.'

That was the last time she took tablets. 'The other times, I got more violent, or more Russian roulette. It amazes me I'm still here. I'd do things like drive round blind corners on the wrong side of the road.'

'How old were you before you stopped?' I asked.

'I don't know if I want to tell you.' There was a long pause. 'Probably not till my thirties. On and off. Not all the time.'

Having her own children made Jane seek help. 'I was going to start damaging other people's lives.' Her job training community workers at Wairarapa Community Polytech was another catalyst. 'Here was me bloody teaching all the stuff that good community workers need to deal with their own luggage. It made me realise I had to deal with some of my own; I'd buried it for too long.'

After the Aroha Trust hui at Kāwhia in 2007, Jane contacted me and said she wanted to talk more about her sexual abuse. She'd been inspired by the other women's stories, by people like Louise Nicholas who refused to be silenced, and by changing attitudes. 'Some of the stuff that's come out about what was going on in that era has opened up a huge can of worms. People can start to see it's not about blaming the individuals who suffered.'

When Jane was a teenager, everyone — including her — blamed her parents for her problems, she said. In hindsight, that was unfair. 'Yes, my home life made me vulnerable. But I had five brothers and none of them went off the rails. All my behaviour was screaming sexual abuse but no one picked it up. If it wasn't for the sexual abuse, I don't think I would have stabbed that boy or been so violent. I was incredibly angry at everybody. I responded by getting off my face, challenging authority. I didn't have any idea what the real problem was.'

Now she did know. At the age of 11, she was sexually abused by a prominent artist who ran workshops for young people and was later convicted of multiple counts of sexual abuse (not including Jane). 'I thought he was interested in my creative ability when all the time . . .' Her voice trailed away. 'He was the one who destroyed my innocence.'

After that, it was as if the dam broke. In the next nine years, Jane was raped by more men than she wanted to disclose. None were family members. None were strangers. She laughed a hollow laugh. 'I felt very safe with strangers.'

Jane's first rape was when she was 13, by the only gang member, a V8 boy. One was a gang associate. The others were 'respectable' citizens: one a St John Ambulance man who drove her home from Girl Guides, another a church worker, another a family acquaintance.

It took Jane a long time to see it wasn't her fault. 'I always felt young and stupid and why did I let that happen? I still have to remind myself sometimes that I was a kid. Having my own children helped. When they were the same age, it seemed horrific. If someone did that to my 15-year-old, I don't know what I'd do. Commit murder probably.'

Everything was stacked against her, she said. 'I was physically mature. There was a constant expectation from men. I had to grow up really quickly because of what was happening at home. I was the only girl. Afterwards, I lost respect for myself. And yes, I started to dress in the way men expected. Kids get attention any way they can, even if it's negative attention. It's interesting though that it was never when I was dressed provocatively that I got raped. It was in trust situations with adults in positions of power. It's like a paedophile: get to know a child, earn their trust, then move in.'

Social workers never identified the core reason for her behaviour, Jane said. 'They let me move into the youth centre house when I was 15 and go flatting when I was 16. They weren't putting me into places of safety.' At the same time, when the court ordered her to go home, she ran away. 'I didn't want to be controlled. There were eight people living in a tiny little house. I'd had a taste of freedom. Dad would board up the bedroom window so I couldn't get out and give me a hiding if he caught me, but nothing stopped me.'

Jane's parents had no idea what was going on, she said. Still, I couldn't understand why they'd let a V8 guy in his mid-twenties take their 13-year-old daughter on a Sunday-afternoon picnic with three of his mates.

She shrugged. 'They must have trusted him.'

He raped her. 'We were in his car and he said if I didn't turn it up, he'd get the others to have a go too and if I told anyone, they'd come back and block me. I lived in fear of him. If I ever saw a car that looked like his car, I'd run a mile. I never told anyone. People say being murdered is preferable and they're not wrong. It destroys your relationship with half the population. It destroys your trust, your sense of who you are, the way you see the world. It erodes your soul.'

When she was 15, Jane wrote an imaginary interview with a rape victim in her diary. It went like this:

'You've been raped, haven't you?'

'Why, how can you tell?'

'It's in your face — it shows. Scared of men, huh? Can't trust them, love them? Always let you down, do they? Scare you in bed — can't respond. They're all the same to you, aren't they? How much of your soul can you bare to them, how close do you let yourself get? Not very much, I'll bet.'

'What can I do — you're right, you know. Can't talk about it — wouldn't understand. It never leaves me, it's there like a shadow, haunting, tormenting, never lets me go. No confidance [*sic*], feel useless, dirty.'

The interview ends.

In the long term, Jane said, her experiences had made her a strong feminist. 'I've channelled my anger into more constructive channels: social justice and empowering people, taking out the vulnerability factor.' But she felt overly protective of her two sons. 'I know sexual abuse can happen to both sexes.'

When Jane finally sought help, her counsellor convinced her to lodge an ACC claim as part of the healing process. After a six-year battle with the department, she won her multiple-claim case on a technicality and received a lump sum payment that she thinks was one of the biggest settlements for multiple abuse at that time.

Jane said she'd never have lodged the claim if she'd known what she'd have to go through. 'There was nothing healing about it; it actually compounded the abuse.' By the time it was over, around 30 people had worked on her case (although she'd been promised that only one person at ACC would see her file), information about her had been mistakenly sent to a member of the public on an office fax machine, and she'd received confidential details about four other women who'd made claims. Worst of all, her lawyer (a woman) strung her along for two years — failing to apply to ACC for a review of her claim, forward her medical assessment report or apply for legal aid — before Jane replaced her and resolved her case. Her new lawyer encouraged her to lay a complaint with the Law Society. 'But I was too heartsick by that time. Everyone seemed to know what had happened to me, and I just wanted to go and curl up in a corner and hide from the world.'

Looking back, Jane was in awe of her parents for keeping the family together during her childhood. 'I think I'm pretty tough, but I couldn't have done what they did. They are so staunch.'

The Māori renaissance healed the rifts between them and today they live next door to her in Ngāruawāhia.

'When I left home, they went through a huge transition themselves and things changed dramatically for Māori in the South Island,' she said. 'The journey they went on meant they were able to stand tall in themselves and that really changed our relationship. It meant that I could start to know who I was and start to live that myself. We've spent 30 years rebuilding our whakapapa, and that's an amazing story in itself. They want their moko to know who they are, where they come from, and we want to make sure that our whānau are never alienated from their roots again.'

Jane believed that cultural disconnection lay at the heart of her childhood troubles. 'If that hadn't been there, I would have had a strength to call on that I didn't have. I think it makes all the difference. If you're secure in who you are and you have that whānau support in those crises or whatever happens in your life, you can hopefully find a much more positive outcome.'

I asked Jane if she'd come to terms with being a fair-skinned Māori.

Her eyebrows shot up. 'A mongrel? I think Kāi Tahu have much more of a profile nationally now, and people can see all these white Māori all over the place. Even a lot of people who might have been staunchly, "You have to be chocolate brown to be Māori", their moko are little Janola kids and so the attitudes have had to change. There's much more acceptance that you can't assume who's Māori and who's not just by looking at someone.'

But she loved going back to Dunedin. 'Down home, I don't have to prove myself. Being white, I've often felt like I have to be a better Māori than anyone else. But I don't give a shit anymore. I know who I am and that's the difference. I know who I am, so it's their problem, not mine.' She jabbed her middle finger in the air and grinned. 'So, you know, the one-finger salute.'

TEN

IN THE DRIVER'S SEAT

Six months after the city council took on the Aroha Trust girls, the city planner advised the town clerk that it 'has been quite successful in that a lot of clean-up and painting work has been done at very little cost to the Corporation which, because of lack of funds, would not have been attempted. On the other side of the picture, these people have been usefully employed instead of being left on the dole.'

Soon after, the street works engineer agreed to employ us to paint handrails round the city because we'd proven ourselves and the arrangement 'should give a good return for outlay'.

Two months later, when we still hadn't signed the contract, he was losing patience. 'My optimism is fast waning,' he wrote. 'The relief team [us] with whom I am negotiating seeks guaranteed 40-hour paid work and I am unwilling to give to this team any advantage over our own employees. At present I have agreed that in conjunction with handrails painting (fine weather), scrub-cutting (damp weather), I will endeavour to find a source of indoor work for wet days.'

Another month and he could barely conceal his annoyance in a memo where he announced that the 'protracted negotiations' had broken down, presumably because we wouldn't agree not to be paid for days when it was too wet to work.

This rare paper trail reminded me how precarious our employment had been. Although the trusts had support from the mayor down, we had to negotiate for work with hard-nosed officials protecting their permanent staff and budgets. Depending on the nature of the job, we attracted a 75–100 per cent government wage subsidy, which was what made us attractive to them. But we were never sure where the next job was coming from, or if there'd be one. We had to fight for rights like a 40-hour week that other workers took for granted. What's more, we relied on the council bosses' goodwill to keep renewing our individual contracts with the Labour Department beyond the usual three-month limit for relief workers, and couldn't afford to get too offside with them.

So we were pleased when they came up with a new job for us, painting the arts centre in the city. It would keep us going for months, there'd be no problem with rainy days — and the colour scheme wasn't orange. But there was something oppressive about the dark wood panelling, grand old staircase and endless, flaking bedrooms of the former hostel. You'd finish painting one room and next door there'd be another exactly the same. Skirting boards began to haunt my dreams.

In the common room where we hung out during smoko, the shelves were crammed with dog-eared board games. A new Aroha Trust girl, about 18 years old, challenged me to draughts. Small and dainty, she wore frilly white blouses with puffed sleeves under her overalls and never raised her voice or swore, hence her nickname Lady Jane. By night, she was a stripper. Her boyfriend, a pimply Pākehā beanpole, wouldn't let her mix with us outside work, but he was happy for her to take her clothes off in front of other men.

The first time we played draughts, she beat me. Quietly, sweetly, convincingly. And the second. I became obsessed: I was the university graduate. We played every day, I watched her moves, I learnt from my mistakes. I never won.

Once I swallowed my feminist principles and went to see her perform at The Purple Onion, a strip club at the top of Cuba Street.

In a cold, half-empty room, a group of men hovered close to the stage. Strobe lights played over the half-naked bodies of young girls in clichéd costumes. I felt glum and jaded watching them wriggle their way self-consciously down to their g-strings to the perky beat of the Village People. But in the middle of it all, Lady Jane still managed to look, well, like a lady.

The other Jane, who'd come up from Dunedin, quickly became known as Honky Jane because of her blonde hair and fair skin. She moved into Abel Smith Street and shared one of the big front bedrooms. 'I remember being really annoyed because the girls were always pinching my clothes,' she said. 'I desperately wanted to have something that was mine, and people would respect the fact that it was. But that was learning to live with other people too.'

Clothes may have been shared, but housework was a different matter. Gini said she paid board and expected everything to be laid on. 'Knowing what happened with the money of the house, what bills got paid, where it went to, who got delegated to do the cooking or the cleaning, I washed my hands of it. I was just in it for myself. But I liked it there.'

Somehow a meal was prepared most nights, usually by me, Annie or Gerry. Gerry at least cared about the house, moaning about the mess and telling people off for turning up the record player too loud when her young daughter was asleep. Not like her younger sister, Rangi, a real party girl.

The meals were basic. Chicken stew. Mince. Boil-ups. Lots of white bread. We ate kneeling on the carpet in the lounge around the big table with sawn-off legs — you could fit more people that way — while Phoebe Snow crooned 'Don't let me down' from the scratchy record player. Renée Geyer was another favourite, especially 'Standing on Shaky Ground'. 'Cos it consistently felt like that,' said Charmaine. 'It was a real hit and everyone jived to it.'

Posters of Che Guevara and Rua Kēnana, block-mounted by Jane, who was good at that sort of thing, hung on the walls. I knew little about

Rua, the Tūhoe prophet, except that he was a pacifist and revolutionary with many wives. But his face drew me in. Side-on, he was strong and soulful, his long hair kinking down to his shoulders.

When we left Abel Smith Street, I took the black-and-white poster of Rua and hung it in future houses; people sometimes mistook him for a youthful Pat. Once, Junior came to visit me with a friend, a man in his forties. I made sandwiches and we sat around the kitchen table. The man smiled a lot but didn't say anything; he seemed rather overwhelmed. Later, we went through to the lounge. When he saw Rua on the wall, his eyes filled with tears and he began to talk: he was a Tūhoe man himself. Over and over again, he expressed amazement that such a poster would be hanging in such a house — a Pākehā house, I think he meant. When he said goodbye, he held my hand for a long time. I was stunned that one small, unwitting validation of his world could bridge the gulf that had seemed to separate us.

On my way home from the hairdresser's, I swung by Brougham Street, the three-storey rabbit warren where Mike Womble, Mike Hancock and an unlikely assortment of other people lived. It was the third in the triangle of trust houses, along with ours and Peter's.

'Anyone home?' I called.

'Up here.' Mike Hancock's elfin features appeared from the mezzanine bedroom he'd built above the lounge. He'd been a welcome addition to the scene since he got back from overseas. Not as buttoned-up as the Wombles, easier to talk to, happy to spend time with us girls. He stayed on the edges of the Black Power, driving a taxi rather than working for their trust.

'Sorry, mate. Did I wake you up?' I said.

'Never mind, I have to cook tea anyway,' he said, climbing down the ladder. 'Hey, look at you.' He reached out to pat the huge, fuzzy cloud of hair that engulfed my face. 'Just like an angel!'

'Hell's Angel, more like,' I grumbled, but I was secretly pleased. Everyone was getting afros, Jimmy Hendrix-style. It was part fashion, part political statement. A few days earlier, Annie had come home with a cute, fluffy halo. But my natural curl had magnified the effect and my hair was now several times the diameter of my head. It stayed like that for months, getting drier and frizzier by the day; the split ends plagued me for years.

Mike yawned. 'I was out driving all night. Just as I was going to knock off, your lot rang up wanting a ride home from The Strip.'

I made a growling sound. 'So that's why Charmaine and Gini fucked off for a sleep in the van this arvo.'

'Next time I'll make them walk,' he said, buttoning his shirt over his skinny chest, tucking the flaps into his jeans and running his fingers through his ginger curls. 'There. All done. Coffee?'

I stood at the doorway of the one-person kitchen as he filled a dented black kettle, fished two mugs out of a stack of dirty dishes and gave them a quick rinse under the cold tap.

'There's someone I want you to meet,' he said. 'She'd be great for your fullas' trust.'

'Really?'

He nodded. 'Her name's Georgie. She's a barmaid at the Waterloo. Smart. Been around. Gorgeous-looking, too.'

'Ha! So that explains the interest.'

He pretended to look hurt. 'Her boyfriend' — he emphasised the word — 'isn't a gang guy. They've got a two-year-old son, but he mostly stays with her parents.'

I retired to the lounge, sat on the couch and wrestled off my work boots. Good old Mike, always on the lookout for us. We could certainly do with some help. Plenty of girls wanted to work for Aroha Trust, but some of them had to have a few clues or we'd all go under.

'Has she got her licence?' I called out. 'I'm sick of driving everyone everywhere.'

'I'm sure I've seen her drive,' he said, coming through with the coffee.

'Everyone *drives*, Mike.'

He grinned. 'Why don't I bring her round tomorrow after work? You can ask her yourself.'

Ko Aotea me Tākitimu ōku waka
Ko Taranaki me Whakapūnake ōku maunga
Ko Taikotu me Te Wai-au ōku awa
Ko Ngā Ruahinerangi me Ngāti Kahungunu ōku iwi
Ko Ngāti Haua Piko me Ngāti Mākoro ōku hapū
Ko Horiana Hohepene Wikitoria taku ingoa

When I pulled up outside Georgie's state house in Hastings two decades later, her 14-year-old son was on the roof, retrieving a ball from a game of cricket in the backyard.

'Kia ora, girlfriend,' she boomed from the front porch as I opened the car door. Lines of tiredness etched her face, but she was still striking in a dark green and gold tasselled top and black trousers, and there was a flash of perfect teeth when she smiled. Two younger children appeared behind her, both as fine-looking as she'd been at their age. She pointed to a house across the road. 'Remember my son? Just a wee fulla in the trust days? He lives over there with his partner and my two moko. I'm a nanny now.'

I shook my head. 'Impossible! That would make me far too old.'

Georgie ushered me into her clean, sparse kitchen. She'd made a lot of changes in the past couple of years: left her partner, taken on her Māori name, Horiana, and started a nursing degree, supporting her five children on the DPB, supplemented by weekend and night work at the hospital psych unit. Her second-year exams were over, but giant sheets of handwritten biology notes were still Blu-tacked to the cupboard doors.

'They remind me of what I've been through,' she said, pointing at them with stubby fingers, the nails bitten to the quick. 'I studied every spare minute. Never again, though. It wasn't worth the risk and it took a toll on me health-wise. I was really becoming run-down. Not eating. Smoke like a bloody train. I felt like a walking zombie. Sometimes I just wanted to borrow somebody's brain for the exam and then give it back.'

Georgie planned to spread the final year's study over two years so she could spend more time with her children. They were behind her decision to train as a nurse. 'I'm no longer going to be a Social Welfare statistic,' she said proudly. 'I'll be able to provide for them, help them with their goals. I'm going to be their rock because I feel no one's offering my kids anything except the dole. They're going to go through exactly what I've been through.'

They saw her in a different light now, she said. 'I've always been a staunch, strong mum. But for me to get an education and be further bettering myself, it's really made them look at me as someone to be proud of.'

'Staunch' was the word Georgie also used to describe her parents' relationship. Her father, of Aotea and Te Āti Awa descent, was a truck driver and freezing worker who had old-fashioned attitudes towards women and liked a beer. Her mother, from Ngāti Kahungunu, was a packer and forewoman for the New Zealand Apple and Pear Board, just like her mother had been.

'There were lots of arguments but never any abuse,' Georgie said. There were also family outings to the country and the river, home-baking, birthday and Christmas celebrations, a stray box of lollies or bananas off the back of her dad's truck. 'They were perfect role models really. They put us in good schools. We always had kai. And warm beds. Even though there was sometimes two or three of us to a bed, we were still warm and happy. We came from a happy home.'

Things were harder in those days, she said. 'People talk about poverty today, but I think a lot of it is self-inflicted. I was brought up in an era where you don't worry about where your next feed's coming from, you get out there and you get it. Or you dig a garden. You find yourself something, even if they're the most mundane jobs. It's all about survival, it's all about where your priorities are.'

The oldest of seven children, Georgie went to St Mary's Catholic primary school where she was one of only a few Māori pupils. Although both sets of grandparents were fluent in te reo, they didn't pass on the language. 'I suppose you have to understand the dilemma in those days, but I feel really ripped off,' she said.

She excelled at sport and by the time she got to Tennyson College, netball was her greatest love. 'A lot of people thought I could have gone a long way. But then, I don't know, I went for a walk on the wild side.' She laughed. 'But I still had the idea that if you looked at a boy and kissed him, you got pregnant. So my mum did really well instilling that one in me.'

Like many of the other women, Georgie was expected to look after younger siblings while her parents worked. It was impossible to study in the bedroom she shared with three sisters, and there were always chores to be done. Halfway through fifth form, she got fed up and decided to run away.

She and a friend hitch-hiked to Wellington with $1.50 in their pockets. When the YMCA turned them away, a guy across the road invited them in. A few minutes later, the police stormed the house, something Georgie was always grateful for. 'Before you knew it, 12 Mob members came downstairs and were told to go outside; we never knew they were up there. We just looked at each other and held on to each other.'

The two young women were taken to the police station. In the cells, a drag queen gave them Denis O'Reilly's address — Georgie still remembered it: 111 Vivian Street — and told them to go there and ask for him. 'He and another Pākehā guy knew we were runaways, but they were really good. We ended up sleeping in their room on the floor, under their protection. That's how we got to know the Blacks.'

But Georgie was not about to become a street kid. She found a job at Bonds Hosiery Factory, and moved in with a Pākehā boyfriend. Her father came to Wellington to look for her, and twice she went back to Hawke's Bay. 'I drove around our street at night. I could see my mother at the sink, and I could hear my father at the table talking to her. I stopped on the other side of the road and I just sat there and looked in.'

But it was a year and a half before she got in touch with her parents and went to see them. 'I was so scared. I hopped off the bus and I could see my mother running to me. It was such a massive reunion.'

I didn't get it. Why would a 16-year-old girl from a happy family vanish for 18 months without telling anyone she was alive?

'I don't know. This was a big adventure buzz for me and I think I just wanted to see what I could do by myself. I didn't mean to hurt them.'

I still didn't get it.

'I'll never forget this cheeky broad standing by the door. She had this scarf halfway wrapped around her face and she stood there leaning back against the wall looking me up and down.' Georgie gave a deep, throaty laugh, her first meeting with Charmaine and the other Aroha Trust girls forever imprinted on her mind.

Mike Hancock had brought her round to Abel Smith Street as promised. The short blue dress, red lipstick and high heels she wore behind the bar couldn't have been in greater contrast to the Swannies, work jeans, boots, scarves and berets that were our daily uniform.

'My first impression was, they'll be wondering who the hell's this suave, hip chick walking into our house,' Georgie said. 'Then I thought, oh, what the hell, this is me, this is who I am.' As for the lounge of girls: 'They looked young, hard, staunch, and like, shit, I hope I never get in a fight with any of them.'

Our clothes were practical for work, but they were also part of a deliberate image. 'We set ourselves apart from a lot of people,' Annie said. 'But we felt good about it. Well, I used to.'

We were especially proud of our steel-capped boots. 'We'd convinced the city council we needed the fur-lined, knee-high variety, primarily because they were the cool boots and we didn't want to be seen wearing these stink ankle jobs,' Jane reminded me. Twenty years later, hers still sat in her shed. 'I just loved those boots,' she said. 'They were part of being a bunch of tough sheilas, a visible emblem that we were powerful, we did have some control of our lives. You know, "Look out world, don't fuck round with me."'

Georgie threw in her pub job and came to work for Aroha Trust. 'I walk through life, I try anything once. Annie and yourself were also the attraction; there felt like there was some good leadership from you.' A puzzled look came over her face. 'Somehow I got roped into being in charge too. I was quite taken aback because I thought, hell, I've only been here for a month.'

I looked at her guiltily. At 20, she'd been older and more capable than most of the girls — and she did have her driver's licence. There'd been no time for an apprenticeship.

Georgie loved working for the trust and got on well with the girls. But trying to keep them in line wasn't easy. 'I would let things go and go and go,' she said. 'Until in the end if people weren't bucking their ideas up and we were supposed to be doing a job, I felt, nah, no more. Then I'd get, "What are you on? What's your problem?"'

'With Charmaine and Gini, I blew. I said, "You go on about how you're treated, about oppression, blah, blah, not given the chance and the opportunity. You can't even bloody sort things out for yourself. You can't even be responsible here. Fuck's sake. Get your shit together." Then Gini would think, "Nah, fuck that, I'm going to the pub." And Charmaine would hang her lips. I remember after I'd done a big spiel at work, got really shitty, three of them didn't turn up the next day. Then I thought, "Well, I don't care." Trial and error. It was, take one day at a time, mate. You don't know what you're going to be confronted with.'

I was relieved to hear her say this. At work, we rotated the person in charge every week. That way, we figured, no one could be seen as the boss and everyone would learn what it was like to be responsible for the group. In practice, it wasn't that simple. Most of the girls had trouble running their own lives, let alone a team of workers. Whenever we arrived at a new school, someone had to meet the principal, discuss what work needed to be done, negotiate where and when we could have smoko. Sometimes I could hardly bear to watch the misunderstandings and prejudices unfold. The girl in charge would be shy and tongue-tied. The principal — already sceptical about women labourers, especially women who looked like PD workers — would think, 'surly and unhelpful'. He would be defensive and patronising. The girls would think, 'racist prick'.

My inclination was to step in and rescue, smooth things over, keep the peace. Annie had no such qualms. 'I think it worked quite well,' she said. 'The headmaster' — it was nearly always a man — 'would come out and he would automatically come and talk to me cos I was white and looked the straightest. I would go, "Oh, I'm not the boss today; she is." They had to go and talk to someone, usually a Māori woman that had a lot of tattoos and dressed in great big heavy jackboots. I wouldn't involve myself because I think I made a conscious decision they had to relate to that person.'

One day, the girls walked out of a school in a middle-class area after the principal tried to make them have smoko in a back room. 'We turned round and said to him, "Well, when we're good enough to have our lunch and our breaks in your smoko room, we'll come back",' Annie said. 'We went and told the guy at the Education Board. I think he was pretty sympathetic. We probably gave him a few headaches, but he was aware of what some people could be like.'

'Headaches?' I asked.

'Maybe we didn't keep to schedules or we'd go missing for a while,' she admitted. 'It was pretty basic, mundane work and it was hard to keep people motivated to the task. I was probably one of the ones who needed to be motivated myself.'

From my point of view, Annie hadn't been the ally I'd hoped for when she started working for the trust. We were hardly ever on the same team: it made sense to spread ourselves around. In general, I liked the renovation work for the city council while she preferred the freedom of moving from school to school with the Education Board, though we swapped from time to time.

But it was more than that. She'd disappear without warning, skip trust meetings, leave me to enforce the rules we'd all agreed on. Much as I admired her democratic instincts, I resented the way she sometimes hid behind them. And it didn't stop the others thinking of her as a leader.

Amelia was clear about who'd been in charge. 'You were,' she said. 'I used to hate it when you used to separate me and Nayda. "*You* go and work at that end and *you* go and work round the corner." Me and Nayda used to whinge at each other and say, "Bloody little bitch".'

Tasi agreed. 'I wasn't really into those decisions; I didn't really have any say in the matter.'

I asked her if she'd wanted a say.

'Sometimes,' she said. Little things had bugged her. 'We'd work hard out and we wouldn't have lunch till later on. Or sometimes it took us a long time to get to work, you know, get around to doing what we were doing.'

Mahina said Tasi used to moan behind our backs. 'I don't know if she was going off at you or Annie: "Those bloody honkies, they think we're just bloody workers. We'll do what we like." At the time we used to think, what are they telling us that for? Why can't they do it their bloody selves?'

Gini had no confidence in her own leadership ability. 'Because I had no qualifications or communication skills, but also because I was so low in self-esteem, no way should I be up in the front line.' For a long time, she baulked at learning new skills. 'We used to mix up all the weed sprays and I remember not having anything to do with the nitty-gritty measuring, purposely trying to cut from the administration side of learning how things work. Just trying to be the labourer at the end. It was too complicated to go there. We left those jobs up to you — and Annie. I was still thinking, you're the white ones, you know how those things go, that's your job. And my job was to cut down the bush or spray the weeds or the physical bits.'

For Gini, learning to drive was the only real incentive to get more involved in the running of the trust. 'I wanted the responsibility of the van, even if it meant having to learn and be an authority. When I learnt to drive, it gave me so much power and freedom.'

Power. Freedom. Responsibility. Driving represented everything Aroha Trust stood for. This matched my own experience of growing up. For all his moral conservatism, my father encouraged his daughters to be independent. In my house, you got your licence — and access to my mother's small car — the minute you turned 15. Letting us behind the wheel was better than having us rely on dodgy young men in even dodgier vehicles, I suspect. The strategy paid off when, in my last year of school, Dad's seizures stopped him from driving: he had a small squad of chauffeurs at his disposal.

In the trust, everyone wanted to drive. Annie and I taught many of the girls. Some got their licences at the time, others didn't sit the test for years.

'I was stuck way out in the wops somewhere,' Gini said. 'My partner had left and I was landed with these children and thought, I need some way of getting around here. I had become a Christian by then, and I said to the Lord, "Come on, I need a car." And he said to me, clear as day, "You get your licence, and I'll get you a car." I took the traffic cop for a drive up Kaikohe, and we got to the end of it, and I said, "Well, did I pass?" He said to me, "You're a bit overconfident, don't you think?" I said to him, "You would be too if you had been driving around for the last 10 years." He said, "So, what made you go for your licence?" I said, "The Lord did, actually." And he rolled his eyes and gave me one of those looks like, oh another one of them.'

As one of the younger girls, Jane had to wait her turn for driving lessons. 'It was a big thing in the trust, a sign of when you hit being considered responsible,' she said. On a quiet Sunday afternoon she puttered nervously along Waterloo Quay in the Red Baron, me issuing instructions, Tasi and Junior egging her on in the back. Behind us came the wail of a siren and flashing blue lights.

'What is it this time?' I muttered. Young, brown faces and battered vehicles were a traffic-cop magnet, I'd discovered. 'Eat the Rich' painted in black across the back doors of the van probably didn't help, although a quick peek inside would have revealed an equally large sign that read 'Eat the People', so the writer was not at all clear about their slogans.

To Jane's eternal shame, the cop told her she was driving too slowly. Not long after, she and Rangi proceeded to prove him wrong, driving our Morris bread van over to Brougham Street one night, where we were having a few drinks.

'We were off our faces,' Jane said. 'I can remember hitting a green Mercedes and trying to back out and hitting the car that was behind me. They were both parked; there weren't people in them, thank goodness.'

After a short visit, they left without revealing their mode of transport. 'We parked the van round the corner in Elizabeth Street and *someone* left the handbrake off,' Jane said. 'It took off down the street and hit the parked cars in front.' The van was written off, but the police never tracked down the culprits. 'But when you guys found out, we were pretty much in the dog box.'

Jane's story reminded me how much I hated trying to manage teenagers not much younger than me, far wilder than most parents had to deal with. The girls nicked the vans — and my Honda 50 — every chance they got. No amount of pleading that someone might get hurt and that we couldn't get to work without our vehicles made any difference. It was disheartening, it undermined our solidarity, and I struggled not to take it personally.

I could never let my guard down. On our way to work one morning, I went to get Agnes from her flat, leaving the keys in the ignition. Immediately, Amelia jumped behind the wheel. 'I thought I was neat cos you'd only shown me once how to drive and I thought I knew it all,' she said. 'Nayda was nutting off: "Idiot! Go on, kill yourself, you clown." I think she came up to tell you to hurry up.'

At work, Georgie looked out the window of a school staffroom during smoko to see the van going around and around the school paddock. 'It was Charmaine. She was determined she was going to learn how to drive. What better place to learn than a bloody big rugby field, eh. So I used to put the keys in my pocket. And I'd get hounded and hounded. I got so good at turning off, cos you had to.'

Charmaine didn't give up. 'I'd wait for Georgie to go for a mimi, and prior to that I'd hoisted the keys out of her jacket. I'd think, she should be on the toilet now, and off I'd go in the van and I'd drive it round all the paddocks. That's how I learnt to drive.'

When Georgie was off work with a migraine, one of the girls without a licence drove the Education Board van and crashed into a bank. Georgie was asked to take the rap. 'I said I would because the guy who covered for us a lot had to go and see his boss,' Georgie said. 'Those were the things we did, I think.' She looked thoughtful. 'That was getting a bit beyond.'

I searched the archived Wellington Education Board minutes, hoping to find mention of Aroha Trust and our escapades. When nothing showed up, I rang our boss. Now retired, he only recalled one story: that the neighbours had complained when the girls sunbathed topless on a field at Johnsonville Main primary school on a hot summer's afternoon. It sounded unlikely to me: our lifestyle trained us to stay well covered. I checked with the other women. None of them remembered the incident either, though one said a principal in Johnsonville had let us use the school swimming pool. It made me wonder if a quick change out of wet clothes had become exaggerated to fit some preconceived notion of us as brazen and lazy.

We were in and out of the Education Board offices, organising the next job, picking up tools, getting paid, nicking toilet rolls from the ladies', working in the library when it was wet. Georgie remembered the few staff who put themselves out: our manager, the wages man, the tea lady. 'She lost her love in the war; never, ever married,' Georgie said. 'Whenever we went into the café, she always used to bring us over a cake. Say, "C'mon, you girls." We always talked to her and it must have been the highlight of her day. Having worked in offices myself, I can see how up their nose that lot can be.'

As usual, I saw things from both sides. To the office workers, we must have seemed foul-mouthed and intimidating, keeping to ourselves and scoffing as many staff biscuits as we could lay our hands on. I could see how our difference might scare them even as I hated the way they looked down on us.

'They made a lot of us have a complex,' Tasi said. 'One time we were doing the morning tea and we had to pour all these people's tea and I was shaking with the teapot. I was nervous because of their attitude. They weren't really appreciative of us. Probably they were going through their problems too.'

ELEVEN

GETTING THE BASH

We'd been hauling heavy slabs of Gib board from the pallet on the footpath onto the high scaffolding in the Newtown Community Centre theatre for what seemed like forever. One girl at each end of the Gib, its chalky edges cutting off the blood supply to our fingertips, our leg muscles shaking with fatigue. Still the stack didn't seem to be getting any smaller. We were well overdue for a smoke and a sit-down.

But our new boss wouldn't hear of it. 'Not till you've finished,' he said. We muttered under our breath. Who did he think he was? No one told the Aroha Trust girls what to do.

It was the first day we'd worked for the slim builder in his early thirties with wavy brown hair and a shaggy beard, who was tougher than he looked. His partner, a quietly spoken older man, was probably planning a peaceful retirement sometime soon. Both Pākehā, they'd agreed to take the city council team on and teach us building skills. In return, we gave up some of our independence.

We spent the next few months clambering around on planks, gibbing and painting the theatre's high domed ceiling and walls.

Banks of dirty, stained-glass windows filtered pastel light across the sloping wooden floor. I relished my bird's-eye view and the orderly, self-contained world up in the rafters, even when I knocked over a tin of cream paint and it splattered like seagull droppings on the church pews below.

For me, the two builders were a godsend. They were great teachers, long-suffering and unflappable. They must have been aware of the chaos behind the scenes, and I suspect they cared about us more than we realised. I liked the physical work, learning on the job and having someone else take charge. Even if the younger one was a bit of a stickler.

'Do it again!' he said, surveying our work after he'd made us repaint a section of the wall. 'I can still see a line where the two batches meet.'

'No one will notice all the way up here,' I grumbled.

He shook his head and walked away. We prised the lid off the smoky green paint and stirred the contents for a full five minutes before starting on the wall for the third time.

When the Education Board girls called in during work hours, he was unimpressed.

'Ten minutes,' he'd say. 'Then you have to go.'

They'd give us sympathetic looks. 'Poor yous, having to put up with that all day.'

I'd roll my eyes and whisper 'slave driver' along with the rest of them. It was so much easier than being the slave driver myself.

At first, Jane was suspicious of our new bosses. 'For me, they were just more blokes; it took a long time for me to trust that they didn't have ulterior motives. But they were pretty amazing when I think back. They were very patient and took us as we were a lot of the time. I don't know how many people would have put up with us. The women were pretty hard nuts; I don't think most of them would take shit from anyone. You had to be pretty careful in the way that you dealt with most of the women in the trust.'

Jane loved renovating old houses under their supervision. 'Some of that work was quite groundbreaking and valuable, and had a long-term effect in terms of my confidence at doing stuff that's considered traditionally male.'

She was less complimentary about the Education Board work, in particular our use of weedkillers. A school in Strathmore hosted a miniature circus while our girls were working there. 'We were spraying the grass the kids were playing on and the horses were eating, which was absolutely horrific,' she said. 'And pouring it down the drains. We had no protective gear whatsoever, no idea what we were playing with. I'm not sure if it was the same day that one of the girls drunk some of the Ban 750 while she was pregnant. After that day I got really, really sick and I thought I was going to die, cos I'd been wearing a big, old, brass backpack that had leaked all over me. Charmaine and Annie didn't know whether to take me to the hospital or get an ambulance or what. I was absolutely bloody crook. But we didn't tell anyone.'

There were other on-the-job hazards too. 'I remember them letting us loose with chainsaws, chopping up all this old wood that was full of nails,' Jane said. 'When I think about it now, I think, "My God, what a bunch of lunatics."'

෧෧

One day at work, Jane and Tasi took to each other with hammers. 'The council guy walked in in the middle of it and didn't know what the hell to do,' Jane said. 'Here's her and me going at it. I guess it's because we were similar in age; it was almost like siblings. Me and her would probably argue the most. A lot of the time that was the only way we knew how to react to things.'

Most of the girls were quick to scrap, though none of them ever threatened me. Gini considered herself just as responsible as her partner, JB, for their fights. 'I used to always blame it on him,' she said. 'But I know now I was a witch. I provoked him.'

She was very jealous. 'He'd just have to be doing anything that would stir up these emotions in me, and I would go up to him and accuse him of having an affair. He'd get angry. We'd forget it. Start drinking. Then I'd come out again. I'd say horrible things, run him down, tell him that when he did hit me, it didn't hurt anyway. I'd really drive him to the extreme. Because he was quite good. He could control his temper until I pushed him over the side. I remember one night he kicked me into this little corner of this toilet in the pad. Saying to him, "Spare it! Is that all you can do? I can't even feel it", my flesh cringing, and all the bruises and the pain that I was in. It was like it was uncontrollable. I was running him down to the max, and he was getting angrier and angrier and angrier. I could hear myself like a broken record. He finally walked out because he had no more energy to hit me anymore. And he was big. He was six foot plus.'

Being bashed felt normal, Gini said. 'Once a month at least I felt I needed a good hiding. My flesh would literally cry out for a bashing. I think it was because of my childhood. I was so used to getting that hiding that afterwards I felt like I was accepted. I felt like I was loved again, because he cared that he'd hurt me so much that he was so sorry. It was a walkway of love. That's how I think to explain it now.'

Junior was the same. 'I'd just take on the biggest person to get a hiding,' she said. 'I had become so addicted, I had to have a hiding. I'd walk into a Mongrel Mob pub and do the fist in the middle of them, knowing that I was going to get a hiding. And I'd get wasted and smashed up. And get home. I just thought if I didn't get a hiding over a couple of months, there was something wrong. I'd better go and look for one. And I would.'

Gini believed that the women were responsible for most gang fights. 'They start bickering among themselves or with another guy, and next thing you know, it's all on.' She started a war on the night of her twenty-fifth birthday — by then the mother of two young children — when she got drunk and shouted, 'Nomads the best' in a pub full of Black Power and Mongrel Mob.

'I'd lost it totally and was just manifesting what I believed to be my heart's desire: giving loyalty to the brothers.' She woke up in an alleyway in a pool of blood. 'I was left there to die. You know those glass jugs — they broke one on my face.' She ran her finger along a long scar on her right cheek just under her eye. Even that didn't put her off. 'I just accepted it like, oh well, what goes round comes round.'

When she became a Christian and married a man from her church, Gini couldn't believe he wouldn't hit her. 'To be in a relationship where he would just walk away made me madder. I'd run after him and attack him so that he would turn around and hit me. When he still didn't, it made me even angrier. I went to the pastor and said, "Look, I don't know how to say this, but I feel I need prayer because my husband won't hit me." It's what I felt in my heart. I was used to a hiding. I deserved one. Why aren't I having one? So they worked me through that. It was like I'd been deceived all these years and now to see the truth of the matter, that you don't put up with hidings, you don't have to get abused, it was foreign but it was good. That's taken some getting used to, but I like it.'

Gini had to work hard to stop the cycle of violence with her own children. Her husband helped, she said. 'It wasn't until I got married that it almost stopped overnight. He takes me through the stage of, "No, don't hit them! No, they don't deserve that. It's only a little thing. Don't worry! It'll fix. It'll mend. Don't!" To have somebody there with you is a big difference. The church were there, but they weren't in my house, in my face, in my bedroom, in my hallway, in my kitchen. Whereas my husband is. He can hold my arms down, stop me hitting them.'

She still got the urge at times. 'I'll clench my fist and look really ugly, but I won't lash out. Even if I'm going up to one of them to grab them by the jersey, 99 per cent of the time I will stop there. It's been a real breakthrough in an area that I really wanted. You get brought up thinking there's no way you're going to take it on into the next generation, and you're doing it all of a sudden. It's a lifestyle thing that's been handed down. Unwillingly. I'm in my forties now and I'm just starting to see out of it. It's one thing to know there is another way, but another thing to actually practise cutting that thing, putting something in its place.'

'Don't look round! The pigs are here,' Gini said. We went into a huddle, pretending we had nothing to do with the Black Power milling round us. Cops in navy-blue uniforms stood in each exit with their arms folded, rocking on their heels. Others worked their way through the crowded Friday-night public bar of the Lion Tavern.

'Evening, girls. How are we tonight?' The cop addressing us was young and officious, with cautious blue eyes.

Gini ignored him and kept talking to Nayda, who'd come to town for the weekend, her belly just starting to show.

'Fine till you lot got here,' Jane muttered.

'You're not 20,' said the cop, his gaze drawn to the gold cross nestled in her cleavage.

'Got an eyeful, you dirty prick?' she snarled.

He flushed. 'Let's see your ID.'

'Left it at home.'

'Get out of here before I arrest you. And you and you.' He tapped Gini and Nayda lightly on the shoulder.

Gini swung around. 'Keep your hands off me, cunt!'

'Watch your language or you'll be spending a night in the cells.' Red blotches were marching up his neck.

Gini took a step towards him.

Nayda stopped her. 'Let's go, pal. There's a bad smell in here.'

'You're fuckin' right there,' Gini sneered, but she let Nayda guide her towards the door. Jane followed.

'You okay?' Mike Womble had come over to see what was going on.

The cop turned to me. 'You too,' he said.

'You can't throw me out, I'm 22.' I fished my driver's licence out of my back pocket and handed it to him. He peered at it in the dim light. 'Full name?' he said.

'Phillipa Mary Desmond.' I tried to say it quietly.

Mike sniggered. I glared at him.

'Date of birth?' said the cop.

'25 August 1955.'

The cop looked doubtful.

'Look, I'll prove it.' I found a dry spot on the bar and scrawled my signature on a serviette. 'There! Satisfied?'

A second cop, who looked vaguely familiar, appeared. 'You're not going to fall for that, are you?' he said to the first. 'She's got that signature down to a fine art.'

Now I remembered. He'd thrown me out of the Cambridge the week before. 'That's because it's mine,' I said, my voice rising.

The first cop screwed up the serviette. 'Out!'

'But that's not fair—'

'Now!'

I waited till they moved away, then fumed at Mike. 'Arseholes! They'd never treat me like that if I was with a bunch of students. What happened to innocent till proven guilty?'

'Welcome to the real world!'

'Are you going to the clubrooms later?'

He nodded.

The cop was bearing down on me again. 'Okay, see ya there!' I said, and took off.

Outside, the girls were standing on the footpath.

'Thought you'd deserted us,' said Jane.

'Bastards! I might as well not have a fuckin' licence.'

'Let's try the Southern Cross,' said Nayda. But the bouncer wouldn't let us in. Too young, too scruffy, too many of us, he said.

'We'll have to go home and get out of our work gears,' said Gini. 'We can have a blow while we're there.'

At Abel Smith Street, I pulled on a cream shirt and black cords and pushed my big toes through the loops of platform sandals that added four inches to my height.

'Hurry up, Pip!' Jane called from the kitchen.

Gini was leaning against the bench with her arm slung over Nayda's shoulder, a silly grin on her face. Jane heated two knives over the gas ring until the blades were red-hot. She carefully placed a small brown chip of hash on one and mashed it with the other. I bent over the knives, breathing in the smoke through a glass milk bottle with the bottom bashed out, and held it till I thought my lungs would burst. Then I doubled over, coughing.

'Fuck, that stuff's harsh,' I croaked when I could speak again. My eyes streamed. My voice echoed in my head. Shadows danced across the kitchen walls. The girls' faces glowed blue and orange through the gas flame. I loved them. I loved Aroha Trust. There was nowhere in the world I'd rather be.

⚭

I stood in the Black Power clubrooms, a small, Spartan house in Murphy Street that the mayor had loaned the boys, pending its demolition for the motorway. Over the heads of the packed-in bodies, Mike Womble passed me a double rum and Coke.

'Thanks,' I mouthed, making a mental note to slow down after this one. At the Black Power disco in the Aro Valley hall the week before, I'd lost count. When I'd lined up the doorway in search of fresh air, I walked straight into the wall and crumpled in a heap on the floor. Gini was beside me in a flash. She picked me up and slung me over her shoulder like a bag of fertiliser, then headed across the courtyard to our house, a couple of minutes' walk away, chatting away to Charmaine and ignoring my feeble protests to be put down. The ground rose and fell like a rollercoaster while I tried not to throw up down the back of her jacket. At Abel Smith Street, she opened my bedroom door and tossed me onto the bed. 'Sweet dreams,' she said, leaving me to cope with a ceiling that spun when my eyes were open and spun faster when they were shut.

That wasn't going to happen tonight.

Around me, 50 voices joined Bob Marley in: 'No Woman, No Cry'. Suddenly I had a blinding insight. I cupped my hands and shouted into Mike's ear. 'I thought he was saying women make men cry. But he's not. He's comforting *his* woman, telling *her* not to cry.' The world tipped from cynicism to compassion, from loneliness to love.

'Amazing what a few drinks can do,' Mike said, giving me the infuriating Womble smirk that he and Peter had perfected. But it faded quickly and, for once, I was sorry to see it go. Mike was the quieter twin, but since he and Annie had split up, he'd been really down. She, on the other hand, was having a ball. Her latest boyfriend was a gentle

Highway 61 guy with a stutter who she was probably with now.

'I'm outta here,' Mike said. 'Same old people, same old fuckin' shit.'

I watched him push his way to the door, wishing I could make it better, then did a quick check round the room and out into the hallway where girls were sometimes dragged upstairs and gang-raped, or put on the block as it was called. I still had enough back-up: Peter Womble was standing with a couple of Black Power guys I trusted, and there were a group of Aroha Trust girls at the end of the bar. I worked my way over to them.

'Fat little prick,' I heard Gini say as I got close. 'Thinks he can come to our house and stick his dick in anyone he wants. I'll smash his fuckin' head in.'

'Ssssh,' Nayda said, putting her hand on Gini's arm, her face grim. 'He's right there.'

Gini pushed Nayda away. Her eyes were bloodshot, her voice insistent. 'I'm not scared of him. He's just a Fat. Little. Fuckin'. Prick.' She emphasised each word by banging her empty glass on the bar.

People were starting to look. We hustled Gini away from the group of guys behind us. She was gunning for the one who'd raped the quiet 16-year-old at Abel Smith Street. But confronting him was out of the question. Not outnumbered like this. Not on his turf, with everyone drunk and stoned. Not ever.

Someone strummed a few chords and a catchy song started up:

> *In 1970, the Black Power went to war*
> *They went to Peka Peka to the rock festival*
> *They stole a little pūhā and they stole a little pork*
> *And they stole a mighty Mark I so they didn't have to walk.*

I looked around at the boys wearing their 'rigis' — short for 'originals' — the prized jeans they never washed and often slept in, split across the knees, patched, safety-pinned, the backsides hanging out, battle-scarred and faithful as a best friend. On the back of every denim or leather jacket was the embroidered clenched fist they'd defend with their lives. Some had sweet, vulnerable faces; others looked world-weary and mean.

The singing reached a crescendo as they punched their fists in the air:

> *Teke te raho,[1] raho te teke, it's the mighty Black Power song,*
> *Teke te raho, raho te teke, it's the mighty Black Power song.*

I broke into a smile. Someone had a sense of humour. The chorus of the anthem of the biggest gang in New Zealand was sung to the tune of 'The Woody Woodpecker Song'.

Across the room, Arthur, the country boy I'd got on so well with when we were both new to the scene, stood folded around a beer bottle, swaying groggily. There was no point going over to him; he was too wasted. He'd gone inside for a few months when the cops caught up with him for whatever he'd been on the run for. When he got out, he was angrier. He moved into Epuni Street with Peter Womble, joined the Black Power, grew an ugly mo. But I'd seen another side of him. I wished I'd taken my chances at the beginning. Secretly, I still hoped we could be more than friends.

Ricki, treasurer of the Wellington Blacks, stood beside Arthur, surveying the room. He was small and spunky, a black beret atop his long curly hair as usual. For once, he was without his shades. I never saw him get aggro. His philosophy was 'make love, not war', though this was not entirely flattering; he didn't get the nickname Ricki Slut for nothing. His poor girlfriend never mixed with the gang or the Aroha Trust girls. She was determined to turn him into a Rastafarian. And she succeeded in the end, I think.

Jane went with Ricki for a while. 'He'd always apologise for being Māori,' she said. 'He wished he was Pākehā. I found that really sad.'

I asked her if she'd told him that she was Māori too.

'No! I didn't tell anyone. But I think that's why I remember it. It

---

1   refers to female and male genitals

seemed ironic that he didn't like being identified as Māori because of his skin colour, and I didn't like being identified as Pākehā because of mine.'

Once, I saw TV footage of the cops bailing up some Black Power members in a quiet street in the middle of the day and telling them to keep the noise down, though the voice-over said they hadn't been making any noise. As the cops got back in their car, one of the boys lashed out. Instantly, Ricki was by his side, holding him back, waving the cops away. He was the peacemaker, an excellent foil for Rei Harris who — as I watched — tipped his head back, guzzled the best part of a pint of Lion Brown and belched loudly.

Rei was a smart leader who steered his troops towards work and political action. He'd set up the Black Bulls, the forerunner to the Black Power, in 1970 when he was only a kid himself, 18 or 19, and was the national as well as the Wellington president of the Black Power. I didn't feel scared around guys like Rei and Ricki, but I wasn't close to them either. I lived primarily in a world of women, both at work and at home. Most of the gang men stayed on the periphery of my life.

Annie was more adventurous. 'You knew most of them and you built up good friendships with four or five,' she said. 'Those four or five were probably in sufficient pecking order to be able to protect you from anything that might be going to happen.'

I asked her what they did together.

'A lot of pubs, a lot of nightclubs. We never went for a picnic in the park or anything. It was all going out.'

Rei's wife was beside him. They had children and lived in a house in Thorndon guarded by Dobermans, where I never went. I didn't often see them together — or any couples being couples. In public, the boys were too staunch to pay attention or show affection to their partners.

'You'd drink at the same pub,' Amelia said. 'But how you got to where you were going, that was your problem. You didn't go together. And then with leaving, it was like, "Don't get in my face, cramp my style".'

She pointed to a photo in my album. She, Nayda and Gini were sitting on the kerb outside Wellington Cathedral, eating crayfish. (Little did they know that, quarter of a century later, their stories would be preserved on the site opposite, where the new National Library, including the oral history archives, was being built.)

'This is a classic example,' Amelia said. 'Someone had dropped the crayfish off at the Lion Tavern. But we weren't invited to go and eat with them, where they were, and join in. It was like, you look after yourself, see you at home, or see you after.'

Sometimes Amelia preferred not to be with the boys. 'They got too conspicuous. Especially the way they dressed and looked and acted. And I didn't like being with some of them, especially when they slapped their ladies around, treated them like dirt.'

When Amelia and her partner were home, his mates could arrive at any time. 'Three o'clock in the morning: "There's a rumble happening." I'd always expect him to be jumping out of bed and getting patched up and going. Sometimes I used to think it was an excuse; they wanted to get him out of there to go to a party. Most times I didn't like it. If I ever voiced it, it was like, "Shut your face". And you had to worry about the things that used to happen when they had rages at their club houses, and you weren't allowed to go or weren't there. You'd hear things. Like new girls going with your man, and all you want to do is find out who that person is and give her the bash. But you never had the balls to do it. I didn't think a boy was worth that much to be fighting in public, rolling round on the ground in my nice clothes.'

The arm's-length relationship between men and women was one reason why Aroha Trust succeeded. Tyrannical as the boys could be, the gang was their primary focus and they were largely absent. This gave the girls a curious freedom. They were used to hanging out together and supporting one another. The trust tapped into a solidarity that already existed.

When we girls were out together, we'd usually end up at The Cave or The Sunset Strip, buying jugs of overpriced Coke and surreptitiously adding our own rum or bourbon. Then we'd move on to The Last Resort or Carmen's Coffee Lounge. Carmen, Wellington's first lady of drag, was a hefty Māori renowned for her sensational breasts and her low-cut ball gowns. In 1977, the year Aroha Trust was set up, she ran for mayor with the backing of businessman Bob Jones under the banner 'Get in

Behind'. Her coffee lounge, nestled beside the Salvation Army in Vivian Street, sported red walls, purple carpet and black leather furniture. Downstairs she served tea and toasted sandwiches; upstairs delights of other kinds. The staff were all drag queens and gay men, young and beautiful.

'Carmen was awesome,' Jane said. We used to go in there all the time and she always looked after us.' When Jane's parents came to visit, she took them first to the public bar of the Royal Oak, 'but this bloody transvestite started smashing this Jap sailor round the head, so I thought I'd better take them somewhere more respectable'.

They adjourned to Carmen's. 'Carmen came and sat down with us and treated my parents as if they were having an audience with the Queen. She did it for me; it was lovely. Behind us the johns and the girls were going up and down the stairs. She even took Mum on a tour of the boudoirs.'

When Bubbles escaped from Arohata, she went straight to The Sunset Strip, where Carmen gave her money to get out of town. 'The queens used to help us, feed us and generally look after us,' Bubbles said. 'I used to go and do their gardens and things they considered too manly to do. We'd get free entry into the nightclub. We'd still be there when it shut at six o'clock in the morning.' The arrangement worked both ways. 'If their clients wouldn't pay them, the boys would make sure they got their money.'

At the end of the day (or night), it was always back to the boys. Our girls were gang girls, defined in relation to the men, particularly Black Power. Living in their shadow. Forever circling them. We might start the night cruising on our own, but it would be rare not to do the rounds of their pubs, clubrooms and disco.

'Excitement!' Annie said, when I asked her why. 'There was always action and things going on.'

'So it was a positive excitement,' I said.

'Definitely. There was always a buzz that goes with it. We were all living parts of our lives on the edge.'

I felt uncomfortable. It was all very well for Annie and me; our edge didn't drop into the same precipice as some of the other girls. But she was right. There was something addictive about the energy generated by the gang, something that pulled us in like a magnet, even as parts of it repelled us. Normal life, by comparison, seemed predictable and boring.

Hillary Watson

Joining forces: We didn't usually work on the same jobs as the Black Power, but here we're building a fence together at a city council house in Newtown. Girls clockwise from left: Charmaine, Rangi, Tasi and Jane. Note who's on the end of the shovels!

Different girls, still on the shovels: From left: Tasi, Rangi, Lady Jane and Georgie, with a member of the Black Power work trust, Te Waka e Manaaki, in the foreground.

A bit of shift work: Evelyn and Tasi (foreground) do a good turn for the Salvation Army by moving furniture. We'd volunteered to help the Sallies relocate their warehouse.

Amelia and Nayda outside the Orange Hall: Ready to paint . . . or skiving off to have another smoke?

Gini cuts grass at a local school: 'I really enjoyed that sort of work. It was outside. It was in the fresh air. There wasn't someone standing over you to make sure you were doing it perfectly, wonderfully, how they expected.'

Happy birthday: Charmaine and Georgie bring out the cake to celebrate Aroha Trust's first birthday at the Aro Valley Hall, August 1978. They're wearing tuxedos (penguin suits, as they called them) 'borrowed' from the Newtown Community Centre. Behind them is Jane's poster.

Candleman (Steve Silestean) was a legend among Wellington's street people. Bubbles: 'He had big shoulders. I could cry on them, sit on them, borrow off them.'

The morning after: Black Power members outside the Aro Valley Hall, where they held their regular Saturday-night discos.

United Women's Convention, Hamilton, 1979: From far right: Waynnie, Rangi and Sis, with three other convention-goers in the middle. Jane (far left), wears a jersey she'd knitted: 'I was so proud of that jersey, eh. That embodied how I felt about being part of the trust and the one-finger salute to the world. Women, I guess, were my whānau, and the trust embodied that. It was like my tūrangawaewae at that time, my place where I could stand tall.'

CITY OF WELLINGTON

Department of Administration and Finance

MUNICIPAL OFFICE BUILDING,
5 MERCER STREET,
WELLINGTON,
NEW ZEALAND.

v1

PLEASE ADDRESS COMMUNICATIONS TO THE TOWN CLERK, P.O. BOX 2199, WELLINGTON

IN REPLY PLEASE QUOTE
60/1378

FOR ENQUIRIES PLEASE TELEPHONE

MR. Knox
724-599   EXT. 896

20th August 1980

To: T.E.P. Workers,
       Housing & Property Branch.

As you know, the T.E.P. Scheme has been stopped. Last Friday
we had a meeting with the Labour Department and they told us
the new rules.

All jobs have to stop, except those jobs which fit into the
new rules.   So far only one job fits the rules, and we are
trying to get the Labour Department to say yes to some other
jobs. This is going to take a few weeks.

Your job will stop on Friday, 5th September. That will be your
last working day unless we tell you otherwise.

By next Wednesday we will know how many people we can employ.

All gorse cutting jobs will stop.

No people under 18 years can be employed on outside work.

From Friday 5th September we will not be able to employ Trusts
or groups except on contract. The Labour Department will decide
who to send us for jobs. No one will be able to come to our
office and get a job. You have to go to the Labour Department
office in Cuba Street.

This is your advice that your last working day with the Council
is Friday 5th September. We will tell you next Wednesday if we
can employ you after then. If we can not give you a job you
should go to the Labour Department and see them about other jobs.
You will not be able to work for one month, so it would be wise
to keep some money.

Sorry about this bad news.

Colin Knox
Assistant Town Clerk

Laid off: Assistant town clerk Colin Knox tells workers on the council's special work schemes (including the Aroha Trust girls), that the rules are changing and they'll all lose their jobs in two weeks. August 1980.

Charmaine, Annie, Gini and Waynnie give a hippie mum the once-over during a visit to a commune in Eltham. It's 1980 and they're living with others from Aroha Trust and Te Waka e Manaaki who've formed a new work co-op on Māori land in Taumarunui.

Pip and Tasi share a moment at Pip's wedding in the Island Bay School hall, December 1980.

On a knife edge: Pat and Pip make the first cut of the wedding cake. Given the unexpected guests, we agreed to keep the speeches short, highlight the merit of bringing people together from so many walks of life, then get on with the dancing.

Speaking up for the unemployed: In September 1984, Jane made headlines. The *Dominion* caption for the above photo read: 'The most talked-about person at the Economic Summit Conference, Ms Jane Stevens, talks with Federated Farmers president Mr Peter Elworthy at the social function which closed the three-day event. Ms Stevens is national co-ordinator of Te Roopu Rawa Kore O Aotearoa (the unemployed and beneficiaries association), and chairman [*sic*] of the Wellington Unemployed Workers Union.'

B 12 Auckland Star, Wednesday, September 19, 1984

Today's woman

A symbol of summit

Jane Stevens pulled no punches

By ROSEMARY COLLINS

Jane Stevens . . . mixing with the millionaires.

THE gilt-edged invitation to drinks at Government House said lounge suits or day frocks. Alone among participants to the economic summit, Jane Stevens had neither.

She worried about it a bit, but had no option. She turned up in what she had been wearing all day — jeans, old running shoes, a T-shirt which read "Fight Unemployment" and with her tattooed forearm covered by a faded denim jacket.

"I was quite scared they wouldn't let me in, but they didn't say anything," she said.

For perhaps the first time, a denim-clad figure representing the unemployed chatted with millionaires, politicians and businessmen in the ballroom of the nation's most important home.

It was all most acceptable. For those chosen to find the answers, the way Jane Stevens looked was a reminder of why they were there — a quest for a more equitable future.

THAT day she had made them all feel distinctly uncomfortable. In a passionate, angry speech, she pointed the finger at the well-fed of the summit and blamed them for the fact that she and thousands of others were unemployed.

The summit catch-cry was sacrifice and restraint, but she told them bluntly they could count her out. Strident and bitterly she demanded more of the cake and said her belt could be tightened no further.

It was poncey to the point of rudeness, and it made the 23-year-old at once the novelty and symbol of the summit.

No one would have dared say so publicly, but normally secure millionaires felt victimised and defensive.

For three days they were in a forum where she made it dubious to be very rich. Their Jaguars and Mercedes remained parked almost shamefacedly out of sight round the side of Parliament Buildings.

The often patronising acclamation which greeted her contribution to the summit surprised and amused the Jane.

She spent day two of the talkathon checking through the list of participants for people her unemployed and beneficiaries movement had approached for help in the past.

"All that rubbish in there about voluntary work being important," she nodded towards the debating chamber with a wry smile. "It's all very well to say this is a terrible problem, but my experience in the past showsthey haven't had that much enthusiasm to do anything about it."

Her list included the Employers Federation, who never replied to a detailed application for help in funding the movement's activities centre, IBM who declined to donate a typewriter, Lion Breweries who declined to donate some beer for a fundraising, and Feltex who alone gave them some seconds carpet.

An offer of a job from one well-meaning employer at the summit after her eloquent speech left her furious.

"THIS is my job," she pointed to her identification tag, which proclaimed her representative of the Unemployed and Beneficiaries Movement of

Aotearoa. "I'm very committed to the work I am doing. It is important."

She grew up in Dunedin's Andersons Bay, one of six children. Her father is a bus driver, her mother works voluntarily running a Maori community secondhand clothing shop.

Jane left school at the end of the fourth form with no qualifications, no ambitions except to earn a wage. She was unemployed for a year.

"I didn't have the qualifications. Most employers didn't even bother to reply. I tried to get on the dole but I was only 15. They told me to go back when I was 16."

She drifted in to one of the country's first unemployed centres, and at 16 found a job in a Fletcher Challenge company, the Great Outdoors factory.

It was to be her only paid job in eight years of continuous unemployment. She held it for a year before the factory closed.

Jane moved north too — to Wellington where she lived and worked with Black Power and the women associated with the gang.

Under the TEP scheme, she laboured for the City Council and government departments until the scheme was scrapped and she was back on the dole.

In 1980 Jane decided to put her years of unemployment to use. She helped set up the Wellington unemployed workers union and is now national co-ordinator of an interim group of 32 such centres around New Zealand.

Jane is one of New Zealand's hardest working unemployed. She is paid the dole for a job involving long demanding hours helping others find work.

Her home is a flat in the Hutt Valley, where one of her three flatmates has just become redundant.

The struggle to gain acceptance and recognition is easier under this Government for her. She has accused the Labour Department of being obstructive and unhelpful to unemployed people in the past, but said Labour's creation of a ministerial employment portfolio has made her life easier.

With satisfaction she told of one senior Labour Department official who regarded her as a nuisance before the election. Last time I saw him he was waving and smiling," she said.

Employment Minister Kerry Burke has already acted on one of the movement's demands — consultation and participation.

But even those cost-free promises crumbled when Jane failed to be consulted about the summit's only concrete move to fight unemployment — the establishment of a high-powered committee of businessmen headed by Manufacturers Federation president, Earl Richardson.

Ominously, she knew nothing of the initiative — sorted out late the night before the summit ended — until it was trumpeted to the nation by the Prime Minister David Lange.

Of her submissions for an increased unemployment benefit and a survival minimum wage there was little or no discussion.

AFTER three days of talking, eating and drinking in the rarified air of Parliament, she goes back to spartan offices off Boulcott St to face the reality of unemployment.

"The summit probably won't improve her living conditions, or those of her flatmate out of work. But in time it could stem the flow of young unemployed beating a path to her door.

"I can't help feeling a little cynical about it, because of my past experience. They have got the chance now to change things. I hope they are not just full of platitudes."

TWELVE

EAT THE RICH

Pat was still working as a builder's labourer, trying to figure out his next move. From Abel Smith Street, it was only a short walk up the hill to his flat near the university. Sometimes, late at night, I took refuge there. We'd curl up in an armchair by the fire in his bedroom, play his Neil Young records — 'Only Love Can Break Your Heart' — and make love in his single bed. There I could recharge, relax, not have to watch how many big words I used. First thing in the morning I'd be off home to wake the girls for work. They hardly knew Pat existed. Still unimpressed with my lifestyle, he never came to our place. The arrangement suited us both, but it was no recipe for a shared future.

Like Pat, Georgie's partner disapproved of her involvement in Aroha Trust. He wasn't a gang guy either and couldn't understand why she'd thrown in a good job to work for us. 'To him, I completely lowered my whole standards,' she said. 'I went from a hip, slick chick to someone who wore gumboots and Swannies. He started calling me a Black Power girl and I wasn't a Black Power girl. I was associated with Aroha Trust. I knew the Blacks, I knew the Nomads, I even got to know some of the

Mongies and Highways. But I never felt that I was affiliated with any of them apart from Aroha Trust. In my eyes, we were a group of women on a positive mission, with good ideas.'

Unable to work things out, Georgie left her partner and joined the eclectic mix at Brougham Street that included the two Mikes. One day I found her and Jane embroidering Black Power patches at the table in the lounge alcove, overlooking a three-storey drop to the ragged lawn.

'What's going on?' I said.

Georgie bit off a piece of cotton with her teeth and grinned. 'We took pity on them.'

I pulled a face. 'Since when were you their flunkies?'

'It's fun,' said Jane, delighted to find any outlet for her creative talents. 'Wanna help?'

'Doubt it! They can do their own dirty work,' I said, but I could have just been reluctant to expose my abysmal sewing skills.

A slim, young Pākehā guy in six-inch heels and red hot pants minced into the middle of the lounge and did a twirl. He swept back his blond fringe, fluttered his eyelashes and pouted, 'How do I look?'

'Cool!' said Georgie. He did look gorgeous, but I couldn't understand why any man would choose not only to adopt the blatant signs of female oppression, but exaggerate them. It was only later that I discovered he came from a similar background to the boys and often harangued them about the way they treated women. He lived at Brougham Street with his gay partner, an older, balding academic film-maker whose father was someone important. The partner made a documentary about the Black Power called *Te Mangu Kaha*; sadly, no copies have survived.

Other Pākehā lived there too: a young skinhead with a squashed face; the softly-spoken mechanic who fixed our vans; and a big-hearted, volatile woman with two young girls who had another daughter to Mike Hancock and brought up Junior's son for much of his life.

Brougham Street was also the headquarters of the Wellington Black Power. There, they had their office, ran their work trust and held their meetings. Bill Maung — a 60-year-old Burmese refugee — was a regular adviser, passing on his combination of Buddhist wisdom and political nous. He wasn't that interested in us girls, though: he didn't seem to know what to make of us.

Along with a few Blacks and the Wombles, Bill pushed for education, work, sport, better housing, and cultural identity. Under his tutelage, the Black Power became increasingly political, issuing press statements supporting the occupation of Bastion Point and referring to themselves as 'a movement, not a street gang'.

The Wombles and Mike Hancock were always banging on about the revolution. One day, in Cuba Mall, Charmaine took them literally. 'We'd just finished this spiel about eat the rich, power to the people,' she said. 'I'd been sitting there like the righteous pupil, taking it all on board. Got my black beret and my little red star embroidered, really dedicated blimmin' revolutionist. Seen this lady pull up in this limousine. She had all these furs on, dripping with rings and diamonds, and she had a chauffeur. I can remember grabbing her by the coat and swinging her up against the window, and the two Mikes freaked out. This is me being staunch to the revolution. "When the revolution comes, you're going to be skinny, skinny, skinny. Eat the fuckin' rich." Then I spat on her chauffeur. My two teachers got quite concerned. Not one of them patted me on the back and went, "Good girl!"' Charmaine chortled. 'They freaked. So did this poor lady.'

Given the range of inhabitants, tensions at Brougham Street were inevitable. After a visiting Black Power chapter blocked a girl at the house, the softly-spoken mechanic packed his bags and moved out. He didn't want to live under a cloud of violence, he told me. But more important, he felt as if he'd be condoning the rape if he stayed.

I often wondered how the Wombles rationalised their involvement with the Black Power, especially when it came to violence. Unlike Denis O'Reilly, they didn't endorse the gang by wearing a patch. But otherwise they were as close as it got; Peter was even on the national Black Power committee.

I always felt protected when they were around and they often stuck up for individual women. Like the night a Black Power prospect followed Jane into the toilet at a party and locked the door, leaving other prospects on guard outside. 'He said it was my fault cos I turned him on,' Jane said. 'I bashed on the walls and screamed the place down. I expected to get beaten up but that was fine compared with being raped. Some of the older guys like Arthur and Peter Womble heard me. They rescued me, took him outside and gave him the bash. Not long after, he went to jail for raping another woman.'

I'm sure the Wombles also challenged the Black Power's treatment of women in general, sometimes at great personal risk. But they faced the dilemma of anyone who works on the inside to bring about change. If they'd made a fuss about everything that went on, they'd never have survived. So they picked their battles and let some things go while they tried to gain enough respect to influence the gang leaders who really called the shots.

There were dangers in this approach. A staunch image was essential: violence was all around us, weakness something to be preyed upon. Over time, they inevitably became hardened and desensitised to some extent — like undercover cops (an analogy they would have hated).

I say this because I walked a similar moral tightrope. At one end were relatively minor crimes like stealing. During the Aroha Trust years, I'd happily accept the booty from clotheslining expeditions, but I drew the line at pinching things myself and I didn't want to be around when the girls did. Once we went to Oriental Bay for the afternoon. As we were leaving, one of them nicked an office worker's handbag. Whipped it off the concrete wall where the young woman sat sunning her feet, eating an ice-cream, talking to her friend. I felt sick at the thought of how her day would be ruined when she realised it was gone. And for what? The money? Maybe, but there were only a few dollars in her bag and we had our own pay packets by then. Habit mostly, I think. Because it was there. Because the girl could. And because she couldn't imagine ever being in that young woman's place. I felt disapproving and tight-lipped, implicated, guilty. Everyone else seemed delighted.

At the other end, the stakes were much higher. Annie never forgave herself for not intervening when she heard one of the girls getting a hiding from her boyfriend behind closed doors. 'I knew it was happening, but I didn't feel comfortable enough to walk into that room,' she said. 'When I saw my friend the next day, I vowed never to do that again. Regardless of consequences, I now interfere. I'm sure there were elements of self-preservation, but it was more that it's not my business, it wasn't happening right there in front of me, it was a private thing.'

The trouble was, the battle lines weren't clear. The boys weren't just the enemy. They were brothers and cousins, partners, mates. We lived with them, met to discuss trust matters, worked on the same council jobs from time to time, partied and pubbed together. Like the women, many had been horrifically abused before becoming abusers and predators themselves. So when the outside world demonised them — and us by association — we closed ranks and came out fighting on their side.

'Get Tough With the Brutal Bash Boys: Unwashed, Unwilling, Unwanted', screamed a headline from the tabloid *Truth* in 1978. The article alleged that the Black Power had scoffed a free feed of lamb donated by the Gear Meat Company and then lay outside in the sun refusing to talk to government department officials who'd met to hear their concerns.

Jane stuck the clipping in her diary and scrawled 'All bullshit' on it. Underneath, she wrote, 'Have you ever tried talking to a room full of people? *They* being in their own everyday environment didn't find it hard to get up and speak as it was a common occurrence in their work, but the *Blacks* were in an alien environment and haven't had the experience and confidence needed for public speaking.'

Jane followed up with a letter to the editor complaining about 'the crap' the reporter had written. 'Either he is incredibly stupid or this was his idea to stir up some reactions from the people involved. Instead of helping the Black Power and others in the same situation, you have told the public that they are not interested in work.'

Aroha Trust and the Black Power were invited to Bruce Stewart's marae at Tapu Te Ranga to meet a Sri Lankan professor of alternative lifestyles. Again, Jane's diary was invaluable. 'It started with everyone giving speeches, mostly in Maori,' she wrote. 'Then the guest speaker got up and talked for about an hour and a half, which got very boring after a while, and the film crew were busy darting in and out, taking films of everyone. After the talks finished, we all had a kai done in a hangi, then more talking began so we finally got away about seven.'

Jane's reference to the film crew sent me scurrying to TVNZ's archives, where I fell into my past. There were the tall irregular wooden sticks that formed a fence round the marae, the women picking pūhā, the steam rising from the hāngi when the sack covers were removed. There were the nuns from next door in long black coats and white veils walking slowly down the driveway in the rain. And there — unexpectedly — was me.

The camera was trained on a young man standing in the middle of a dim room lit by a single bulb, the cord weaving through the rafters. On the wall behind him was a dartboard. He was singing 'Tatōu, Tatōu E' while another young man strummed a guitar. I was in the background, puffing on a cigarette. I looked young and fresh-faced. Not the least bit tough.

During the break, I lined up behind Mike Hancock for the steaming meat and vegetables laid out in wire crates on long trestle tables.

Peter pushed in front of me and started talking to Mike. Then he looked over his shoulder. 'Are you going to tell everyone about Aroha Trust?' he asked. It felt like a challenge.

'Not in front of the cameras,' I said. *And not in front of you.*

He smirked. 'Not scared, are ya?'

I piled my plate with the rich, smoky food, and wished I could think of something clever to say instead of blushing madly as I always seemed to do around him now.

'You *should*,' Mike Hancock said, more gently. 'How else will people find out what you fullas are doing? It's pretty cool, you know.'

I took a bite out of the tender grey pork. Aroha Trust didn't feel cool, it felt disorganised and messy. Not like this place, steeped in something bigger than itself. Not even like Te Waka e Manaaki, inspired by the Black Panthers and the tradition of the Māori warrior. Who were *we*? Just a bunch of girls driving round in vans, pretending we could do men's work. Getting pissed and stoned on the weekend. Arguing over clothes and who was going to be boss for the day.

We were into the same 'black is beautiful' and guerrilla politics as the boys, but almost all the role models were male: Malcolm X and Che Guevara overseas, Syd Jackson and Tame Iti at home. The thing that most united us was our experience as women. Where were our heroines, the ones who looked like the girls and talked their language?

Simone de Beauvoir, Betty Friedan and Germaine Greer, who'd inspired me at university, spoke to a white middle-class audience about sexual liberation, freedom from household drudgery, financial and political equality. But our focus was more on survival. Oppression in the gang scene was basic and blatant: rape, hidings, orders to stay home, cook a feed, keep your mouth shut. In spite of this — or perhaps because of it — many of the girls were stauncher than most feminists I knew.

I looked around at the crowd of young men. There was no way I could say all that here. Annie waved at me from across the room, balancing a plate of food on her knees. For all her charisma, she wasn't one to jump up in public and make a speech. Beside her, Tasi, Junior and Jane had their heads down, eating. They wouldn't say anything either; they hardly said boo in our own meetings. This time, I didn't blame them.

Someone was shouting, 'Get up! Get up! Now!'

I opened one eye and stared directly at a policeman's crotch. He was short and stocky and his navy pants strained against his thighs. I buried my face in the pillow.

'Get up!' he said again.

I swung my feet onto the floor, pulled a blanket around my shoulders, and sat shivering on the edge of the bed. Two cops with their backs to me were tipping everything out of my drawers. The big hand on my bedside clock pointed to five. That meant I'd been home from the

Black Power disco for three hours. I covered my eyes, trying to clear last night's rum-induced fug from my brain.

It was the second police raid of Abel Smith Street in 24 hours. At the same time the morning before, they'd tried to muscle their way in without a warrant but Annie and Jane had sent them packing. This time they came prepared. The warrant was for a stolen flag, presumably the red and yellow one they'd seen hanging in our hallway, the one Annie had brought back from her trip to China. When we didn't open the door fast enough, they booted it down.

Once inside, they ignored the flag and ransacked every room. Anything would do: stolen goods, drugs, runaways. Half an hour later, facing the prospect of leaving empty-handed, the stocky cop who'd shouted at me picked up two library books sitting beside my bed.

'Whose are these?' he said.

'Dunno!' I said. The books were Annie's.

'I don't believe you. Where'd you get them?'

I shrugged. 'They were here when we moved in.'

He opened one and read aloud, 'Nursing School Library, Wellington Public Hospital,' and a date. He narrowed his eyes. 'This is six months overdue. Tell me whose it is or I'll arrest you for theft.'

I'd never been arrested before. I felt sick and slid out of the room, saying I needed to use the toilet. It was hard to believe he was serious.

Annie was in the hallway berating another policeman for the mess they'd made of the house. I pulled her aside.

'Tell him they're mine,' she said. 'I don't care.'

'Well?' said the stocky cop, backing me up against the wall.

Annie and I have different recollections of what happened next. She says *she* told him the books were hers. I think *I* did. It doesn't matter. I should never have put her in the position of having to own up to them. I watched in horror as they arrested her instead of me, locked her up for hours, then laid charges. She was quiet when she got home, said they'd threatened to break her fingers when she refused to let them take prints.

That afternoon, sleep-deprived and jittery, we smoked some dope and went to the wedding of a Pākehā student we'd hired over the university break. It was Annie's idea to employ her under the same relief work scheme that employed us. We needed someone to do the accounts, apply for grants, get us organised. Bubbles was our secretary, but she was pregnant again and about to move out to the Hutt.

The student was mousy and well-meaning. Thinking back, it was good of her to invite us all to her wedding, a small gathering of family and friends. Another day it might even have been okay. But that day the world was divided into *them* and *us*. We stuck to ourselves, exploited her hospitality and left in a hurry, united by the experience of policemen breaking down our door and trashing our house and carting people off for no good reason.

For court, Annie put on her good-girl clothes and got a lawyer. I didn't go with her. I might have had to drive the girls to work or maybe I just couldn't face it, knowing it should have been me. The magistrate discharged her without conviction. But by then I'd learnt that fear could make me betray my best friend, and it was harder to live with that than to be done for something as ridiculous as overdue library books. When I tell Annie this, she laughs and says it wasn't my fault, but then she was never one to hold a grudge.

Except, perhaps, against the cops. In those days, her attitude to the police was 'very anti', she said. 'Based not so much on what was done to me, more on what was done to other people. I saw a lot of confrontations that were created by police, a lot of violence and unreasonable behaviour from police. No, I was not a cooperative person towards them at all.'

Once, the cops threw her in the gutter when she was trying to calm things down outside the pub. 'I look quite straightish, and people were astounded, and reacted badly to that happening to me. There was no need for it.'

Another time, she was pulled over driving the Red Baron and taken to the police station. 'Because' — she look bemused — 'well, it's very weird, because of nothing. They reckoned I had outstanding fines and they kept me there for about five hours. I wasn't allowed to go in the beginning, and then I was. I don't know why I was there, but they just kept me there.'

Georgie, who — like Annie — had no criminal convictions, was also hassled constantly after she joined Aroha Trust. 'No matter where you were, if you were just driving on the road, you got pulled up. Questioned. Whatever. The police thought nothing of us but Black Power or Mongrel Mob wenches doing a political stance in order to get money out of the government for a cause.'

Georgie's worst experience was being chased home from a party with a load of girls yahooing in the back of the Red Baron, after she'd opted to be the sober driver. 'I thought, I've just got to get into Brougham Street, get them home, get them home. I got to the door, and I don't know if it was Gini or Tasi, pulling them in the door, and the cop was on my other hand, pulling me out. The rest of the police were up at the van by the girls, and they were arguing and carrying on. In the end, I managed to get inside. And Brougham Street had a thousand escape routes.' She gave a wicked laugh.

It didn't affect Georgie's attitude to the police as a whole, though. 'Only the certain few. I always thought they're there to protect you, they're there to serve you.'

I feel less forgiving. It's true the girls weren't always innocent or well behaved. But over and over again, I saw harassment out of all proportion to their conduct. The police never let up: they hounded and heavied and provoked us every chance they got. Nor did they ever acknowledge our efforts to provide work and safe houses and hope for their clientele, or offer to help. Their only answer was to lock 'em up. They were just another bunch of bullies we had to deal with — in some ways the most dangerous, certainly the most powerful.

Walking back from Carmen's to Brougham Street in the early hours of the morning, Jane, Annie, Charmaine and some of the boys were stopped three times by the police. The third time, they tried to arrest Jane for being a runaway from Miramar Girls Home. The boys formed a circle to protect her. They were almost home when three more carloads of cops arrived, blocking the road and footpath. Again, the boys surrounded Jane. The Wombles — used to outsmarting the law — invited two cops inside, got Jane out of the way, then told them to leave, they were on private property.

The following night, the same two cops arrested Jane in the Cambridge and put her in a cell with a Mongrel Mob guy. 'I thought he was gonna do me,' she wrote in her diary. 'It was a real heavy scene cos the pigs were really aggro to me cause of the shit that went down at Brougham Street. Lucky for me the Mongie was really out of it and even though the pigs kept calling me a Black Power bitch so that he could hear, he was too out of it to get me. Then I got a gun stuck in my face by one of the pigs cos he didn't like me yelling to get me out of there — he told me to fuck up or he would shoot me. But I was lucky cause when the new shift came on, they freaked out and said, "Why is she in the cell with the Mongie?" and I got shifted.'

In court the next morning, Jane's biggest concern was two buddha sticks she'd hidden in her gumboot flap while she was in the paddy wagon. 'I was really dumb to keep them in my boots specilly [*sic*] when they did do a body search but when I said how smelly my boots were, they left them alone,' she wrote.

The Wombles got her a lawyer who complained about police harassment and her treatment in the cells. The judge dismissed the case but, in hindsight, he protected the police, Jane said. 'It meant their actions were never examined.'

Junior said she was arrested more than a hundred times before she was 20. Gini got picked up constantly too. 'Disorderly behaviour. Assault. Abusiveness. When I look back, silly little things: returning to licensed premises, being in a stolen vehicle, receiving stolen goods, getting caught with a bullet of marijuana which I couldn't swallow because it was tinfoil.'

When the police wrongly accused her of throwing a Molotov cocktail, Gini rang Steve Silestean, who ran a candle factory and was known as Candleman. 'I swore black and blue that I had never done it. Nobody believed me. I mean, this is my word against the police. And Candleman stood by me. We got a lawyer and I got acquitted. It almost made the police want to get me even more. Just being with that crowd of people, they automatically label you one of them. So you take on those labels whether you deserve them or not. Before you know it, you're blinkin' criminal number one.'

Candleman, a Jewish immigrant with snow-white hair and a neatly-trimmed beard, was a legend among Wellington's street people. He gave them work in his factory, money when they were broke, and advice, whether or not they asked for it.

Gini described him as the most influential adult in her life. 'He was always accepting you for the good, the bad and the ugly. Always lecturing you if you'd done something wrong, like parents do. Always going on about life and what you've got to look forward to and how you're going to get there. They were very boring lectures at the time, but when I think back, they must have had an input for me to actually stop and change things around.'

Candleman's generosity seemed never-ending. When they were homeless, he set Gini and JB up in a flat with their two young sons. Later, he financially supported her first overseas trip to Israel as part of a Christian kapa haka group, 'another turning point in my life'.

He had big shoulders, Bubbles said. 'I could cry on them, sit on them, borrow off them.'

Annie was particularly close to him. 'He was a very unusual person in that he was very accepting of all kinds of people. I came to see him as a mentor, another father figure. As our friendship grew, I would quite often stay with him and his partner in the weekends. They were my little haven from the world when it got too much for me.'

Candleman was the father Charmaine had never had. He was the first person to take her to a restaurant. 'I just about smacked over the waiter cos he went to take the bottle to pour my drink, and he popped it beside my ear and gave me a fright. I was just about ready to whack him in the head. And Candleman goes, "No, Charmaine, that's his job."' She laughed. 'He taught me restaurant etiquette. It was about getting me used to that world. No table is too good for you to eat off.'

Candleman also bought Charmaine her first dictionary and introduced her to classical music. They'd argue for hours about things

Māori without him ever getting defensive like other Pākehā, she said. Every year, he sent all her children birthday cards. When times got tough, she'd ring him and say 'Shit's hit the fan, mate', and they'd talk it through. 'He was another mountain and another gift that's been in my life.'

Jane and Gini got off charges because of people like Candleman and the Wombles, who knew how to work the system. Many young people in their position don't have such contacts, which may be one reason why, today, around half of all youth offenders are Māori. Andrew Becroft, the same youth court judge who railed against the detention of young people in police cells, told a police conference in 2005 that over-representation of Māori is 'probably the most pressing issue confronting all of those who are involved daily in our youth justice system'.

The statistics are troubling. Young Māori are five to six times more likely than non-Māori to be convicted of crimes. Even when comparing young people with the same offending history, they're more than twice as likely to get convictions. They're also likely to receive more severe sentences which researchers attribute, at least in part, to 'increased vigilance' by the public and police. Like many things in life, you get what you focus on.

That vigilance can have a lifelong effect. 'All those things that I did when I was young and stupid and thought I was great and knew it all — it's like they're a scar forever,' Gini said. In 2000, IHC refused to employ her to look after a boy with an intellectual disability 'because I've got this assault charge on police when I was 17 and stupid and young, and they're not that quick to forgive.' The irony was that Gini still looked after the boy, with his parents' blessing. She just didn't get paid for her work or acknowledged by IHC.

Bubbles looked into getting a job in Social Welfare. 'I was informed because of my criminal record that the only job available to me would be as a tracker,' she said. 'That's a person that takes kids at risk away for the day and becomes their friend. Well, that's all voluntary work. Why study for a degree that was going to cost me three, four, five thousand dollars and all I could do was take a kid out on a walk?'

Bubbles' criminal record also prevented her working in an old people's home. She snorted. 'I says, "What am I going to do? Bail up all these little old ladies and pinch them and take them home?"'

Nor was she allowed to move to Australia when her children were young, and she had to apply for a visa to visit her daughter and mokopuna who now lived there. So did her partner. 'There's two of us in one house that are not eligible to trip around the world. If I won the Lotto, I'd be highly pissed off.'

Since I recorded the women's stories, new Clean Slate legislation allows many people's criminal records to be disregarded after seven years. That's enabled Gini to be employed as a social worker. But the legislation doesn't apply to overseas travel. It would still be a bummer for Bubbles if she won Lotto.

Not long before she got out of jail for the last time, Bubbles tattooed 'HELP ME' on her arm. 'Until then, it was a haven that you didn't have to worry about nothing, it was all done for you,' she said. 'The hard part was getting on with everybody else. Well, I didn't care about anybody else so they didn't matter anyway.' But now things had changed. She was 19 years old and three months pregnant.

Bubbles described herself as 'profusely tattooed from head to toe'. Dark ink drawings were scrawled on her face, back, arms and hands, legs and feet. I pointed to the words, 'property of Wellington Black Power', on the inside of her left arm. It was hard to imagine Bubbles being anyone's property.

She grinned, unfazed. 'When I have a blood test, I say to the doctor, "Just stick the needle into the B; that's where the vein is."'

All the Aroha Trust girls had tats except Annie, Georgie and me. Most were home-made, a mish-mash of letters, words, symbols, and pictures, some deeply imbued with meaning, others little more than doodles. Alone in prison cells, furtively in girls homes, with drunken bravado in grotty flats, they marked themselves and one another's skin like taggers faced with a blank wall. Amelia explained how it was done.

You tie a needle to a matchstick with cotton, leaving the tip free, she said. 'Heaps of cotton to absorb the ink, so when you dot, it's like a swab and it's pushing the ink down.'

'What sort of ink?' I asked.

'Indian ink. Easy to get. Foolish too. You had to worry about them turning scabby, going septic. My hand festered up. It was sore for a week. You know, it went rotten, not being very sterile and all that. Doing it too hard in one place, and not enough in another place. It gets so you can't see where you've poked. By the time you think you've finished and wipe the blood and the gunk away, you've only done half a side. Oh, it's sore after a while. What a clown I was in those days.'

'So why do it?'

'Just to keep up with the times, I suppose. People were tatting themselves and you were classed as quite staunch.'

Amelia's last tattoo was 'Aroha Trust '77' inside a heart. 'Meaning that was all my world,' she said. 'Friends I really cared about, wanted to always be with. That was the highlight of my life.'

Gini had 'Aroha Trust' tattooed on her arm too. Her first tat was an N on the second finger of her left hand when she was 16. 'I was starting off doing N for NZ, but it was too sore.'

She had a few dots here and there, a cross on her left thumb 'because it was probably the easiest sign', and an S on her wrist, the first letter of a boyfriend's name. On her forearm, one under the other, were the names of the three siblings who'd stuck together after their mother died: Gini, Ringo (Tasi's nickname) and their Nomad brother.

On the underside of Gini's left arm was 'MUM'. 'I remember doing that tattoo drunk and out of it, and thinking it was like a mark saying to me that I missed my mother. That was part of that grieving that I'd held; that was the way I got it out of my system.'

Further up was a large fish, like a whale. Gini had traced around a jigsaw puzzle piece when she was bored, then tattooed Nayda's name through the middle of it. On her upper arm was a Māori design that covered up a swastika. 'I never knew what it stood for, what it represented, but liked the look of it — so there I went, did it on my arm. And it wasn't till years later that I went overseas to Israel and found out what it was all about, white supremacy. And here I am, after all these years hating Pākehā people and having this sign on my arm and realising what it exactly meant — I could have slapped myself.'

Gini, generally so immune to physical pain, still cringed at the agony of applying tattoos. 'It was almost like mutilation and a way of expressing for me the hurt inside that I didn't know any other way to get out.' She regretted them now. 'You're labelled for life. People judge you by what you look like. I've got a green dress on, but it looks like it's got long sleeves because it all just carries on. I feel it in people's eyes, the first time I meet them. I see them reading me like a book, saying to themselves, "Oh, she's one of them, we'll watch out for her."'

Charmaine felt the same. 'You have to get strong if you have tattoos, cos a lot of people judge you. I can read the thoughts in their mind, I can see the words: wrong, criminal, jail, trouble. A whole lot of things that aren't true.'

Like Gini, Charmaine saw her tattoos as a form of grief, 'a whaka-papa in my life, a whole journey of a child that was misunderstood'. All her tattoos were on her left side. 'The right-hand side is your masculine side, and to survive through those days, you had to use a lot of masculine energy. So the feminine side's all been dealt to.'

She pointed to a bird on her forearm. 'Tattoos speak another language. A lot of people that have gone to jail, or spent a lot of time in the system, will have that bird. We all look at each other and we know where we've come from. It's the symbol that one day we will be free.'

Further up Charmaine's arm were a flower and a heart drawn by Nayda. On her left leg was a half-finished chain with missing links, and the words 'Bay of Plenty', that she did herself in the girls home in Christchurch. 'This one is a really, really powerful statement,' she said. 'People were never asking me where I was from. It was about the broken link, and that I came from the Bay of Plenty. It had to be in Pākehā; that's what they could read.'

Jane's tattoos were still getting her into trouble in her thirties. One night she went to a party at the mayor's house to celebrate her partner's re-election to the city council. 'This real right-winger who I hate got onto council and he came in,' she said. 'Of course I was rarking him up, but he got very abusive. He started attacking me and saying I didn't deserve to have children because I have tattoos and all this sort of shit. It hit a raw nerve. Him and his mate. So I just went up to them and smashed their heads together. That was very satisfying.' She laughed. 'My kids saw it happen which was a tough one, but they actually thought it was the right thing to do because they were so obnoxious.' She paused, then added, 'I'm not really proud of resorting to violence. I think I've got it under control most of the time.'

Since then, Jane has had laser treatment to remove the tattoos on her hands. Although time-consuming and expensive, lasering gives much better results than the old method of surgery and skin grafts that often left scars worse than the original tattoo, like Mahina's pale, ropy necklace.

Many of the other women were also considering getting rid of their tattoos. 'Not because of the wrong reasons of the system pressuring me,' Charmaine said. 'For the reasons that I've passed that place, I no longer need those pictures to remind me.'

Bubbles had mixed feelings about her tattoos. 'The ones on my hands, yeah, I regret. The others I don't because they can be hidden away if necessary, which I don't think's necessary any more. People are more talkative to you in the winter, and then summertime comes and you're walking around in a singlet and they freak right out.'

Her appearance had always come at a price, she said. 'Work prospects are pretty dull when you're covered in tattoos and a ring in your nose which you won't take out.' She worked in a shearing gang, and some farmers had even banned her from working in their woolsheds, though her reputation as a hard worker usually won them over in the end.

Like the other women's, Tasi's tattoos were a mixture of the profound and meaningless. Now that she was a Christian, she was opposed to marking the body but philosophical about what she'd done before she knew better. 'They're a testimony of where I've been, what road I've taken. And a testimony to other people, especially to a lot of street people.'

When I recorded her story in 2000, Nayda had no plans to remove her tattoos either, although she'd covered up 'lots of rubbish' on her arm with roses and butterflies, and her former Mongrel Mob partner had coloured in the words 'Black Power'.

Until she saw people staring at her, she'd forget about the star on one cheekbone and the dots on the other. But they were part of her, she said, and she had no regrets. 'I did when I was in my twenties and I'd go home and see my other friends and they'd go, "Gee, you've got tattoos", and they worked in offices and that sort of thing. That's when I used to feel uncomfortable. Not now.'

THIRTEEN

SURVIVAL SKILLS

On the plane to Dunedin, the first leg of my trip to Kaitangata to record Annie's and Bubbles' stories, I sat next to a television station sales manager.

'Fantastic!' she said, when I told her what I was doing. 'You can tell me something I've always wanted to know about gang women.'

'What's that?' I said.

'I've always wanted to know about blocks!'

I groaned. Charmaine's warning that she wouldn't be part of anything that fed into middle-class preconceptions about gangs flashed through my mind. 'I'm not really planning to go there,' I said. 'There's enough sensationalism around gangs already. It'll just encourage more gang-bashing.'

'It's what everyone wants to know,' she said.

'Rape's rape, isn't it, no matter how many men there are. There's no need to spell out the gory details.'

She shook her head. 'There's something special about blocks.'

An air hostess interrupted us with trays of food. I peeled back the tinfoil and prodded a greasy square of lasagne with my plastic fork. I hadn't asked any of the women if they'd been blocked. They'd tell me if they wanted to, I figured. So far no one had, although they'd described near-misses and other victims. But I couldn't ignore the woman beside me for the whole flight.

'What exactly do you want to know?' I said reluctantly.

She rattled off a quick list: 'Where the word comes from. If they're part of gang initiations. What happens. Who decides.'

'I'm not an expert on gangs or their pecking order,' I protested.

She sniggered at the unintended pun. 'You should still ask them.'

I looked out the window: below me a cotton-wool carpet tinged with pink, above an infinite blue sky. I was never blocked, nor did I ever witness one. It's like a tsunami: if you're that close, you'd better start running. They happened anywhere. Inside flats and houses, in backyards and gardens, at gang pads and parties. Always out of sight, never far from the girls' minds.

At the Black Power disco, a ripple would go round the room. Everything seemed the same — the music still bounced off the walls, the flickery strobe light still lit up the slow-motion dancers. But you could smell the danger, sense the backstage shuffling. Sometimes you'd even see the secret signal used by the Blacks: the closed fist of one hand, side-on, smacked against the open palm of the other. You'd look around for the victim. If she was lucky, you might be able to warn her, get her out of there. Usually, though, she was surrounded, or she wouldn't listen, or she'd already been whisked away.

'I'm interested in ordinary things too.' The woman's voice dragged me back. 'Like where the women live. If they take their kids to school. Who cooks? What they eat.'

'Thank God for that!' I laughed. 'It'd be a shame if all the stories I've recorded went to waste.'

'Keep in touch,' she said as we walked down the gangway. 'It'd make great television.'

On the bus from Dunedin to Kaitangata, I made up my mind to ask Bubbles about blocks. If anyone understood gang rituals, it'd be her. I went over what I already knew. Sometimes it was a girl the boys picked up from the pub or a party, who had no back-up and didn't know how to handle herself. The common view was that these girls were asking for trouble.

Gang members divided women into three categories just by looking at them, Nayda said. 'One, you're really easy. Second one is you're a really good person and you're not there to' — she lowered her voice — 'fuck them all. And the third one is, "Oh, she's all right"; they'll leave you alone, they won't try and hang around. Some women would be really big mouth, and they'd be the type the men'd probably want to beat up.'

But it wasn't always girls who behaved badly who got blocked. As a street kid squatting in Tinakori Road, Charmaine remembered young Black Power members coming over from Walton House. 'We all used to run and hide — behind chests of drawers and washing machines, outside — because they had horrendous reputations for rape. They took whatever they wanted and we were too young to combat that.'

Evelyn used almost the same words about the Nomads. 'They would come in and just pick whoever they wanted. We'd run across the road and they were over there ransacking the house and whoever's asleep, we'd hear them screaming because they'd been raped or blocked.'

Tasi told me about one woman from a rival gang whose underwear was hung up on a stick. 'They were waving it around like a flag, like defeat, cos she was the opposite to this gang that raped her. And she wanted to commit suicide.' Women never talked about it, she said. 'Back then, you didn't want to ask too much because you didn't want them to replay the whole scene.'

Sometimes it was the girls we knew, our friends, who were put on the block, some of them repeatedly. 'The Black Power disco turned out to be pretty heavy,' an entry in Jane's diary read. 'Four girls got blocked — the same ones as usual.'

We did our best to keep one another safe. Rule number one in social situations: stick together. Rule number two: stick together more. When you go to the toilet, always take someone with you. At the Black Power disco, never go outside alone where you could get picked off without anyone knowing. The Wellington members might not touch you, but what about visiting chapters? Never go to a party or the clubrooms without back-up. If you have a boyfriend, be sure he'll put your safety ahead of the bros. If you're not sure, only go out with other women (the more the better, and even then be wary) or men who have the standing and decency to protect you.

Nayda identified other rules for survival. 'Don't come across as too feminine. Don't bend over in front of them. Watch what you say cos it might lead them on. I think, too, the jeans and the bush-shirts made me feel better, like I was hiding my body. Like I'd almost become male, the dress anyway. The dress was like a shell.'

Our clothes weren't just practical for the physical work we did. They didn't just make us feel staunch. They were an essential part of our protection. Even when we dressed up, most of us covered up.

Charmaine put it this way. 'I wasn't allowed to be a woman, I wasn't allowed to be attractive and I wasn't allowed to be feminine if I wanted to survive without being raped.' That's why lots of girls wore two pairs of jeans, she said. 'So if they have a hard time getting through the first pair, you can fight them off and they'd have to try and get through the second pair.'

None of these rules was foolproof. Not long before she started working for Aroha Trust, Nayda went to Auckland with Bubbles to stay with a friend. She discovered an ex-boyfriend from the Black Power was staying there too. 'He was quite civil. I thought, this is good, it'll be all right, he's not going to hassle me in any way.'

During her visit, Nayda started going out with a young Black Power prospect. One day, Bubbles went to town. 'The music was playing,' Nayda said. 'We were all in the sitting room. And some visitors had come; I'd met them in Wellington. My ex came out of his room and he said to me, "Come here." And just the way he said it, I knew something was wrong. I could feel the tension in the air. He said, "Come here." And I said to him, "No!" And he came over to me and punched me in the face, grabbed me, threw me on the mattress in the lounge, and by this time my nose was bleeding and I'm looking at my boyfriend who's a prospect. Then my friend's partner comes in, and he had that look in his eye, like' — she took a deep breath — 'rape. It dawned on me what they were going to do. All I could do was look at my boyfriend and he *wouldn't* do anything or didn't *want* to do anything. My nose was bleeding, it was bleeding really fast, there was blood everywhere.

'My ex said to me, "Get in that fuckin' bathroom and clean yourself up. Bi-itch." I took off in the bathroom and I was thinking, I've got to get out of this. Survival, eh. I turned on the cold water tap and it ran really fast so there was a *ssshhhhh*.' She mimicked the sound of running water. 'I closed the door. This is an old house, an old bathroom. I was thinking, for the life of me, plee-ase, open, open. For what my life was worth, man, I just got this window open. He goes, "You better fuckin' hurry." I said, "I won't be long." And I was out that window, man. I just left the tap running, blood everywhere. I just took off out the window. I got it open and I ran. Went up the back flat, knocked on the door cos there was this young couple there. The wife was home. I knew her husband worked. She saw me and she let me in. I was so grateful to her.

'If he'd come in that bathroom, or I walked out of that bathroom back into that lounge, I was dead meat. Another thing, when I look back at it now, my friend knew what was going on. But then I suppose this is where that male thing comes in. It's like, "Shut your mouth, don't you say anything".'

Her new boyfriend knew too. 'I thought, fuck you, ya fuckin' arsehole. Wouldn't save me. But I can understand now why he didn't. He's prospecting; he's not meant to try and stop it. But I thought, you mouse.'

Nayda hid in the neighbour's flat until the next day, when she knew the boys had gone. 'You could hear their boots walking around the house.' I imagined her listening through the wall, jumping at every sound, waiting until it was safe to go and find Bubbles. And I thought about the courageous woman who sheltered her, not knowing if gang members might burst in at any moment and take their revenge on both of them.

Bubbles and Nayda packed their things and left at once. 'Bubbles says to me, "Look, I'm sorry." I'm going, "I got away, I'm just glad I got away. That I'm not another, *oh, you remember when so-and-so got blocked*. There's no one talking about *me* like that."'

I realised that it was as important for Nayda to have been spared the public humiliation as the actual ordeal. If she'd been blocked, it would have been her good name in tatters, not the reputations of the young men who did it.

A few weeks later, the friend's partner rang Nayda to borrow some money. 'Thirty-four dollars, that's what comes to my mind, to travel from somewhere to somewhere. I said' — her voice became a high-pitched shriek — '"What a fuckin' cheek." I slammed the phone down. Thought, ya bastard, I saw that look in *your* fuckin' eye.'

The experience knocked her. 'I was very wary after that. Very wary. My next relationship wasn't like it should have been. I wasn't very open with him, I wasn't giving of myself. Even the sex bit. I could have been a sack of spuds. It was strange.'

Back in Wellington, having a young Black Power boyfriend didn't protect Nayda from the older guys. One night, when he was away, she slept with Rana at Epuni Street. At dawn, she woke to find the same senior gang member who'd raped the quiet 16-year-old at Abel Smith Street standing at the foot of the bed.

'I said, "He isn't here"' — meaning her boyfriend — 'but I knew something was wrong. He said, "That's not why I'm here."'

The first time Nayda told me this story, she said she pinched Rana to make her cry and scared him off. A year later, she paid me a special visit to tell me what had really happened. She hadn't pinched Rana. Rana hadn't cried. The guy hadn't been scared off.

'He got on top of me. It was silent.' She put her hand over her mouth to demonstrate how he'd shut her up.

I looked into her eyes, usually so expressive, the light gone out in them.

'I just let him. I had to. I didn't want Rana to wake up.'

What Nayda didn't know until afterwards was that she was already four months pregnant.

After dropping my bags at the motel, I met Bubbles and Annie for dinner at a local steak house. We were all quiet. I put it down to nerves and tiredness. I'd seen Annie a few times since the trust days when she'd breezed through Wellington, but not Bubbles. They both did hard, physical work: Bubbles in the shearing sheds, Annie at the freezing works and as a wool classer. They looked older, lined. Annie bemoaned the arrival of middle-age spread. Bubbles had lost weight though she still looked formidable in a pink t-shirt and black vest that showed off her tattooed arms.

'I absolutely wouldn't put on anything red till recently,' she said. Red was the Mongrel Mob colour. Other than that, she dressed as she always had. 'Black bra, black undies, black socks, black shoes, black jeans, maybe a different coloured t-shirt, orange and black normally because that was the Black Power colours. And blue denim jacket. I don't give a damn about clothes. I could quite happily wear my shed clothes to town if they were all nicely washed.'

In her mid-thirties, Annie had moved home to Kaitangata to be near her mother when her father died suddenly. Bubbles followed soon after, just as she'd followed Annie to the Wairarapa in the early 1980s when trouble struck.

As Bubbles drove me back to the motel in her souped-up Falcon, I asked how she and Annie became such good friends.

'When I met Annie, I didn't even like her,' she said with a chuckle. Annie had turned up to a wedding at Walton House, the short-lived, Black Power/Mongrel Mob pad, with a man she introduced as Peter Womble, and the next night with someone she called Mike. 'I thought, this lady's lying to me, she's full of crap, this is the same egg she was here with last night. I got an instant hate on for her.'

When Bubbles found out that Mike and Peter were identical twins, she didn't bother to apologise. 'I'd probably written myself off real badly and I didn't care,' she said. She was angry at having driven all the way to Whanganui that day to get custody of Rana, who was staying with relatives, only to find the judge had rescheduled the hearing because she arrived late.

Soon after, Bubbles was evicted from Walton House when she put another girl in hospital after a fight. A friend took her round to Mike and Annie's community house at Brougham Street. Again, Bubbles wasn't impressed. 'There was this little old man in this chair who was calling me all these disgusting names and was yelling and screaming at me and poking his finger, and I'm thinking, oh, what the hell's this house?' But she had nowhere else to go and — more important — Annie offered to help her get Rana back.

'I had to prove I could look after Rana. Annie came with me to court and held my hand. We tried to do everything properly besides the fact that I'd dropped a trip the night before with friends and was quite utterly off my face sitting in the courthouse just saying yes and no to anything and everything. All I wanted was my daughter back. I didn't really give a damn about any of their processes.'

It took a moment for her words to sink in: that even with Annie's support, Bubbles had jeopardised the thing she wanted most in the whole world for a trip. I tried to imagine why. Bravado? Fear of failure? Fear of success? An inability to think ahead? It didn't make sense. I wondered how Annie had reacted; she was never afraid to speak her mind.

'She's probably the only person who could've blown me up in those days and I'd have listened to her,' Bubbles said. 'A few times I wanted to dong her. But I thought, shit, she's so little, she'll fall over and then I'll really feel mean.'

We pulled up outside my motel. 'What time will you be up?' I asked. We were going to spend the next day recording her story.

'About half past five. I always cook breakfast for everyone before they go to work.' Bubbles' partner was a shearer, and her youngest children, 16-year-old twins, were rousies.

I glanced at my watch; it was midnight. 'Take your time,' I said.

All night I dreamt that I was dragging my tape recorder through mud. I kept forgetting a crucial technical step and none of the women's stories were saved. I'd wake in panic, tell myself all I had to do was put the tape in the machine and press 'record', then sink back into the nightmare. It was a relief to hear the alarm go off and, when Bubbles knocked on the door, I was waiting.

To me, the word 'bubbles' conjures up frosted glasses of champagne, a long soak in a hot bath, breakfast cereal — not the heaviest woman in the Black Power scene. The nickname was acquired at the age of nine, when she exercised horses in the paddocks near her Auckland home. Overhearing that one of them, a pony called Bubbles, was about to be put down, she crept back after dark to rescue her. 'Put a bridle and a saddle on her, and her cover, and away we went. From Takapuna to Devonport, which is a long, long way on a Shetland pony in the middle of the night. I got stopped by the police at about four in the morning. When I got home, it was "Oh, Bubbles, eh." It just stuck.'

The only girl in the family, Bubbles was used to roaming around at night with her five brothers. 'It probably induced a life of crime later on, but we were just kids jumping out our windows and picking apples off the trees and going to the bakery over the road and grabbing a hot loaf of bread.'

In Bubbles' early years, the family lived on a farm in Kaikohe, where her father was the manager. She loved animals. One Christmas, there was a leg of pork with crackling. But when Bubbles went to feed her pet pig, he was gone. 'Charlie the pig was on the dinner table, so I felt quite sick and horrible and hated my mother,' she said. 'I classed Charlie as my friend.'

Another time she tried to bury a dead calf. 'We thought it was so sad. We covered it in sacks and flowers and were having a tangi for it, and got a crack from our father. I remember him saying it was stupid and that animals get born at night-time and die, and it was a farm animal not a pet.'

That hiding was one of the few things Bubbles remembered

about her father except that he was tall and dark, with wide shoulders and big hands. 'He came in and out, made more kids and took off again. He was never a major feature of our life and eventually left when I was about eight.'

Bubbles' mother, a Pākehā, later disliked Māori. 'Whether that was caused through what our father had done to her, I couldn't tell you. I do remember butcher knives flying across the room into her favourite picture, and her screaming and yelling and all of us getting ordered to bed. I don't remember much after that so I'm wondering if that was the last time he was around.'

Bubbles said she still loved animals. 'Our cats, our dogs, they all get buried properly and have tangis. We've always had as many animals as we could put up with. Animals aren't judgemental like people. As long as you look after them and feed them, they'll love you, no matter what.'

Bubbles' mother worked as a typist to support her six children and later trained to be a teacher. 'I think my mother would have been a really intelligent woman and had a lot of skills to offer.' She was a brilliant knitter, something she passed on to her daughter.

Otherwise, there was little feminine about Bubbles' up-bringing. 'Because we lived in a lot of hand-me-downs through financial difficulties, there was no little dress to get handed down; it was a pair of boxer shorts and a t-shirt. And I used to always have short hair when I was little, so I presume I looked as much of a boy as the boys did when we were all heading out the door. I used to get the shits up about little girls and their pigtails and their pretty little bows on their dresses, and made a beeline to be more nasty to them than anybody else.'

Bubbles and her brothers stuck together, good practice for her later gang days. 'If we played cowboys and Indians, I'd always have to be the Indian because he got killed. I remember being tied up to trees and willow arrows being fired. In those days, girls didn't play rugby, but I used to play and get kicked off the rugby field and told that it's not feminine, and used to play knife games and splits and did more boy activities than I ever did girl activities. I was quite a ruffian.'

Bubbles loved school. 'Got away from home. Didn't have to do chores. You could draw things; they had all the bits and pieces you needed.' With brothers in classes above and below her, no one picked on her. She excelled at sport: rugby, netball and swimming. Looking at her broad shoulders, I could see why. 'I could have been the model pupil if I had persevered in my behaviour. I still like school now. I haven't stopped trying.'

After Bubbles' father left for good, the family moved to Northcote. Bubbles hated her new school and leaving the farm, but it was a bonus being closer to her English grandmother, the only person she had happy memories of. 'She was beautiful, a little short round old lady that had lovely biscuit tins on the old sideboard.' Bubbles and her younger brother had often gone by bus to stay with her in Devonport for holidays. Now they could catch the ferry to visit.

The children spent hours playing behind their house in the bush that stretched as far as the harbour. One day, three of them built a cave in the side of a sandstone hill. When they crawled inside, the front collapsed. It was several hours before they were rescued. 'When the candle went out, we started getting scared cos it was getting quite stuffy in there. The local policeman dug us out. I can remember those big huge muddy boots of his giving us all a swift kick in the butt, and being taken home practically by the ear. That would have been one of my first meetings with a policeman, who I decided was no-go. If anything, he saved our lives, but we didn't see it as that. Policemen from then on were considered the enemy.'

On Bubbles' ninth birthday, her grandmother died. 'After that I started going off the railway tracks. I didn't really worry about anybody concerned with my family. Even later in life, other than ringing my mother up to say she's getting another grandchild, there's been not much communication at all.'

When her mother got a new partner, a teacher like herself, Bubbles hated him. 'He probably took away the bare amount of time our mother had. I think he was really good to all of us. When I look back now, my behaviour would have been quite appalling. If we all drove the poor man away, it's understandable.' Once he gave them money to call him 'Dad' in front of his friends. 'All the boys did, "Dad this, Dad that", and I walk in and go, "Mr T", and was quickly exited from the room and wasn't allowed to come back.'

The arrival of a baby boy made things worse. 'I felt I was the girl and I was owed more time than him. If anything had happened to him, I probably would have laughed. I couldn't stand him.'

Bubbles became increasingly out of control. 'I thought we missed out on everything. We didn't have toys and we didn't have things that other kids had, and that was a major part of me cutting loose and doing and getting the things that I wanted myself. I made a vow to my children that they'd never go without. But it's totally unrealistic. Now that I'm older, I can see how hard it must have been. Those were the days when there were no government handouts and no help whatsoever from any departments because they didn't exist. If you were a solo mother, you went to work and you looked after your children.'

When she became a mother herself, Bubbles often had to rely on the Domestic Purposes Benefit. 'It's okay when people really need it,' she said, but she was scathing of women who deliberately had children to get it, and especially those whose partners were working or could work.

'The other thing I vowed never to do was to hit my kids,' she went on. 'I remember going to school and not being able to sit down on the seat cos your legs were too sore where you'd got the strap or the jug cord or anything else that was in the immediate vicinity. I also felt that, because of the person I am, that if I ever did hit them, they'd probably get more than I could ever bargain to control.'

The closest she'd come to violence was grabbing her 16-year-old daughter's cheeks, she said. 'That freaked her out enough to give the correct answers and deal to the situation immediately because she knew I was beyond control. When I'd really had enough and I knew I'd hurt them, I'd leave. I'd walk down the road and have a cigarette or sit in the park.'

Bubbles' own mother took more drastic measures, making her daughter a state ward when she was 10. 'She had to choose which children to let go away so she could exist with the others — her choice was myself and my younger brother,' she said flatly.

'We were obviously getting into a lot of trouble. I remember the Social Welfare turning up and we went into my room and packed a bag. I was sent to a farm with these two old people who were probably lovely. But all I wanted was my brother and familiar surroundings and as soon as I was able, I packed me a bag, took some food and disappeared.'

Bubbles nearly made it home, 100 kilometres away, before she got caught. 'It took about three days. I walked, hitch-hiked, jumped on a train one part of it, on a goods wagon.' At night she slept out. 'Loved it. No worries. I even feel at home in the dark now. After eight, she's all go.'

Bubbles spent the next nine years in and out of institutions: Allendale Girls Home, Kingslea, Arohata, Christchurch Women's Prison. For a long time, she hated her mother but now she was more understanding. 'She would have been at her wits' end and that would have been the only answer.' In those days, she said, parents had to sign you over as a state ward to get you into a girls home, and gave up all rights to your care. 'You didn't have the options they have today — you know, we'll take them back home and we'll see if this works and that works. Then it was: you're a state ward, goodbye.'

Bubbles' first impression of the Black Power was that 'they were very rude, obnoxious, dirty and absolutely yuk'. She was 17 and on the run from Arohata. When they tried to stop her getting into a Wellington nightclub, she punched one of them in the face. 'And they went, "This woman's got balls, she's all right."'

Introductions over, she felt at home with the gang, much as she had with her brothers. 'Heaps of boys doing boy things and things I like doing. Pinching cars. Ragey parties. Going out to prearranged fights at prearranged places and I already had my big head up the front. I'd be one of the boys and be away. I dressed like them, lived like them, could fight like them, so went with them. We were classed as the juniors cos we were all young. And for some unknown reason, the seniors thought they could control us, but they soon found out they couldn't. Which erupted years later into a new gang called the Nomads.'

Bubbles found men easy to relate to. 'The women were just someone to screw, cook and leave at home.' In her early gang days, she didn't have a boyfriend. 'They were mates to hearty party with and go hard with. Nah. Wasn't interested in the sexual side of it, thank goodness.'

'Why thank goodness?' I asked.

'The lifestyle some of those girls had was terrible. Like the men leaving them at home and going out for weeks on end. And other women. Blocks were really common then. Gang rapes. Nah, it wasn't me.'

I thought of the sales manager on the plane and dived in. 'Did gang members have to take part in blocks?'

'Most of the guys did. If they didn't, they'd probably be called the wimp of the wimps. A lot of people would probably be quite disgusted, but even that side of it didn't worry me. Keep on drinking and ignore what was going on somewhere else.'

I took a deep breath. 'Were you ever blocked?'

'No! I think if I didn't have breasts, I could have easily been one of the boys.' She looked over at me. 'Was I nice when you met me?'

'You were to me,' I said, remembering how relieved I'd been; having Bubbles as an enemy didn't bear thinking about.

'I was quite nasty when I first got out of jail to a lot of people. Probably my way of crowd control. Go away!'

I went back to blocks. Bubbles didn't know where the word came from. Nor did anyone else I asked, though several people suggested it referred to a slab of meat on a chopping block at the abattoir.

There wasn't a particular ritual around them, she said. 'Someone was there who shouldn't have been there. Everyone would get so pissed, and if one of the guys had picked up a girl from the pub or something — a lot of the time, it was the guys that already had girlfriends so there's no way you could take her home — they just got dropped off at the pad.'

'Would it happen to regular girls in the gang?'

'No. Girls that belonged to men were protected. Utterly. But if you were just there for a look, God knows what would happen to you.'

I had one last question. 'Did you have the power to change what was happening?'

She shook her head. 'No, not really. I don't think I would of either. I don't think I ever had a conscience about what happened to other people.'

It was a sentiment she repeated a number of times. 'Never been a people's person.' And, 'Because I was a loner, I didn't want to contribute to anyone else's well-being or not-so-well-being.' And again, 'No conscience. No worries. No ties.'

I asked her if she'd cared about herself.

'Oh yeah,' she said. 'I was number one in my life and made sure I acted accordingly. As long as I was all right and a few immediate friends were all right, the rest of the world, who cares?'

Having children forced Bubbles to think beyond herself. She was particularly close to her oldest daughter, Rana. 'My buddy. She's a lot like me. She likes coming and going, she doesn't give a damn about authority, but she does care about other people whereas I really didn't for a long time. Even now I can flick people at the drop of a hat.'

We finished talking in time to go and pick up Bubbles' partner from work. Outside the motel, she discovered she'd left the car lights on and the battery was dead. A look of fear — fleeting but unmistakeable — flashed across her face. She's scared of him, I thought, feeling shocked and sad: the biggest, toughest woman I ever knew is afraid of her man. We borrowed jumper leads from some guys in the next unit, started the car and arrived at the shearing shed to see him wrestling his final sheep for the day, his lean, muscled arms slick with sweat.

One person that Bubbles never flicked was Annie. That night she cooked tea for both families in the shabby, comfortable house owned by her and her partner, a shearer who was working at the freezing works because of a bad back. A television set that no one seemed to watch snowed in a corner of the open-plan living area. Facing it was a dentist's chair posing as a La-Z-Boy.

Bubbles spent most of her time on the phone jacking up rides and the next day's work for her twins. It struck me that their lives were more interconnected than mine and my teenagers': they all worked together, knew the same people, lived in the same small area.

Bubbles' partner set his bong up on the low coffee table, and Bubbles and Annie's partner joined him. Standing at the stove, Annie pursed her lips and tossed the stir-fry harder. I was glad they didn't invite me to have a smoke.

Annie's daughters, 11 and nine, were a welcome distraction, displaying the same bright curiosity as their mother. A few years later, the older one stayed with me in Wellington. I pulled out the Aroha Trust photo album and left her to look at it. When I came back, tears were streaming down her face. She pointed at two old photos of Bubbles. In the first, she was coming through a doorway — big, mean, lunging at the camera — while a boy beside her raised his fist in the Black Power salute. In the second, she sat on a stereo speaker in front of a rusty corrugated-iron fence, one bare foot in the air, a bottle of Lion Brown pressed to her lips.

'Aunty Bubbles looks so heavy,' Annie's daughter sobbed. 'Now I can see how hard it must be for her to change her life around.'

The next day it was Annie's turn to talk. I'd been looking forward to comparing notes with my old friend, but it was surprisingly hard work. She remembered little about setting up Aroha Trust and not much about day-to-day events. 'I think I had an idea and the time was right for it to happen and it just happened,' she said. Then, when I pressed her, 'Actually, Pip, I think you did a lot of it.'

She was equally vague about Abel Smith Street. 'I can just remember it being very chaotic, a lot of in-and-out traffic all the time. That part of life was quite a blur for me,' she said, rolling her Rs in a Southland drawl. Yes, she said, she'd always played an important part in the houses she lived in. But she couldn't define her role except to say, 'I wasn't the organiser.' On that at least, we agreed!

Annie was a visionary, leaving other people to worry about the details. Drugs may have also contributed to her vagueness. 'I saw myself very much as an experimenter of life,' she said. 'Things were there to be experienced and enjoyed. I was never much of a drinker, I get sick. But I was taking a lot of pills and smoking marijuana. Everyone was doing it. And we were into that nightclubby, dark side of life.'

When she got pregnant, Annie gave up dope for good, put off by the damage she saw it doing to those around her. 'I think it robs people of their motivation and inspiration,' she said.

She deflected questions about her personal life, both then and now. I knew she'd always been a private person, but I sensed a deeper unhappiness that she couldn't share. The only time she really relaxed was when she was talking about ideas and the wider world. While working in the shearing sheds and freezing works, she'd finished a sociology degree and begun a social work diploma. 'I have an appetite for knowledge, I love to know things,' she said.

She enjoyed living in Kaitangata, where her mother was like a second mum to her girls. 'The initial starting point is, "Oh, you're Alfie and Jeannie's girl." It's very easy and it's very nice because it's those ties of kinship. I know I can live in a big city, but it's a nice environment for my children to be in.'

Financially it was hard, though. 'I think New Zealand society has polarised into extreme haves and have-nots. I put myself in the have-nots. Financially, I'd have to struggle to do a lot of things. Really struggle. At the same time, there are thousands and thousands of people in much worse situations than me. All the people I know do it relatively hard. Our society has moved from one where you're measured by how much you care for people to how much can I have for myself. I'm very opposed to that.'

Annie's parents were both Pākehā, of Scottish and Irish descent. She and her older brother grew up on a sheep station just out of Palmerston, where her father worked as a general hand and her mother was the housekeeper. There were always other children to go swimming with, build huts and climb trees. Two or three times a year the family would make the hour-and-a-half trip to Dunedin by car for supplies. The rest of the time they joined in the local fun. 'I can remember dancing with my father, standing on his feet.'

When I first met Annie in the 1970s, she took me to stay with her parents. I was a bit scared of her mum, a no-nonsense Southlander, but her dad seemed delighted in his only daughter and called her Bernadette Devlin (as my father did me). He brought home muttonbirds for me to try and laughed when I couldn't force down the oily meat. 'Good, more for me!' he said, but I felt like I'd failed some sort of townie test.

Annie's father was president of the Ocean Beach Freezing Workers' Union before she was born and shared his political passion with her. 'My whole upbringing has been in a socialist, Labour Party, left-wing environment,' she said. 'I recall from quite young my father talking to me about the subordination of the individual for — I forget the last bit — but it's basically for the betterment of the common good. I see all the community things that have developed in my life coming from those attitudes and ideas.'

Although he'd left school at 14, he wanted his children to be well educated. 'He was a man ahead of his time. He encouraged me to step outside the normal mould that girls get married and have children, and that's life. He was a lot deeper than that, which was unusual for a man of his origins.'

The independence that Annie's father fostered at home went down less well at school. 'I was just alive and sparky and in the thick of things.' Once, when a teacher bullied her, she organised a group of girls to sit on the monkey bars outside the staff room singing:

'We hate you, Mr Ferguson, oh yes, we do
We hate your black suit and your red car too.'

After a short stint at boarding school, where she was always in trouble, Annie's father sent her to East Otago High School where she passed five School Certificate subjects but failed University Entrance 'because I hadn't done any work'. The family moved to Kaitangata and Annie lasted a term at South Otago High School before quitting college. She began nursing at Balclutha Hospital but took off to Dunedin without finishing her training. 'I just wanted to get out and see this world that I thought was waiting for me.' When she abandoned nursing in Wellington to work for Aroha Trust, I hadn't realised it was for the second time.

In Dunedin, Annie ran a drop-in centre in the Octagon as a community volunteer. 'Looking back, I was just too young,' she said. 'It was all full-on and adrenalin-rush sort of stuff.' But it connected her to community networks all round the country and people like Denis O'Reilly, who was working with the Black Power in Wellington. In need of a change of scene, she moved north, into Walton House — the combined gang pad where Denis was living — and out again just as fast.

'There was a lot of violence, and there was a lot of violence towards women,' she said.

'Was the violence—?'

'It was rape,' she said abruptly. She never saw it happen. 'You just heard about it, you just knew. And I felt unsafe. That I didn't have enough credibility to be there and survive.'

Candleman gave Annie a job at his factory and she moved into Brougham Street. One day she got home from work to find a woman about to be blocked. 'I just went, well, I'm going to have to put myself on the line. And then my friend arrived back, a woman friend who had a lot of standing, and went, "Right, what the fuck do you think you're doing in my house, doing this?"'

That friend was Bubbles. The block never went ahead.

'Was it common for a woman to have enough influence to stop a block?' I asked.

'No!' Annie said. 'Women didn't have a lot of say.'

I was relieved to get home from Kaitangata and kiss my own kids. My visit had challenged my sense of self and shone an uncomfortable light on my Pākehā, middle-class, city ways. Both Annie's and Bubbles' partners were rural, uneducated Māori men who smoked too much dope. Both women had privately confided that they were worried about the other's health and relationship. Bubbles had been in hospital with a wool abscess. Annie looked worn out from work, study, motherhood and lack of money. Both were still heavy smokers.

But my unease went deeper. I'd been hurt by Annie's guardedness and shaken by Bubbles' insistence that even now, she only cared about the small group of people closest to her.

A few days later, a newspaper article caught my eye. A six-year-old British boy had shot and killed another child. The article said that a small child raised with anger or neglect from the first hours of life will not feel for others' pain. It quoted a child psychologist: 'Empathy is the basis of moral behaviour, and it is laid down in the first two years.'

Ah! Empathy: the ability to walk a mile in someone else's shoes. That was the word I'd been looking for when Bubbles talked about her indifference to most people.

Two years! What a small window to create the basis of moral behaviour. Even if it were bigger — the Jesuits say, 'give me the child until he is seven, and I will show you the man' — the clock is ticking from the moment we're born.

Ultimately, I couldn't judge if one woman's upbringing was better or worse than another's. I only knew what they chose to tell me. Nor could I assess the relative importance of nature versus nurture, or why some women seemed more resilient than others. Having said that, a number of the Aroha Trust women were horrifically abused as children yet seemed capable of broad empathy. I wondered if that was because someone special had loved them when they were very young, given them a blueprint to love others.

Bubbles' mother seemed overwhelmed rather than indifferent. But Bubbles never spoke of love or tenderness in her early life, apart from her grandmother, who for the most part lived a long way away and died when she was nine. What happened if a child was starved of affection during those crucial early years when they were learning whether it was safe to trust the world?

Bubbles had worked hard, raised children, extricated herself from the gang scene and bought a house with her partner. She had no regrets, she said. 'I think I'm quite fortunate I've had such an action-packed, busy life and I'm still alive and my head space is still normal. Cos a lot of our friends have died or they're absolutely nuts cos of the things they've put into their bodies.'

But childhood seemed to have taught her that she couldn't count on other people. 'If I'm in control of my own life and my own little circle, I can change that and make that better,' she said. Trust was the flip side of empathy, it seemed. And a large dose of love was needed to kick-start them both.

On a rainy Sunday evening, I joined a small group standing in front of Farmers department store in Wellington's Cuba Mall. Inside the window, four Australian guys had set up house for two weeks as a stunt for the International Arts Festival. Apart from a private toilet and a hip-high stripe painted strategically across the shower cubicle, everything they did was on view.

Two teenage boys in orange hoodies and low-slung jeans shuffled to the edge of the group. One of the men in the window touched his shirt, which was also orange, then pointed at the boys' hoodies, as if to say, 'Look, same colour!' The boys stood there sullenly. The man pointed to their baggy pants, then tugged at his fitting, lime green trousers and gave a thumbs-up sign: 'Hey, mine are better!'

The boys couldn't resist. One of them flicked up the bottom of his jeans to show off Nike socks. The man looked thoughtful, then rolled up his trouser legs to reveal burgundy ones. The boys whispered to each other, then pulled off their beanies with a flourish. Underneath, both had short hair, dyed blond. Beaming, the man removed his crimson hat to reveal a completely shaved head. The audience clapped and the boys walked off with wide grins.

The exchange calmed me down. The little things we have in common, the things that make us human, could override our differences. All you had to do was focus on them.

☗

The phone went. It was Annie. We hadn't spoken since I left Kaitangata.

'I've rung to apologise,' she said.

'What for?' Annie wasn't the apologising kind.

'I'm sorry about the bong. We were really embarrassed.'

We? Annie's partner had seemed happy to join in. 'Don't worry about it,' I said, disappointed that she thought I was too straight to cope with people smoking dope.

'Bubbles' man knows that no one smokes inside my house,' she went on.

'You don't have to explain.'

'It was like he was saying, "Stuff your rules! I'll do what I like in front of your Pākehā friend!" That's what really pissed me off.'

'Oh,' I said. 'Thanks. I did feel some pretty strange vibes. I thought it must have been me.'

'Nah. There's a lot of shit happening down here that I can't talk about right now. I'm sorry you got caught up in it.'

'Are you okay?'

'Yeah, I'm fine,' she said briskly. 'Now, who are you going to visit next?'

FOURTEEN

PUSHING BOUNDARIES

I wanted to drop acid. It'd be the first time. Jane — more experienced in such matters — agreed to go halves on a tab and promised not to leave my side.

Apart from marijuana and alcohol, I didn't do drugs. There was no way I'd throw handfuls of coloured pills down my throat: unpredictable cocktails of uppers and downers, pinkies and rollies that could fry your brain cells a hundred different ways. Especially not after a girl fatally overdosed on prescription drugs that a young man stole while he was staying at Abel Smith Street.

I didn't know the young man was there: Junior and Tasi had hidden him in their bedroom. In court, his lawyer argued that 'he had fallen in with a group of undesirables and was easily impressed by them'. In her diary, Jane underlined 'undesirables' on the newspaper clipping, and wrote, 'these words are meant to be all of us'. She sounded rattled. 'Boy, he must have creamed it to the judge. He bowled off the chemist's while he was staying at our place and everyone started popping pills. It could have easily been one of our girls that died of an OD. None of them knew how to handle them properly, including him.'

Pills made people crazy. Hallucinating on pinkies, Mahina thought she'd pushed one of the boys out the window at the Newtown Park flats. 'You know how high they were. And I thought I'd killed him. Then Tasi and Evelyn and I went into a fruit shop and they reckoned I pulled everything off the shelves. I don't remember doing that. It was like you lost three days of your life. I stopped after that because I couldn't remember those three days. I think we were doing a job in Newtown, I don't know if it was at a church. I left the water going and it flooded the building out. So Tasi told me.'

But acid was different. To me, it seemed cool rather than stupid. At university, I'd scorned the politicos who decried marijuana as escapist but didn't apply the same test to alcohol. I thought they invented pious reasons not to do things because they were afraid. Fear narrowed your mind. It closed you down. It stopped you living life to the full. That was not going to happen to me.

One Friday after work, Jane and I carefully halved a tiny square of paper dipped in LSD. I let my half rest on my tongue, light as a postage stamp, and felt my throat tighten. I forced it down, then waited anxiously for writhing snakes, dripping faces, an irresistible urge to jump off high buildings. We walked to the Cambridge. As I sat on a stool peering into my beer, goldfish appeared: fluorescent, jumping-jack flashes of light cavorting in the amber liquid.

Pat turned up. He told me he was leaving town, going to Canterbury University to do Honours.

'I'm tripping,' I giggled, mad with relief that the world had become a magical place, not a Dali nightmare.

'So am I,' he said.

'I was surprised — usually he stuck to alcohol — then relieved: he wouldn't be able to disapprove. For a moment, or maybe an hour, I was distracted by the smooth sound of JJ Cale sliding like lava out of the jukebox, the frolicking of the goldfish, Gini's — or was it Georgie's? — laughing breath on my ear: 'Pip, eh!' When I turned back, he was gone.

He hadn't been high, he told me later; he'd just said that. As usual, our paths had collided and veered off awkwardly.

⚮

That night, Jane and I went to a party at the Highway 61 pad, behind the Cally, a pub by the Basin Reserve. 'It was in a really neat but crazy place down the back of this flat,' she scrawled almost illegibly in her diary when she got home, still speeding. 'Before we came inside, we had a joint and then another and another and another, and the whole place really freaked us out. I can still hear the music playing and all those big, fat bikies towering over me all dressed in the dirtiest disgusting clothes they could find.'

I wouldn't have gone to a Highway party on my own or just with Jane, but it was okay because the Wombles were there, and the Blacks and the Highways tolerated each other. There's no way I'd have gone to a Mongrel Mob party under any circumstances. They and the Blacks were out-and-out enemies, and although I didn't take sides, the Mob were unlikely to stop and check.

It worked like this. Broadly speaking, our girls were gang girls. As a group, we were linked to Wellington Black Power through their work trust, Te Waka e Manaaki. But we insisted on our independence, and girls from any gang (or no gang) were welcome to join us.

'We actually cut across the boundaries of different gangs,' Annie said. 'It wasn't our problem, it was the men's problem.'

Within the trust, rifts never occurred along gang lines. 'That was the thing about it,' said Georgie, one of the few women with a non-gang partner. 'A bunch of women who got on so well, and yet each and every one of them went with different members of different gangs. We might have had our moments, but they were more family-orientated moments with the two sisters and stuff like that.'

Outside the trust, things were more complicated, not least because of the girls' shifting allegiances. They generally went out with guys who wore patches, but they weren't always particular about which patch.

When Charmaine fell in love with Paddy, a member of the Highway 61s, 'every whānau or Black Power in town took it upon themselves to challenge me,' she said. 'They'd watched me grow up from age 12. The times I'd run away, they'd always been there protecting me and looking after me in the best way they knew how to. So they naturally assumed that I was being preened to push out these little Black Power babies. I was being saved for the right day in their own funny little, strange, ownershippy minds.' She gave her trademark cackle. 'I got challenged and stuck on meat hooks all over the place for that decision. But I stood phat to it. I'd go, "Blacks are brothers, not lovers." I'd say, "Hey, it could have been worse. He could have been a Mobster. Smile!"'

At that time, the Blacks and Highways got on all right, she said. They could drink in the same pubs and many of the old Highway men had gone over from the Blacks, including Paddy, 'cos he wanted to ride bikes and they were more into whānau'. Still, it took guts for Paddy to be with Charmaine. When he fell asleep at the Black Power disco one night, I saw Rei hack off his long black hair and one of the boys boot him in the head as he lay on the floor.

For a group of guys that were anti-establishment, the Black Power had a strict hierarchy and a surprising number of rules. This didn't suit all their members, particularly the juniors who became more and more rebellious. In the days before Aroha Trust, Bubbles identified with the rebels. 'The Black Power had changed to wanting club fees and doing as you were told and having jobs,' she said. 'We were totally against that. So it was decided that you have your money and your games, and we'll go somewhere else and do our own thing.'

The juniors' philosophy suited Bubbles better. 'Nothing to do with structure in those days. Didn't want to conform to anything that anyone else wanted.' She was close friends with their fearsome leader Dennis Hines, their bond cemented when he came to her aid in a pub fight and they both did time for it. 'He's still travelling the same path,' she said.

'He's been New Zealand's most notorious criminal, but I see another side of him. He's just a big soft teddy bear and a really, really nice person.'

Around the same time as Aroha Trust was set up, the disaffected juniors formed a breakaway gang called the Nomads. Gini's partner JB and her brother were members. 'I think a lot of those other gangs wouldn't touch me because of how terrifying the Nomads were,' she said. 'My brother was, in his own way, a man of his word. If he didn't like anybody and he was out to get them, they would know. They'd be in the hospital, he'd go and visit them and stab them. It was that sort of reputation that stuck with each member of the Nomad gang. People wouldn't dare look at them sideways because of the consequences.'

Like Bubbles, Gini saw another side to the Nomads. 'They've got that tough exterior but deep down inside they're human, just like the rest of us. They cry and have family problems. They don't show it because they're too hard. To get into the heart of that person is like going into outer space. It's going where they don't let people go unless you're close, intimate.'

I asked her how that made her feel as a partner.

'It made me feel stronger and secure in that person. And because the gang is like a family unit, you feel secure in its atmosphere.'

Charmaine said Gini's brother always looked out for her. 'On my sixteenth birthday, he sent me a switchblade with a note saying, "I hear you've been doing a lot of hitch-hiking; you might need this".' She laughed. 'Other girls were getting pretty dresses and make-up when they turned 16, and I got a switchblade and a bong.'

At first, we managed to juggle the different gangs at Abel Smith Street. It wasn't unusual to have Nomads in the lounge, Blacks in the bedroom and Highway 61s knocking on the front door. Even individual Mobsters would visit and be made welcome.

As time went by, tensions worsened with the Mob and — because we were Black Power-aligned — we lived under constant threat of a hit on our house. When rumours flared, the boys would stand guard for a night or two before drifting away again and leaving us to fend for ourselves.

With the Nomads, the lines were more blurred. They had close links both with the Black Power and with some of our key girls. It was impossible to keep them out of our house and out of our lives.

Jane never felt safe at Abel Smith Street. 'It was meant to be for the women of the trust, but quite often partners were there,' she said. 'It was like a railway station really. I didn't feel like I could go to bed at night and feel safe. The Nomads might arrive. Or I might be attacked or raped or beaten up, or whatever.'

I was surprised to read in her diary in April 1978, only a few months after we moved in: 'Fuck, things are getting really heavy lately. The No Brains came round to Abel Smith Street the other nite.' (No Brains is what we called the Nomads. That, or Mads.) 'Just walked in, smashed a few things, made themselves a feed without even asking and left again. We really shit ourselves. Me and Pip and Tasi were the only ones around.'

I hadn't realised they'd started bothering us so soon. Their visits became more frequent. One day, Gerry had just finished making boil-up when four of them walked in, helped themselves, and sat in the lounge eating our tea.

Out in the kitchen, sick of being scared, I muttered mutinously — loud enough for them to hear — that there were no free feeds at our house, then flounced off to my bedroom.

Tasi put her head round the door when they'd gone. 'D'ya know who that was, Pip?'

'Fuckin' Nomads! Think they can come in and take whatever they fuckin' well like.'

'Yeah, but do you know who the guy at the front was?'

I was too steamed up to care. 'Mean fuckin' bastards! As if we haven't got enough mouths to feed. And there's no money left in kitty.'

'That was Dennis Hines. He just got out of jail.'

As I was digesting the fact that I'd just scolded the leader of the meanest gang in town, Gerry barged in. 'Guess what? They brought their plates out to the kitchen and I was shitting myself cos I was the only one there. But they rinsed them and left them on the bench. They left this too.' She held out a wad of notes. Enough to feed us all twice over.

At Easter, I went to stay with Pat in Christchurch. We hitch-hiked down the West Coast, sometimes glaring at each other with our thumbs out on opposite sides of the road. Although I was 12 inches shorter and three stone lighter than him, I insisted on taking my turn to carry our only pack as we climbed the steep hill out of Balclutha — just as every other self-respecting feminist of my generation insisted on paying her own way, opening her own door, putting on her own coat. A carload of local boys wound down the windows and gave us the fingers as they zoomed past. 'La-a-azy ba-aa-astard!' the driver shouted at Pat, his words stretched out on the wind. No one stopped to pick us up.

As evening fell, we arrived in Twizel to stay with a friend who was working on the dam. We sat on the doorstep of his single men's cabin until someone told us he was on night shift. In darkness, we unrolled our sleeping bags under some trees on a gentle slope, and Pat wrapped his arms around me to keep me warm. During the night, I slid down the slippery pine needles and woke thinking he was gone.

At Lake Hāwea, we played pool with the farm boys. I'd spent hours hunched over a pool table in the Dunedin youth centre, and could hold my own. The drunker they got, the more the farm boys tried to impress me, the only woman in the bar. I laughed at their favourite trick, staggering around with the tip of the cue balanced on their chins. In bed, Pat accused me of chatting them up. It was just a bit of fun, I said angrily. And, anyway, I could do what I liked.

We didn't talk about Aroha Trust or the Black Power. If Pat worried about my safety, he didn't let on — or perhaps he knew I wouldn't want to hear. He had his own problems, was disillusioned with university the second time round and lonely in a new city. I didn't ask if anyone else warmed his bed when I wasn't there. Free agents don't.

On the last night of my stay, he slipped *Blood on the Tracks* out of its cover. 'I want to play you two songs before you go,' he said quietly. Bob Dylan's raspy voice cut through the silence: 'We always did feel the same, we just saw it from a different point of view.' Then he moved the needle forward to 'If You See Her, Say Hello'.

❦

Back in Wellington, I got sick. When a fever set in, I crawled home to Mum. She brought me cold flannels and hot soup, and didn't ask any questions. While I was convalescing, Annie came to visit.

'I'm moving out of Abel Smith Street,' she said. 'There's too many people. And I'm worried about Charmaine. She's too young to be around all that shit. Jane's coming with us.'

I could hardly believe it. Annie was abandoning our women's house, the one we'd worked so hard to set up, the one we'd only been in for six months.

'Are you leaving the trust?' I asked, almost too sick to care.

'Nah, I'll still work for the Education Board. I just want a quiet place to come home to.'

I thought about Abel Smith Street without Annie. We weren't getting on that well. We'd had a bad fight when she'd waltzed in late on her cooking night, saying Candleman had taken her out for a sauna and a feed. She didn't even apologise.

I had mixed feelings about Candleman. He was unfailingly kind to me — I still have the dinner set he and his partner gave me when I got married — but I kept my distance. The last thing I needed was another father figure, and I was a little suspicious of any man who took girls less than half his age to saunas. I might have been a bit jealous too.

'We waited for you for ages,' I yelled. 'There wasn't any food in the house.'

'You can cope for one night,' Annie shouted back. 'I'm not your nursemaid.'

'You could have let us know.'

'I wasn't near a phone.'

I could hear myself becoming hysterical. 'Selfish bitch! You come and go exactly as you please. I'm always the one who's left to pick up the pieces.'

'Chill out, Pip! No one died of starvation. Fuck, you're uptight.' And she swung her bag over her shoulder and walked out.

In some ways, it'd be easier at Abel Smith Street without Annie. If she wasn't around, I wouldn't count on her and she wouldn't be able to let me down. It'd be good for Jane to be more independent too. She was my silent shadow, painfully shy and lacking in confidence. I couldn't imagine the two of them getting on, but that was their problem.

'Your mother's going to hate me for leaving you,' Annie said at the door. 'Remind her that one day you'll want to leave too. It might help her understand.'

I was surprised that she cared what my mother thought. I wondered if the message was intended for me.

By the time I got back to Abel Smith Street, Annie, Jane and Charmaine had gone, and the place was a tip: muddy boot prints tracked through the house, dirty plates spilling out of the sink, maggots squirming in the rubbish. I borrowed Mum's vacuum cleaner. We would clean up. We would start again. Everything would be all right.

That night I left the vacuum cleaner in the hall when we went to the Black Power disco. By the time we got back, the long metal pipe had disappeared. We never locked our door and one of the boys, it seemed, had picked it up on his way to a stoush with the Mongrel Mob.

There was no way I could explain this to my mother. To my surprise, Shorty, a member of the Nomads, offered to help me look for it. He was young and beautiful, even in gang regalia. Intelligent too. In other circumstances, he could have been a pin-up boy for Māoridom, with his blue kerchief tied around his neck, a thin, silver bangle on his arm, and a trilby hat perched cockily on his head. Instead he has spent most of his life in prison.

On a sleepy Sunday afternoon, Shorty drove me from one gang

house to another, asking hung-over, indifferent people if they'd seen the pipe. I felt ridiculous trailing after him, then I thought about Mum and kept going. Finally, we ran out of places to look and he dropped me home. He seemed as glum as me that we hadn't found it.

I headed to my bedroom to hide out. And there it was, lying in silver splendour in the middle of my crumpled sheets. No one knew how it had got there, or they weren't saying. I didn't care. All that mattered was that someone had appreciated this was an emergency. At stake was not only my good name with my parents but, more important, the Black Power's.

I was pulling weeds along a school driveway in Porirua, enjoying the easy monotony of the work and the hum of conversation around me when Arthur's name came up. I listened more closely.

'You two seemed to be having a good time last night,' Evelyn said to a new girl.

The girl rocked back on her haunches and grinned. I caught the word 'spunky' and saw her eyes flash.

Evelyn giggled. 'I thought you already had a boyfriend.'

'That egg!' the girl said. 'Arthur's more my style, don't you think?'

My head began to pound. No, not Arthur! I'd been biding my time, hanging out with him whenever I could, waiting for him to make the first move. But the girl was pretty and feisty, and she lived at Epuni Street as Arthur did; I didn't stand a chance.

Pull yourself together, I told myself. You can't be jealous of a 16-year-old street kid who's fallen for a gang guy a few years older. I jabbed my trowel into the hard earth and tried not to care.

On the way home from work, we called into Takapuwāhia Marae to talk to Greg Whakataka, a carver who'd been at the Mōkai work co-op hui. It was the same marae where Gini and Tasi's mother had been laid out when she died, though I didn't know that then.

As we approached shyly, Greg looked up from his work bench, his black hair pulled back into a ponytail that highlighted his handsome profile. He showed us what he was working on, then launched into a story about wanting to build a traditional waka with no nails and navigate it from Tahiti to Aotearoa by the stars. Finally he asked why we'd come to see him.

We were from Aroha Trust, we said, pronouncing 'aroha' as if it had no 'h', as most of us did. We hoped he'd help us design some t-shirts.

He looked puzzled. 'Why did you call yourselves Arawa Trust?'

We shrugged. It seemed obvious.

'Have you got special links with Te Arawa?'

We stared at him blankly.

'The iwi?' he said.

'We just thought it meant love,' Georgie said.

'Oh, you mean "aro-ha". Say it properly!' he ordered.

'Aro-ha,' we repeated obediently.

He smiled for the first time. 'Now, what's this about t-shirts?'

They were blue, the Black Power colour, though I'm sure that's not why we chose it. On the front, in black, was a gourd edged with a koru design, representing new life and hope. In the middle of the gourd were a slasher and shovel, their long handles crossed, symbols of our work and socialist ideals. The words 'Aroha Trust' were curved around the bottom. At the top, two clasped hands stood for unity and sisterhood.

The t-shirts were part of our growing confidence. We formed a netball team and played on Saturdays at the Hataitai courts. I was centre, Georgie starred as goal attack, and there was plenty of other talent. Sometimes the boys would come and support us, just as we watched them play league.

We formed a basketball team too, and played at the YMCA. It was the first time for most of us. Georgie roped in a tall Pākehā photo-grapher from The Big House, another community house in the city, to be our coach. The usual chaos prevailed. Instead of sewing our numbers on the backs of the blue t-shirts, 'we pinned them on, stuck them on, glued them on,' Georgie said.

The photographer had trouble passing on the rules around non-contact. In one game, Charmaine was subbed off after five fouls. 'When a player gets sent off, you clap,' Georgie explained. 'That clapping means good game, good sportsmanship. But Charmaine thought everyone was clapping to say, "Yeah, get off, you bitch." She turned around and gave them the fingers and told them to get fucked.' Georgie laughed loudly, exposing her perfect teeth.

Our own house. Our own vehicles. Our own t-shirts. Our own sports teams. Aroha Trust was becoming a force to be reckoned with. We were also building up a reasonable reputation as workers. In May 1978, assistant town clerk Colin Knox — who I later discovered was Māori — told the mayor that the city council was pleased with the three work trusts employed under the government's Temporary Employment Programme: Bruce Stewart's, the Black Power's, and ours. He described the relationship as 'robust' and said the trusts 'are developing into an important agency in the city because they seek and provide for young Maori people an alternative to theft, alcohol and violence which is the preoccupation of many who come to the city from other areas'.

Making a somewhat dubious distinction, he told the mayor that 'groups working towards weekend revelry still have the opportunity to seek unemployment assistance but not under this scheme'. What did he think *we* did on the weekends?

At the same time, he singled out Bruce's trust as the most stable and ended on a note of caution. 'There has been little publicity of the scheme, and until there is a history of progress on the part of more than one trust, I believe we should say little, but give what support we can to the groups which are making a real effort to come to terms with life in the city.'

On top of our regular work, we landed a council contract marking out traffic lanes with reflective catseyes. The council's relief work coordinator, a tall, middle-aged Afro-American, helped us win it. He was an ally in the bureaucracy, but I wished he'd stop asking me to marry him.

The contract was good for our morale and for Aroha Trust's kitty. The $1500 was a big boost to the communal funds that paid for our vehicles, sports uniforms, trips away and emergencies. Even more important, it was a small step towards self-sufficiency and 'real' work. Our heavy reliance on relief work put the trust at risk: if the government cut the scheme, or changed the rules, our base would be destroyed.

There was some glamour involved too, at least at first. 'Here we were, this group of young women, putting catseyes on the main roads of Wellington,' Jane said. 'That in itself was like "yoo-hoo". Doing things like the road people normally did. Putting out the dunces' hats and working right there in the middle of the road, and being able to shut off bits of road. That was really powerful.'

One Saturday, though, things were not going well. Using a putty knife, Jane mixed the two components of the special glue together, then smeared the thick grey paste on the bottom of a stack of catseyes. Carefully measuring the distance between each one, Georgie, Tasi and I placed them on the road: four round, one square; four round, one square. The work was hot and slow. There were no white lines to guide us, and no second chances. The glue hardened like cement on contact. Once the catseyes touched the asphalt, they were there to stay.

I crouched down at road level and surveyed our handiwork. The lane we'd created along Victoria Street looked like a gently curving snake. We had 4000 catseyes to lay. At this rate, we wouldn't be finished by Christmas. But it was hard to concentrate. In spite of the bright orange cones, cars kept trying to nose their way into our work space. It was only a matter of time before one of us got skittled.

'Partly because we were women, a lot of the drivers didn't take any notice of us, and so we had to start putting the dunces' hats closer and closer together,' Jane said. 'I can remember being incredibly frustrated and leaning in the window of this car with my putty knife and saying, "If you don't fuck off, I'll slit your throat." You tried to be reasonable as far as you could, but you resorted back to form when nothing else worked. The funny thing was they seemed to stop doing it. I don't know whether word got around Wellington, but at that stage anyway, they stopped coming through.'

'Gizza smoke, Pip?' said Junior.

I shook my head. 'Buy your own!'

'I would but I'm skint.'

'Tough! Buy a carton on payday so you don't run out.'

'I will. Cross my heart. Go on! Just one!'

'Uh-uh.'

'Ple-ease! I'll pay you back. Promise.'

'Nah!' I walked off before she wore me down. I'd got hard. If I gave in, everyone would want one. Maintaining my own nicotine addiction was expensive enough without propping up a dozen other girls'. Besides, it was time they learnt to think ahead.

I struggled with my meanness. I believed in sharing. And if the girls had smokes, I knew they'd share them with me. As Hunter S Thompson observed of the Hell's Angels, they operated a system close to pure communism: from each according to their ability, to each according to their need. The principle had seemed compelling when I studied Marx at university, but that was before I discovered I'd always have the cigarettes, the girls would always have the need.

Their relaxed attitude to possessions was more practical than dogmatic. They'd never had much and were used to going without. Life was too chaotic to keep track of personal belongings. Forward planning was not their forte. When they were flush, they threw money around like confetti at a wedding. If we didn't get their rent and $10 weekly contribution to the trust kitty the minute they got paid, it would be gone on food and cigarettes, booze and drugs, new jeans, music, court fines if they were about to be locked up.

Monday and Tuesday were like Lent. We'd have starved at work if we hadn't collected money in advance for lunches. (I smoked in front of them, but I drew the line at eating.) We'd head off to the dairy and buy tinned corn beef, tomatoes and white bread for sandwiches, orange cordial, biscuits for morning tea. For those who didn't live in a trust house, it might be their only meal for the day. Then it would be Wednesday and the sun would shine again.

Collecting money was one reason we always met at Abel Smith Street on payday, but it was not the main one. With two teams working in separate locations, we needed time together to build unity. As well as day-to-day work matters, there were always wider issues to discuss: unfair treatment by a headmaster, union stopwork meetings, police harassment, girls getting raped and beaten up.

When it came to running the trust, we sometimes made it hard for ourselves. Like many women's groups at the time, we refused to have formal structures or delegate decision making. That was the way power-hungry male organisations worked; we were not like that. Instead, we rotated the chairperson at each meeting and left the note-taking to whoever felt like it. Sometimes no one felt like it and no notes were taken.

What we didn't realise was that there are always hierarchies. Not naming them doesn't make them go away, it makes them go underground — as the women subconsciously understood when they remembered me and Annie as being in charge. Instead, we created a layer of ambiguity around roles and leadership that I later heard described as 'the tyranny of structurelessness'.

Still, our democratic instincts were basically sound. All their lives, the girls had been bullied, ignored, told they were useless. Our philosophy was to believe in people, give them a say, encourage everyone to be a leader.

When Annie studied to be a social worker, she realised how innovative we'd been. 'Aroha Trust was a true alternative to mainstream practices and structures,' she said. 'We created that without having any of the theoretical knowledge about different ways and different kinds of organisations. We used a consensus-based rule-making process without knowing all these things. We just did it because it was the right way.'

At first the girls held back in our meetings: no one had ever asked for their opinion before. But gradually they became more confident and outspoken.

Jane spelt out the change in her diary: 'We've been talking about a lot of things lately and it's made me think a lot about people's lives. The most important thing is what they feel, what comes from the heart and in their head. That's the most difficult thing to see because it's only rarely the barrier is let down and feelings are let free. And it's no wonder it's like that. Having them abused a few times, you learn to keep them to yourself. For me, I find it so hard to say what's in my head. I blame that partly on my life at home and partly on past experiences.' She'd crossed out the next phrase: 'and the rest on me'.

'All I ever wanted was to be loved and to have someone to listen to me,' she went on. 'That's why I think I took all my frustrations out on other people by beating someone up . . . I was screaming out, somebody love me, listen to me, try and understand me. All I got was a nite [*sic*] in the cells and people telling me I was a smart little mole who couldn't keep her hands to herself and should be locked up away from innocent people.'

School was no better, she wrote. 'I had the brains enough to go to university — if I spent five years doing something I hated. I went from top academic to the no-hopers class just because I couldn't fit in so in the end I was expelled from two schools for stabing [*sic*] someone and fighting. For the person who can't learn in a classroom situation there is no hope. You become a dropout to the rest of society. And you start to believe it so you act like one. Well, this is my story. It's one that could be fited [*sic*] to untold people — a lot of whom are in prisons around NZ. Now with the trust, I've got something I belong to, I've got some direction. And I'm just starting to be able to talk to people. What has been destroyed is slowly being rebuilt.'

FIFTEEN

MAN TROUBLE

I spent the evening at Epuni Street hoping Arthur would appear. I'd heard that he and the pretty young girl had split up, he had to go to court the next day, he'd probably go inside again. I needed to say goodbye.

When he didn't show up, I drove home slowly on my Honda, looking for him in the shadows, only to find he'd been at Abel Smith Street all along. Everyone else drifted off to bed and I went into the kitchen to make a cup of tea. While the kettle boiled, I watched him through the doorway, pacing up and down the lounge as if he was already in a prison cell, pausing only to look at the poster of Rua Kēnana. Finally he sat on the couch, with his elbows on his knees and his chin in his hands, staring at the carpet.

'How many sugars?' I called out.

'Four,' he said.

I handed him a mug, then went over to the record player and put on Bob Marley to try and soothe him. We smoked my last two cigarettes.

He tapped the ash into the palm of his hand and rubbed it along his jeans. 'Don't let me keep you up,' he said.

'Where are you sleeping tonight?' I tried to keep my voice neutral.

'I never sleep.'

'Worried about tomorrow?' I said lamely.

His lip curled. 'I don't give a shit. Inside. Outside. It's all the fuckin' same to me.'

His words winded me like a punch in the stomach. Don't say that, I wanted to shout. People care about you. I care about you. Isn't that worth something? But it seemed cruel and pointless to try and persuade him his freedom was important just as he was about to lose it.

'I need smokes,' I said.

His face softened. 'Addict!'

I grinned. 'I'll give up tomorrow.'

'C'mon then.'

My heart did a little dance.

Outside it was freezing. The dairy round the corner was closed. So was the takeaway bar down the road. Arthur unbuttoned his long woollen army coat and wrapped it round us both. He was not much taller than me and only a little bigger. I nestled my head into the side of his neck. His hand rested heavy on my shoulder.

When light rain began to fall, he drew me closer. Our hips nudged in time to our footsteps. His voice whispered in my ear, dissolving months of wishing I'd been braver when we first met. I hoped there'd never be a shop that sold cigarettes. That we could move softly through the empty streets forever, away from the complications of gangs and prisons and race and class, safe in the cocoon of his big coat and the curtain of rain that shielded us from the harsh world beyond.

'Have you seen Arthur?' Mike Womble's voice was brusque, almost accusing.

'Not since this morning.' I cradled the phone against my ear in the Newtown Community Centre office, grateful that he couldn't see my cheeks flush.

'He didn't turn up for court,' Mike said. 'The pigs are after him big-time. There's a warrant out.'

I picked at a dot of green paint on the receiver. Thank God he'd taken off after I left for work. I couldn't bear to think of him going back to jail. How could anyone bear to have their partner, lover, friend, child whipped away at the bang of a judge's hammer? Like a sudden death without the public sympathy or support. Guilt by association. No space for grief or anger or loneliness; no one to rally around and help pay the bills or mind the kids. I wanted to rage against the futility and powerlessness of it all.

'If he shows up, tell him to get in touch, eh?' Mike said. 'He's only making things worse for himself.'

I knew it was good advice. Arthur couldn't run forever, and when the cops got him, they'd make him pay for the trouble he'd put them to. He'd probably try to take a couple of them down, knowing he was going to get a hiding anyway, and that would make it worse.

'He won't risk coming to our house while he's on the run,' I said, hoping I was wrong.

I wound my way up Maupuia Road in the Red Baron, past ordinary houses tucked into an ordinary-looking suburb. Glancing into people's front yards, I wondered if you ever got used to living with 120 locked-up men towering over you in the same way that you got used to living near the airport or the zoo.

Gradually, the houses petered out and the road narrowed. The scrubby hill on the left dropped steeply to the sparkling, turquoise harbour, a million-dollar view wasted on prisoners in paddy wagons with blacked-out windows, and their anxious visitors.

I'd been to girls homes and borstals before, but this was my first prison visit. I parked the van and followed everyone else — women with kids mainly; a smattering of older people, parents, I supposed — through a gate in the high, grim wall topped with rolls of barbed wire. There was a quiet camaraderie; no one was judging anyone else here.

A warden in dark green trousers and shirt checked my name off a list and searched my bag, taking out the cigarettes and fruit I'd brought for Arthur. He'd get them later, he said. Another used keys from a bunch on his belt to open metal gates and escort me into a bare room dotted with tables. Above us, small grilled windows let in scraps of bright blue sky. There was an urgent hum of voices, bodies leaning in, hungry eyes memorising loved ones' faces for another week.

Arthur was sitting alone, looking young and vulnerable in prison overalls. Healthier too: clean-shaven and clear-eyed.

'You didn't have to come,' he mumbled as I pulled out a chair opposite him.

'How are you?' I asked, regretting the question as soon as it was out.

'Fine,' he said, but his eyes slid away.

I did most of the talking. Every topic seemed fraught. I said Aroha Trust's first birthday was coming up, then remembered he wouldn't be there for the party. Told him the boys had had a run-in with the Mob, and saw a wistful look cross his face. Mentioned that Jane had got off her charges the weekend he'd helped protect her from the cops, then realised no one had been able to protect him.

'You don't need to come again,' he said when our time was up.

I watched glumly as he was led away, passive, cowed. It seemed impossible that anyone in that sterile place gave a damn about him or saw his potential. I feared that every day he spent in there, his despair would grow, his self-belief shrivel.

Back on the road, I wound down the window and blasted my face with fresh air, fretting about the meaning of Arthur's final words. Was it worse to have reminders of the outside world than be left alone? Did visitors add to his humiliation? Didn't he like me anymore?

As I rounded a corner, two guys stood on the grass verge thumbing a lift. I hadn't noticed them in the visiting room, but there was only one reason anyone would be on that hill on a sunny Saturday afternoon: we were part of the same club. Grateful for the distraction, I pulled over.

'Thanks, pal! It's fuckin' hot out there,' the first guy said as he clambered into the front seat beside me, followed by his mate. 'Who've you been to see?'

'Just a friend.'

'Same! That place freaks me out. I couldn't hack being locked up all day.'

'Me neither,' I said. 'Imagine being told what to do every minute.'

'Yeah. And not even being able to see the outside.'

'I'd miss the bros,' said his mate.

The bros? I darted quick looks at my passengers. There was something familiar about their manner. With a jolt, I realised they were both wearing red t-shirts. Was that a tattoo of a bulldog's face disappearing up the sleeve of the one closest? Everything fell into place. They were Mobsters, I was sure of it. They'd seen me talking to Arthur. Even if they hadn't, the Red Baron branded me as a Black Power girl. It was a set-up.

I gripped the steering wheel and chattered frantically, sure that at any moment they were going to hijack the van and force me off the road. The winding hill seemed endless, every corner an opportunity for ambush. When we came to houses again, I relaxed a little, though the man mowing his lawns and the woman bringing in her washing only increased my sense of isolation. No one knew I needed to be saved.

Somehow I kept talking till we got to the bottom. 'Where do you want to get out?' I asked.

'Newtown, if you're heading that way.'

I nodded, dreading the moment I'd have to stop: they must have decided to wait and jump me then. Finally, I had to pull over. The one nearest put out his hand. I flinched, waiting to feel the knife at my ribs, then extended my own reluctantly.

'See ya next week, maybe,' he said.

'Maybe,' I said with a weak smile.

The two of them dashed across the road in front of a truck, gave the driver the fingers when he blared his horn, and turned to wave at me. I replied with three short toots and hurtled back to Abel Smith Street, shrieking as I walked in the door. 'Guess who I just picked up!'

No one was particularly concerned or impressed at the time, from memory. But 27 years later, when I told my daughter Megan, she burst into tears.

'Mum, don't you ever do that again!' she wept, pregnancy perhaps making her more protective than usual.

I laughed and wiped her cheeks. 'Look at me, Meg! I'm fine. It was a long time ago. They were friendly. I was just paranoid.'

She refused to be placated. 'Never give two guys a ride on your own! Promise me! I don't care who they are.'

It was Friday night, about nine o'clock, when a bunch of us girls pulled up outside the Tramways Hotel. Ricki, the Black Power treasurer, and Peter Womble were having a shout. They were off to Hawke's Bay on a three-month leadership course set up by Denis O'Reilly to bring new, young leaders through the ranks of the work co-ops.

Gini and Agnes were going too. We'd chosen them to represent Aroha Trust, paid their costs out of our communal kitty, and agreed to cover Gini's court fines while she was away. They'd only be on the dole, half of what the rest of us earned doing relief work.

The public bar was full of Samoan men. The boys hadn't arrived so we bought our own drinks and leaned our elbows on a high table.

'You'll forget about us when you meet your flash college friends,' I kidded Gini.

She made a face. 'Nah, I'm coming back every weekend. I'm not staying up there with a bunch of eggs I don't know.'

I knew how nervous she was about leaving, but I hoped she'd make the most of it. She was so volatile: hard-working and helpful one minute, bullying and out of control the next. Still, I was going to miss her. And Agnes. They'd leave a big hole in Aroha Trust. We just had to hope it would pay off in the long run.

We'd lost some other girls recently as well. Amelia had gone to live in Huntly with her boyfriend, and Gerry had packed her things and gone back to Whanganui. Between the cops and the gangs, she said, Abel Smith Street wasn't a good place to bring up a child. I agreed, but I was sorry to see her go. She'd been one of our hardest, most reliable workers.

'There's JB,' Gini said, smiling for the first time since we'd arrived.

Long time, no see: Georgie, Charmaine, Pip and Junior meet for the first time in 20 years at Mike Hancock's tangi, Ōtaki, Labour Weekend, 1997. We decide to hold an Aroha Trust reunion the following year.

Ready for take-off: Jane, Tasi, Pip, Nayda and Gini celebrate the first Aroha Trust reunion in a stiff southerly at the top of Mount Victoria. The others have just agreed to let Pip record their stories and write a book about the trust. Labour Weekend, 1998.

Farewell, Mike: Tasi and her son, Nayda, Gini, Georgie, Pip and Jane attend Mike Hancock's unveiling in Ōtaki, Labour Weekend, 1998, during the first Aroha Trust reunion.

Jane (far right) still giving her trademark salute to the world. Beside her is Gini, with Nayda in the shades. Mike Hancock's unveiling, Ōtaki, 1998.

Tasi's a more relaxed Christian these days. When this photo was taken at Mike Hancock's unveiling in Ōtaki, 1998, her religious beliefs stopped her from cutting her hair or wearing trousers.

Junior, with her wide, gentle smile, Westport, 2000. Her dream is 'to have a big house full of kids that haven't got homes. All my life that's all I wanted. A home.'

Evelyn and her beloved cats, Taupo, 2000. Moe mai rā e hine. Rest well, sister.

Bubbles, c 1990s. Leaving Wairarapa and the Nomads behind 'was probably the best decision I ever made in my life. Just get the hell out of here and try and start all over again, and be normal'.

Gini in her volunteer firefighter's uniform, Whangārei, 2000: 'It feels as if my life is so full. I never would have thought it would have come out how it has. And I'm so grateful for it.'

Nayda on her fortieth birthday. In 2008 she finally made the break with gang life. Her personal experience has prompted her, along with a number of other Aroha Trust women, to lodge an historical claim with the Waitangi Tribunal on behalf of all Māori women affected by gangs.

Amelia, 2000: 'I'm a bit long in the tooth to be kicking around with gang members. But it's all togetherness, going out to the beach, no patches. That's what we do here.'

Gini and her koro, Paipera Akuhata, at the graduation ceremony for her social work degree, 2008.

Jane, with Tainui kaumatua Buddy Te Whare and his wife Faye (left), Jane's parents (right) and her younger son, at the graduation ceremony for her postgraduate diploma in not-for-profit management, 2005. Buddy has since passed away. Jane: 'Although he was a very senior kaumatua, he always had time for everyday people. He was a close friend of the Māori Queen and said final prayers for her on top of Taupiri Mountain. He was carried up and down the mountain in a chair by members of the Mongrel Mob, something he cherished and often joked with me about.'

Judgement day: Pip, Georgie and Annie prepare for the second Aroha Trust reunion at Jane's bach at Kāwhia, where the fate of *Trust* will be decided. Labour Weekend, 2008.

Georgie supports Pip as she talks to the other women about writing *Trust*. Kāwhia, 2008.

Bedtime reading: Gini and Georgie study their copy of *Trust*. Kāwhia, 2008.

Amelia and Gini catch up on old times at Kāwhia, 2008.

Charmaine weaves lilies out of flax from Jane's hillside garden for the Ellerslie Flower Show, where she later won gold. Kāwhia, 2008.

Mahina and Tasi read *Trust* in Mahina's lovely farmhouse kitchen. Mahina missed the Kāwhia reunion because she was lecturing on New Zealand native plants at Kew Gardens in England.

To sign or not to sign: Annie considers her publication consent form as Pip explains what it means. Kāwhia, 2008.

Tino rangatiratanga: Thirty years after Aroha Trust was formed, the bonds of friendship remain, the t-shirts are back, and the women's pride in being Māori has gone from a slow burn to a forest fire. Kāwhia, 2008. Back row: Amelia, Nayda, Tasi, Charmaine. Middle: Jane, Pip. Front: Georgie, Annie, Gini. Absent: Bubbles, Junior, Mahina.

He was coming through the swing door with half a dozen of his Nomad comrades. I felt uneasy. JB was always polite to me, but I didn't trust the Nomads. I could feel the tension in the bar rise.

I turned to Jane, all curves and pale skin in a yellow halter-neck top and low-slung jeans. A solid silver bracelet covered the large flower tattooed on her right forearm.

'Let's get outta here if the boys don't come soon,' I said.

She nodded. 'I reckon. This place is starting to give me the shits.'

Just then, one of the Samoans walked past and pointed at Jane's bracelet. She gave him the fingers. He clamped his hand on her arm.

'Get your fuckin' mitts off me!' she snarled, shaking him off.

JB looked over. 'Leave her alone, cunt!' he called out.

The man was joined by his mates. JB put down his drink and took several deliberate steps in our direction. Heavily outnumbered, the rest of the Nomads followed, clutching handles of beer and half-filled jugs.

JB stood in front of the man. 'I thought I told you to fuck off,' he said.

I have no stomach for violence. At the first whiff of it, my body clenches and a silent scream forms at the back of my throat. The week before, Jane and I had clambered on top of the piano at Flanagan's to avoid an all-out brawl. Luckily, everyone had been so busy laying into one another with fists and pool cues, they hadn't noticed us trapped up there. But this time we were right in the line of fire.

We made a run for the door just as the jugs started flying. A photo in the newspaper the next day showed holes in the walls, glass littering the floor, a twisted table lying with its spindly legs in the air like an upturned beetle. An arrow pointed to the door we'd escaped through, where a few minutes after we left, a young man was fatally injured as he fled. He was 16 years old, out prospecting for the Nomads for the first time.

'It's this gang problem again,' the public relations manager for Lion Breweries told the newspaper. But the Samoans didn't wear patches or colours, and it was one of them who beat the young man to death with a piece of timber when he got caught in the crush of people trying to get away. The beating lasted a full five minutes, according to one witness.

The man who killed the Nomad prospect was a 41-year-old matai, a prominent member of the Wellington Samoan Catholic Association and founding member of the government's Samoan Advisory Council. A profile of him in the newspaper after he was convicted of manslaughter read like an obituary. His legal counsel, top criminal defence lawyer Mike Bungay, said it was a tragedy seeing him in jail. 'He spends most of the time reading the Bible.'

The reporter acknowledged the man was a heavy drinker, but said going for a drink 'could be seen as part of his role as matai, providing a restraining influence of [sic] young Samoans unused to booze'. A photo showed a beaming man with white teeth and crinkly eyes in a jacket and tie, holding up a glass of beer after a 1970 beer-drinking record attempt. The caption repeated a comment in the story from a colleague: 'He could take it okay.'

The irony of these comments seemed to have escaped the reporter and editor, but it was not lost on Jane. In her diary, next to the article, she wrote, 'Well, as you can see, the man's been made out to be a hero — for killing a boy.'

Charmaine, 15 years old, not long out of Weymouth Girls Home, made a direct link between the prospect's death and Jane's clothes. 'I remember this Samoan guy harassing her for her body and one of the Mads stood up for her and pulled her back and said, "Leave her alone", and the brawl started. So in my mind, very young mind, very unsafe to dress like that. People die. That's how I interpreted that whole night. You dress like that and people die.'

I asked Jane why she'd dressed so provocatively in those days. 'I think it was part of the value I placed on myself, or what value I saw people placing on me as a person, that men just saw me as a body,' she said. 'I played up to that because that was all I thought I was worth. But I rebelled against being treated as a sex object as well. There was a real contradiction going on, knowing intellectually that I should be able to go out and wear what I like and not be harassed, but at the same time knowing men were only after one thing and living up to that expectation.'

Later, she came up with another explanation as well. 'I think it was actually my way of protecting myself from dodgy men. It sounds odd, I know, but what it did was flush them out, gave me a way of identifying where the possible danger would come from. The flaw was that the real danger was from those I usually didn't suspect.'

Whether Jane's clothes flushed out predators or encouraged them, going out with her was one long, tedious wolf-whistle. In Dunedin, late one night, a carload of young men slowed down beside us and matched our pace as we walked home. Jane's long, fur-trimmed coat was unbuttoned to reveal a green satin hipster skirt and tiny pink top, an ocean of bare skin between. I was in jeans and a jacket to keep out the cold and because my Catholic upbringing ruled out flaunting the flesh.

The driver wound down his window and suggested we get in.

'Fuck off!' said Jane with her usual tact, thrusting her middle finger into the air.

The young men became more persistent. When a second carload arrived, we crashed through shrubbery to get away from them. They trained their headlights on the bushes, trying to make us come out. In my panic, I sliced my hand open on the sharp leaves of a flax bush. It was absurd and frightening. Eventually they gave up and went in search of other prey. But we crouched there for a long time, just in case.

Another late night in Dunedin, the cops picked the pair of us up. 'They were cruising in their meat wagon and they ordered us to get in the back — like we'd done something wrong,' Jane said. 'Two of them got in with us in their winter great coats and helmets. They said they were going to take us home, but they drove around the wharves for a while, which were all dark and deserted. The cop driving would slam on his brakes and we'd go flying off the bench seats and the other cops would land on top of us. Then they'd all crack up laughing. It was just a chance for them to have a good grope.'

Surprisingly, since it was the first time I'd been in a paddy wagon, I'd forgotten about this incident until Jane reminded me, and I don't recall being groped. Perhaps I gave the cops the benefit of the doubt when we were thrown around, or maybe I wasn't their target. Either way, it confirmed her fears that all men — including the upholders of law and order — were after her body. None of them could be trusted.

Back then, I stopped trying to convince Jane that life might be easier with more clothes on. In some ways, I admired her guts. My arguments seemed weak and subservient, even to myself. Why shouldn't she be able to wear what she liked? Wasn't it a woman's right to choose?

Still in Dunedin, a Pākehā man came up to her at a disco and asked her to model for him. The next day he rang, pestering. I tried to talk her out of it. When she wouldn't listen, I went along as chaperone. He drove us to Blackhead, an isolated beach on the south coast, where Jane had nearly been raped once before. It was a bleak Sunday afternoon. Seagulls wheeled and jeered above us; even the surfers had abandoned the chopped-up water.

The man started snapping shots of Jane. After a few minutes, he offered her $20 to take off her top, and pulled out pages of photo proofs of other young women, naked and semi-naked. 'See!' he said. 'There's nothing to it.'

I retreated to a log and sat with my head down, scuffing my toes in the sand. I felt like a voyeur, in cahoots with the man.

He called me to join in.

'Doubt it!' I said.

'Come on, Pip!' Jane said. 'It's easy money.'

I looked at her full breasts, flat stomach, slim young hips sliding into her jeans. My body was not perfect like hers. 'No way!'

'You've got a nice body too,' the man said, as if reading my mind. 'You shouldn't be ashamed of it.'

Suddenly, I stood up, unzipped my jacket, pulled my jersey over my head and unhooked my bra. Nervous at first, then exhilarated, I twirled and posed and laughed with Jane as the wind whipped our skin pink and numbed our faces. Then the man wanted us to take off our jeans. By that time, I didn't care, but Jane was adamant. 'No!' she said.

As he drove us back to town, shame took hold of me. I told no one, and Jane and I never talked about it again. I'm still not sure what possessed me. If I was taken in by his flattery and practised seduction. Enticed by the prospect of earning as much in half an hour as I usually earned in a week. Sick of being sensible. Acting out of solidarity with my mate.

What I find hardest to believe now is that I never stopped to consider where the photos might end up. Years later, Jane recognised the man's face in the newspaper. He'd been convicted of possessing and selling child pornography. 'I was fuckin' horrified,' she said. 'It was quite depressing to see how easily you can be duped into doing that stuff as a kid.'

Fair enough — she was only 15 when it happened. But I was 20. Old enough to know better, you'd have thought.

Here's the thing. The man with the camera on the beach wasn't in a gang. Nor were the carloads of hoons who stalked Jane and me in the bushes, the cops who threw us round the paddy wagon, the Samoans in the pub.

When it comes to terrorising women, gangs aren't the only culprits. Nayda told me that almost all the women she knew had been abused, physically and emotionally, both in and out of gang relationships. Both of her long-term Mob partners were violent, but so were some of the other women's partners who weren't gang members. On the other hand, Charmaine's Highway 61 boyfriend, Paddy, was never abusive. 'He had the ultimate respect for women,' she said. 'The gift he gave me was that he made the bar so high.'

When it comes to killing people, gangs aren't alone either. The Nomad prospect's death in the Tramways was not a one-off. After a scrap in the same pub three years later, members of the Eastern Suburbs Rugby League Club tracked down the leader of the Wellington Mongrel Mob and beat him to death too.

I wondered whether blocks made gangs worse than other groups of men. Yes, insofar as they openly condone, encourage or demand such behaviour. But not all do, and I only had to think of high-profile policemen and elite sports teams to know the divide wasn't that simple. The conditions for pack rape, researchers tell us, are male bonding in a powerful subculture based on teamwork and aggression, often fuelled by alcohol. Lots of male groups fit these criteria.

Jane saw all the men who raped her as being in gangs. 'Gangs of men from the church, police, all those places where men find the power to be abusers. At least when they wore patches, you knew what you were up against and could take steps to keep yourself safe. It was the men I'd been told I could trust who turned out to be the most dangerous.'

SIXTEEN

BLOCK BUSTERS

Aroha Trust was one year old. It was cause for celebration. 'Because we'd survived, we'd done it, we were pretty cool,' Annie said. 'I think begrudgingly, even the men saw that as well.'

We threw a party at the Aro Street Hall, where the Black Power held their discos. For once we were in charge, inviting all our friends and supporters. More than 100 people turned up, including the assistant town clerk and his wife who worked in the Prime Minister's Department, Candleman and his partner, outsiders like my brother, some of the queens from Cuba Street and members of several gangs.

When I asked the women for their best memory of Aroha Trust, almost all of them chose this party. Georgie recalled it in impressive detail. 'We made this big pact that we were not going to drink and we were not going to get stoned and we were going to be perfect hostesses,' she said. 'And we were going to get dressed up. In white shirts, tails, jeans, black pants, whatever. And we got my partner to decorate the hall. He did all the posters on the walls. Spraypainting. On one side he did a whole scene of the sea and a big lighthouse. And I cut out the windows because I'd pinched a set of those orange council lights on the side of the road that flicker on and off. And I decided this was going to go behind the lighthouse and it looked awesome. Really awesome. On the stage we did the wall in tinfoil. Mike Hancock was supposed to do us some bamboo pipes because we got dried ice. And we blew up heaps of balloons and in them we put the paper you get from punch machines, all those round bits, and glitter. We filled the balloons and hung them up on the ceiling. And had a big cake. Do you remember the cake?'

'Where did it come from?' I asked.

'Wasn't it your mum?'

Of course! How could I have forgotten? She'd made it herself and got a bakery to decorate it with the Aroha Trust t-shirt design, but somehow the instructions got muddled up and it arrived with pink icing instead of blue.

'That cake was beautiful,' Georgie said, holding no grudges about the icing. 'And we had this really neat band, and two of the Blacks as bouncers, and one of the Wombles as the barman, plus we were behind the bar. The whole night was a success because—' She looked at me. 'I don't know. Did we have the rule that there were no patches?'

'I don't know if we could have enforced that,' I said, thinking of another time I'd tried and failed.

'I'm sure we stated that we wanted no patches,' she said. 'I can't remember, maybe there were patches. But that was the best night. It was a magical moment for me because that party went off with a hit. No violence, no abuse, no fighting. And the good thing about it too was Charmaine's man turned up on his bike and he wasn't hassled and he was from the Highways, him and another one. I don't even know if Zip and Zap turned up; one was Highway and one was Nomad, two brothers. Yeah, and we had some of the Nomads there. Plus Ricky Punk. Well he was a hard-out skinhead, wasn't he? It went off without a hitch. The band played till three or four in the morning. Everyone had a really massive time. We all stayed straight and sober like the perfect hostesses. And whenever women went to the toilet, we went in droves — two, three, and that was the way it was. And there was no hassles.

I can't remember a fight. I can't even remember a brawl outside cos there was none.'

Other women remembered the party equally fondly. It had been a sign of our growing confidence and independence. We were creating our own future; we didn't need the boys to make things happen.

'For a lot of us, it was a source of real strength,' Jane said. She too helped decorate the hall, drawing a huge poster of the clenched Black Power fist. But it was not a blind endorsement of the gang. She encased it in the life-giving gourd and koru pattern on our t-shirts, and surrounded it with the words, 'Power to the People'.

Just before 10, on the night of the party, we left Tasi to keep an eye on the beer while we went to pick up the band from the Southern Cross that Georgie had sweet-talked into playing for us when the pub closed. By the time we got back, Tasi was gently snoring, her head inches away from a speaker blaring out 'Dark Side of the Moon'. The band walked straight onto the stage, tuned their instruments to Pink Floyd and finished the song before the crowd realised the music had gone live.

At midnight they struck up 'Happy Birthday' as Charmaine and Georgie carried in the cake ablaze with candles. Both were dressed in tuxedos — penguin suits, they called them — 'borrowed' for the occasion by a number of girls from the costume cupboard at the Newtown Community Centre. Charmaine had a white carnation in her buttonhole, Georgie a yellow one.

The band started up again with 'We Are Family'. Junior and Jane pulled Gini onto the dance floor. It was unusual to see Gini up dancing, but tonight everyone was high on Aroha Trust. Other girls joined in till there was a line of young women in black trousers and white shirts stretched across the hall, arms linked, legs kicking left and right in perfect sync. Georgie leapt up and swiped at a bunch of balloons. One exploded with a bang, showering the dancers with glitter and confetti. Everyone cheered.

Watching from the sideline, Annie and I beamed like proud parents.

'Here's to us,' I said, waving my rum and Coke in her direction.

She clinked her glass against mine. 'Not bad for a bunch of girls, eh.'

The lounge at Abel Smith Street was packed, the painters in speckled overalls and sandshoes, the scrub-cutters in Swannies and steel-caps. The sour smell of sweat mingled with tobacco and refried chips. All the Aroha Trust girls had come straight from work, but there was none of the usual banter and bickering. This was an emergency.

'Are we all agreed then?' Annie leaned back in her chair, hooked her thumbs into the front pockets of her jeans and stretched her thin legs out in front of her. A cigarette dangled between the fingers of her right hand, threatening to spill a caterpillar of grey ash onto the carpet.

There was a silence as thick as the haze of cigarette smoke that lay over the room.

Georgie's strong fingers flew through Charmaine's hair, creating tiny plaits that she finished off with coloured beads. 'I must be fuckin' crazy,' she said slowly, 'but I'm in.'

'Me too!' said Gini, thumping the arm of the couch with her fist. 'If we keep letting them get away with it, they'll just go on treating us like shit.'

I looked at her in surprise. I'd never heard her speak up like that before, at least not when she was sober. Perhaps the leadership course was working, even if every time I turned around, she seemed to be back in Wellington.

Annie flicked her ash expertly into the neck of an empty milk bottle. 'What about the rest of yous?'

I was all for taking action too, but I kept quiet. We needed to hear from the girls who didn't usually say much, the ones the boys were most likely to target.

Charmaine's face disappeared behind a large bubble of chewing gum. She popped it loudly and dragged the sticky strands back into her mouth. 'Yeah!' she said. 'Enough's e-fuckin'-nough! Who do the cunts think they are?'

'How is she?' asked Georgie.

'She's okay,' said Mahina, who lived with her. But we all knew better.

'Fuckin' animals!' Jane said.

The girl they were talking about was our workmate and our friend, the latest in the growing list of Black Power casualties. Over the weekend, without us knowing, she'd been put on the block. She wasn't an obvious victim. She was strong and stroppy and smart, with a young child and a big laugh. What's more, she worked for Aroha Trust and we'd dared to believe that gave our members some protection. We were wrong. As a group, we felt powerful and united, but the boys were still casually picking us off whenever they wanted.

'So what are we waiting for?' said Tasi.

There was nervous laughter, but it was clear that everyone approved of the plan. Doing nothing had become unbearable. Our anger outweighed our fear. The blocks had to stop.

Looking back, Gini still savoured the solidarity we'd built up. 'I was real supportive of us as a women's trust to stand against all those blinkin' horrible things that the boys thought they could do and get away with,' she said. 'I was prepared to go all the way — regardless of whether we were going to get our heads knocked off, or discriminated, or whatever. Because by this time I had formed another family with the' — she paused for emphasis — 'women. That's probably when I started to realise there was such a thing as women's lib. Thinking, yeah, these guys have got no right to do this. Let's make a stand together.'

The make-up of the trust made it possible, Gini said. 'There's no way an individual could have did it. There's no way a European woman could've did it. And for us, the Māori women, without the European women, we wouldn't have been able to do it either. We needed their guidance and know-how to be able to come together as a group to form that unity and strength to hit those guys with what we knew was right. It was a real strong time. I felt like I was part of a group of women that were going somewhere.'

On a mild October evening, we arrived at Brougham Street, still in our work gears. Our plan was to confront the Black Power at their weekly meeting. We'd be on their turf, outnumbered four to one, but they'd never have agreed to come to us. Although my heart was pounding, I was glad we'd decided to do something: our silence seemed to condone their dreadful deeds. And I was oddly optimistic. Blocks usually happened in a secret, wordless, boozing frenzy that stripped the victim of her humanity along with her clothes. If the boys had to face us — in daylight, sober, as a group — surely there was no way they could try and defend the indefensible. Who knew? Some of them might even back us up.

In hindsight, the women identified three kinds of gang men: a tiny minority — no more than one or two — who we'd all found completely trustworthy; a disputed group, the majority, who'd protect some women and hurt others or let them be hurt; and a small, treacherous bunch who, given half a chance, would set up almost any girl to be blocked or bashed.

Although we'd warned the boys that we were coming, they arrived late and then made us wait. We paced up and down the hall outside their office, chain-smoking and exchanging small, anxious smiles. Finally, the door opened and we filed in silently. 'We were all really quite scared, but we thought, nah, we couldn't let them see the fear,' Charmaine said.

All the chairs were taken: they'd left nowhere for us to sit together. Eyes down, we stepped over jackboots and jeans and found a small space on the floor wherever we could.

When I recorded their stories, most of the women remembered little about this meeting except the solidarity behind our challenge and the reaction it provoked. The boys came out fighting. How dare we tell them what to do! The Black Power didn't take orders from women. Girls who ended up on the block were scrubbers who asked for it. As for their own missus, they'd treat her how they fuckin' well liked. And if she had a mouth like ours, well . . . The guy who said this slammed his fist into the palm of his hand.

One by one, we tried to stick up for ourselves, feeling our confidence drain away in the face of their contempt.

'If women were equal to men, they'd have been born with balls,' barked Rei, their president, as if that settled the matter.

I was stunned. This was New Zealand 1978. It had never occurred to me that the Blacks might uphold their right to brutalise us on the grounds that we were inferior. And I didn't think that Rei really believed that either. He understood oppression, spoke out when it affected workers and poor people and Māori. It just suited him to play the thug when it came to women and act tough in front of his boys.

The to and fro of the discussion — if it could be called that — is lost to me now. All that remains is the twist in my gut when I think of sitting cross-legged on that floor, jostled on every side by young men with raised fists on their backs, trying to find the words to persuade them that it was wrong to rape women just because they could.

At last — perhaps to get rid of us — we won a begrudging concession. The Wellington Blacks would not bash Aroha Trust girls or put them on the block. All other women remained fair game.

Buoyed by this small success, Jane challenged Rei about the fresh bruises on his wife's face. 'I said to him, quite out of character, you know, "How can you be such a hypocrite and say that no one's allowed to beat up any of Aroha Trust, but it's all right to beat your wife up?"' She laughed. 'I remember thinking that was incredibly brave — or stupid — of me.'

After the meeting, I felt deeply despondent about Aroha Trust's ideals. Being singled out by the boys for special treatment (presuming they kept their word) felt like a betrayal of women outside the trust, a classic case of 'divide and rule' used by oppressors everywhere to retain power. No matter how strong we were, how right, it seemed that nothing we said or did had the slightest effect on gang culture. The only option for women who didn't want to be viewed as punching bags was to get out altogether. With that realisation came guilt. At any time, I could go: there was another world waiting for me. But what of the other girls? Where would they go? This *was* their world.

Looking back, Jane was more upbeat. 'I can't imagine anyone else seeing it as progress,' she said. 'But in that situation, getting them to formally agree that they weren't allowed to rape members of Aroha Trust was quite a big step forward.'

That wasn't the end of the matter. 'At the next Black Power disco, we had made a compact that the first woman to be dragged out of the hall, we were going to attack the man that did it,' Charmaine said. 'We were so serious, you could feel the vibrations. And they freaked, cos it was the first time they had seen us not drink, not drug. We stood in the corner all night long with our steel-capped boots on, crowbars up our sleeves. We did not move one muscle. And they knew we were serious.'

No one else remembered the crowbars, including me, though I'd never have been in the running to wield one. However, I decided that what Charmaine said was true, at least symbolically. The Aroha Trust girls had flexed their muscles. The boys were on notice to treat women better. They knew we were watching them.

They started calling us 'Aroma Thrush', a name we hated, although it suggested we had them rattled. After that, they got more cunning, Charmaine said. 'They didn't do the blocks at the discos — where they used to happen consistently — but maybe they'd do them away from the eye. But they started to stop in the sense of how common it was. They were actually quite threatened by our stance. So then it went further: they didn't want their wives mixing with us.' She gave her machine-gun cackle. 'There was something there — you couldn't pin it down and you couldn't name it — but it was there enough for them to know that they couldn't pull it over us. So it did make a ripple; it made a big ripple.'

SEVENTEEN

SPACE INVASIONS

Junior pleaded with me on behalf of one of the Nomads. 'Please let him stay! Just for a few days till he finds another place.'

Against my better judgement, I relented. To my surprise, we got on well and he was the perfect guest. Until the night, that is, when we sat in a grim, quiet circle in the lounge while he ran the tip of his pocket-knife under the tender chin of his impossibly young girlfriend. She didn't belong to Aroha Trust and it was lucky we were there — or perhaps the performance was for our benefit. No one dared move. The thought flashed through my mind: someone is going to die here.

Suddenly he put the knife away and laughed. *Only joking.* The room emptied and everyone fled into town to get drunk. Except me. I went to bed, pulled the latch across my door as usual. Almost asleep, I heard a gentle knock. Without thinking, I got up and opened the door a crack. And there he was, standing in the hallway with a lopsided smile.

'What's up?' I said. Perhaps he was going to ask if I had a spare towel or where the bread was kept.

'I'm coming in,' he said softly.

I stared at him dumbly.

He said it again, this time more forcefully. 'I know you'll hate me in the morning, but I'm coming in.' There was a roar in my head like the sound of the sea, then nothing except our two bodies on either side of the door, our eyes locked in the endless black space between. *Coming in. Coming in.* I considered calling for help, but there was no point; I knew I was alone. I braced one foot futilely against the wood, and gripped the door handle till my knuckles bulged, trying not to let him see the flimsy op-shop nightie that hugged my breasts and thighs. The icy lino chilled the soles of my feet while, from a distance, my mind observed, 'Ah, so this is how it feels when you're about to be raped.'

The pressure from the other side of the door increased. *Coming in. Coming in.* I pushed back, frantically calculating the number of steps to the sash window on the far wall (four) and the precious seconds it would take to fumble under the curtains, haul up the frame with both hands and flee through the back gate into the lane that ran alongside our house. But I knew I wouldn't make the first move. He'd catch me and pin me to the bed before I got out. Besides, I'd been scared of windows like that since primary school when the nuns filled our heads with stories of them falling like guillotines on naughty girls who tried to clamber out of them.

The black walls of the room closed in on me like a coffin. 'You don't want to do this,' said a faraway voice, soft and soothing as a mother's, followed by his name over and over, like a mantra. I recognised the voice vaguely as my own.

He looked through me as if I wasn't there.

Coming in. Coming in. Desperate, hopeless, I drilled deeper into his eyes, but all I could find was emptiness, a place of no feeling or connection. Every cell in my body, every nerve and muscle, every breath, every scrap of willpower rallied to my defence; I'd seen the knife at that young girl's throat.

And then suddenly, miraculously, for no apparent reason, he ground his fists into his eyes like a small child and shuffled his feet.

'What am I doing here?' he asked, his head bowed.

'You should go now,' I whispered. Not too many words. Nothing that might reawaken the monster. He let go the door and I pushed it shut in his face, dragged the latch across and pressed my ear to the cool wood. There were muffled sounds on the other side, footsteps down the hall, the slam of the front door. I listened for a long time, then turned away and crawled back under the sheets. There I lay, curled-up and quiet. I had survived.

By morning, it seemed like a bad dream, something I must have imagined or at least exaggerated. I didn't hate him. How can you hate someone who isn't there? But now he hated me. He stayed on at Abel Smith Street, lurking, reproachful, as if *I'd* been the one who'd terrorised *him*. I couldn't make him leave and I didn't think of moving out myself. I'm not sure why. It was my home. I was needed there. I wouldn't give him the satisfaction.

Annie was the only one I told. I felt foolish for opening the door when he'd knocked. And I was scared that, if word got round that I'd been talking, he might come back and finish off the job.

'Bastard!' she said, looking worriedly into my face. 'But you're okay, aren't you?'

I nodded. I was fine. We both knew that close shaves didn't really count.

Gini and Agnes were in Wellington again, this time to present a submission to the Select Committee on Violent Offending as part of their leadership course. We went to support them. Afterwards, National MP Marilyn Waring invited us upstairs to her office for a drink.

'I can remember the newspapers got on to it,' Jane said, 'and this doorman saying, "We never let Black Power in here." This staunch, staunch doorman standing at the front of Parliament. And everyone was already *inside* Parliament.'

From then on, Marilyn, only two years older than me, took a special interest in Aroha Trust. 'We'd go to Bellamy's and we'd go into her room and she was quite outspoken,' Charmaine said.

Georgie couldn't believe how cheap the food was. 'You only had to pay two dollars something for a big feed.' She grinned. 'It's a pity you had to have a Member of Parliament to get in, or else I would have gone there every day for lunch.'

Two decades later, in a letter of support for me to record the women's stories, Marilyn recalled 'some extraordinary interactions' with us. 'There had certainly been nothing like the trust before, and what enormous guts you all had,' she wrote. 'I remember conducting you for a day around Parliament. I remember the stories some of the members told — of being chained to a bed and locked in a room all day while the boyfriend who did this was being rehabilitated on one of Muldoon's work trust schemes.'

For Jane, already interested in politics, it was an exciting time. On one of our visits, Marilyn brought Muldoon in to see us. 'He made the mistake of saying his granddaughter's birthday was on Suffrage Day, and Charmaine exploded: "For us, it's women's suffrage every day!" He didn't know what to do. We were all pissing ourselves laughing at this little rotund man with this very famous face. He left quite quickly. That felt powerful, because we weren't used to dealing with decision makers, power mongers.'

It wasn't the first time Muldoon had met some of the Aroha Trust girls. Two years earlier, he'd shouted the Black Power at the Royal Tiger pub, then partied at one of their houses. Bubbles described it as 'a glorious night', during which Muldoon briefly swapped his suit jacket for a gang patch, knocked back whisky and water and threw his empty glass over his shoulder. Bubbles recognised the type: 'A man with obvious power, but at the same time he was just a drunk like everybody else.'

Gini and I walked home along Abel Smith Street after dropping off the Education Board van at the end of the day. Like most of the girls, she walked low to the ground, leading with her hips, as if her centre of gravity was in her pelvis. Long, slow, swaggery strides, while I scurried along beside her.

'How's the course going?' I asked. She was heading back to Hawke's Bay for the umpteenth time that night.

'I still dunno why you picked me,' she said.

'You were the best, that's why.'

'Being in the classroom's stink, but I like the stuff we do outside.'

'Yeah? Like what?'

'We built this cool barbecue last week. And before that we learnt how to drive a tractor. I nearly got my HT licence but I had a hangover the day they did the test.'

'Bugger!' I said, as much for our sake as hers. The trust was still crying out for legal drivers. 'How's your house going?'

'Not bad. I had to give one of the boys the bash, though.' She laughed at my pained expression. 'He's such a fuckin' big mouth. Don't worry! Agnes saved his arse. She said, "Just beat him up a bit, not too much, cos we've all got school tomorrow".'

I laughed too, grateful that the story had a more or less happy ending.

Deep in conversation, I took little notice of the two young women coming towards us until the bigger one blocked my way.

'You're Pip, aren't you?' she said.

'What's it to ya?' I forced my feet to stay where they were and tried to match her sneer.

'You've been telling lies about the Nomads.'

I didn't recognise her or her mean-looking mate, but anyone sticking up for the Nomads could only mean trouble. 'I don't tell lies,' I said, hoping Gini would step in and save me.

The girl folded her beefy arms. 'Fuckin' oath you do! You've been slagging us off. We've heard.'

She was right about that. I was always ranting about the way the Nomads barged into Abel Smith Street, ate all our food (they never left money again), and stood over the young girls on payday and took their wages. Two were sleeping there now and there was nothing I could do about it. I'd asked the council to find us a new house, but there seemed little point in shifting when they could just follow us.

The girl took a step forward. For an instant, I pictured myself writing on the ground, bleeding and humiliated. Then she jostled past, bumping my shoulder. 'Any more lies, honky, and you're fuckin' history.'

Afterwards, Gini didn't say much and I pretended it was no big deal either. I knew her loyalties were torn between Aroha Trust and the Nomads, me and her boyfriend JB. Still, her reputation as a fighter was legendary, and few people — men or women — were willing to take her on. Just by standing there, she'd been my guardian angel.

We were chopping gorse at a Hutt Valley school on Friday afternoon when we got word somehow that all the Nomads were moving into Abel Smith Street. We rushed home to find the front door wide open, the house deserted, and a stack of unfamiliar blankets in the hallway. We flung clothes and valuables into the van before they came back. The bigger stuff would have to wait.

As I carried out an armful of LPs, Junior pointed to the blankets.

'What about these?' she asked.

'Chuck 'em in!' I said. 'Serve them right!'

She tapped my Honda, parked beside them. 'And this?'

I loved that scooter, but this was no time to get sentimental. 'I'll come back for it,' I said.

We stored our belongings at a friend's, making sure we hadn't been followed. Then I took refuge at Brougham Street, leaving the other girls to scrounge beds for the weekend; we'd regroup on Monday.

Mike Hancock fussed around me while he cooked tea. Tam cranked up Jimmy Cliff on the record player and handed me a fat joint. I pulled my chair closer to the fire and lost myself in the pale yellow flames dancing over a bed of fierce, orange embers.

Now that I'd stopped running, I felt giddy with relief. That we'd got out of Abel Smith Street in time. And that things had come to a head. I had no idea how — or if — we'd get our house back; I wasn't sure I wanted it. But I'd worry about that later. For now, I just wanted to soak up the warmth and safety of Brougham Street, a haven I'd always loved.

It crossed my mind that I could move in there instead of setting up another place. But then what would happen to the other girls?

The front door opened with a crash, followed by the stomp of heavy boots down the hall. The fire fizzed, then flared, as a blast of cold air flowed into the lounge. In the doorway stood half a dozen Nomads, silent and menacing. Peter's dog, Che, ran towards them, barking. One of them took a step forward. Staring straight ahead, he swung his left leg back and aimed a vicious kick at the dog with his steel-capped boot. Che flew through the air and landed with a thud against Tam's chair. His high-pitched yelps pierced the silence.

'Shut that fuckin' mutt up before I do,' the Nomad said quietly.

Tam bent down and stroked Che's head, crooning to him like a baby. Gradually the yelps subsided and the dog lay still, apart from an occasional shudder the length of its body.

'Where's our fuckin' blankets?'

The Nomad's words hung in the air for a moment before colliding in my mind with months of pent-up grudges: their constant harassment at Abel Smith Street; my near-rape; the girl eyeballing me in the street; our frenzied packing a few hours earlier; the mindless cruelty to the dog. How dare they demand their measly blankets when they'd taken everything we had, including our peace of mind?

'Well, where's our house?' I blurted before my instinct for self-preservation had time to rally.

'Give us our blankets,' he said, focusing on me. 'We know you've got them!'

Taking the blankets had been stupid, I could see that now. But if I owned up, he'd make me go and get them. There was no way I was leaving the room with him and his henchmen.

I looked around for support. Tam was running his hand up and down Che's side as if searching for injuries. Mike Hancock had disappeared into his loft after tea. Mike Womble was dozing in an armchair. I willed him to wake up: surely no one could sleep through a visit from the Nomads. He gave a small snore. The other boys and girls dotted around the room were all too young and scared.

'They're not here,' I said, light-headed with fear and marijuana.

'What about us? You've taken our whole house. When are you going to give that back?'

The rest is a blank. All I remember is that they left, saying they'd be back. 'And those blankets better fuckin' be here.'

It wasn't because I'd stood up to them, I know that, although I'm glad I did. Brougham Street was Black Power territory and picking a fight there could have started a war. The blankets can't have been worth it.

Stoned, strung-out and needing to be held, I turned to Tam when they'd gone. He was sweet and tender but my heart wasn't in it. Far later than was fair, I changed my mind.

'It's not you,' I said. 'There's someone else.' I'd had a letter from Pat: he was still unsettled in Christchurch; he hoped I was happy; he thought about me a lot.

'It's okay,' he said. 'You should do something about it, though.'

'You sound like Annie!' I said. She often asked me how I'd feel if Pat got himself a serious girlfriend.

'He won't,' I'd tell her, confident beyond reason.

'Don't count on it!' she'd say. 'You can't expect him to wait forever.'

Not forever. Just for a bit longer.

❧

The following weekend the Nomads raided Brougham Street again. This time, only a few young girls were there. Terrified, they hid in Mike Hancock's loft.

'We could hear them below us rampaging around, smashing and breaking things,' Jane said. 'It was a watershed to do that to the Black Power headquarters. But they didn't find us. As soon as we got the chance, we ran through the kitchen and down the stairs. I remember running up the side of the house and taking off in the car, all of us squashed into one Morris Minor.'

It was nothing compared to the mayhem the Nomads wreaked on Abel Smith Street. After a few days, our landlord called in the bulldozers.

Driving past and seeing the house reduced to rubble, I made a mental note to ring Mum and Dad and tell them I was still alive.

Junior was there at the end. 'All the Nomads jumped through the windows because the door was padlocked,' she said. 'We thought we could go back there and crash the night, but not so. There was no roof. When we came back, there might be no walls. So we had a party inside. Reminiscing. End of the old house. See ya later! See ya later!'

My first reaction when Junior told me this was to feel betrayed that she'd partied with the enemy. For me, in spite of everything, there was still a big distinction between the Black Power, with their rules and relative order, and the Nomads, hell-bent on anarchy. But for her, one gang was much the same as another.

'A lot of heavy shit had gone down with not only the Nomads but with the Black Power,' she said. 'Our women were just losing cos we were so young. A lot of us were 16, 17, 18. The older ones could handle it, could stand their ground, but the younger ones couldn't. The older women tried to help us but it was a lost cause.'

Junior didn't remember frantically packing up Abel Smith Street to escape the Nomads. Nor, to my amazement, did any of the other women I asked. For me, the experience had been harrowing, bizarre, unforgettable. For them, it was just another house they'd had to leave in a bit of a hurry.

Not even Annie shared my animosity towards the Nomads. 'They were all right,' she recalled, perhaps because she wasn't living at Abel Smith Street when they tormented us, and Shorty, one of their members, was her pet. Still, I was hurt she'd forgotten what they put us through. It seemed a sign of how far apart we'd drifted by then, although there were many things Annie didn't remember. Her forte was always in looking forward, not back.

What Junior hadn't forgotten was being homeless afterwards. 'Everyone had places to go and I didn't,' she said.

Poor Junior. I didn't know that at the time or perhaps I'd been too spooked to care. Jane invited her to stay at the flat she shared with Annie and Charmaine, a kindness Junior never forgot. But Shorty, Junior's boyfriend at the time, arrived and tried to get into Jane's bed, then broke her nose and front tooth when she stormed out of the room and he thought she was going to tell Junior.

Junior left. 'I thought it would be better if I hit the streets again instead of getting all the crap,' she said. For her, there was no such thing as a safe house.

EIGHTEEN

GROWING PAINS

The council came up with another home for us in Thorndon, a sedate, well-to-do suburb that felt like the wrong side of town. By day our backyard rang with the shrieks of girls in gym frocks and bobby socks the same age as ours who attended the prestigious college next door.

Tasi and Evelyn came out of their boltholes, Gini arrived back from her leadership course, and Jane joined us. Three Black Power members moved in as well to protect us from another Nomad invasion. It felt like defeat — what had happened to *girls can do anything?* — and it increased the risk of a Mongrel Mob hit. But I didn't have a better idea.

On the first day, Tasi put her foot through the floorboards in the lounge. The carpet sagged over the hole and we learned to avoid that spot. But overall the house was solid, with lots of bedrooms upstairs and living space below. I slept out the back in a small room off the kitchen with its own narrow staircase, the maid's quarters in grander times.

I enjoyed the new set-up more than I'd expected. Food stayed in the fridge. I stopped jumping every time someone came through the front door. At night, we'd sit around listening to music. The long-haired, sweet-faced Black Power mascot — at 17, the gang's youngest member — spent an evening teaching me to roll tobacco into cool, white cylinders so I could save on tailor-mades. It seemed a long time since life had been that ordinary.

Another chance came up to confront the Black Power about the way they treated women. TVNZ wanted to make a documentary challenging gang stereotypes, and Rei asked us to go on camera to support them. 'The boys wanted the trust women to say we thought they were all lovely and they were all wonderful,' Annie said. 'We had decided as a group that we would not. Because that wasn't the case, and they hadn't done a lot about it.'

Sensing some bargaining power, however, we agreed to meet at our new house, got out our big aluminium pots, went searching for pūhā along the Hutt River, and asked Marilyn Waring and Colin Knox's wife from the Prime Minister's Department to back us up.

'I can remember these two middle-class Pākehā women trying to eat pork bones and Māori bread on their knees, and we were pissing ourselves with laughter cos they didn't know how,' Jane said. 'Laughing at that, but not really at them cos I think we had some respect for what they were trying to do as well.'

Marilyn never forgot that meeting. 'I remember the room as one of you began, "Okay, you guys, we've invited you here tonight to tell you there are to be no more rapes and no more beatings",' she wrote in her letter of support years later.

One after another, the girls spoke out, demanding change. 'It wasn't people like me who could be vocal,' Annie said. 'It was women they hadn't expected to say anything who got up.'

In spite of this, the boys still refused to denounce violence against women, so we refused to go on TV with them.

Imagine my surprise, then, to read an article in the *Listener* 12 years later saying that a resolution formally banning rape was put to the 1977 National Black Power Convention and passed a year later, and that Rei was 'the initiator and the enforcer' of that ban.

I checked and rechecked my own dates. We first challenged the

Wellington Blacks about blocks at Brougham Street a few months *after* the resolution banning rape was supposedly put to the convention. We challenged them again just before it was passed. But I'd never heard of such a ban and I never heard the boys admit that rapes and blocks were wrong. I went back to the women. They knew nothing about a ban at that time either. What they all remembered with great clarity was the courage it had taken to make a stand, and the resistance we'd met at every step.

Whatever the correct timing, by the early 1980s rape had been outlawed in all Black Power chapters, at least in theory. A decade later, Rei's new partner and other women set up a support group called Pae Arahi o Te Manaaki: Movement towards Caring and Dignity, to work with the boys on domestic violence and other issues.

But it was not until 2008 that Aroha Trust's role was publicly acknowledged, when lifetime Black Power member Denis O'Reilly wrote in his blog on 'New Zealand Edge': 'Aroha Trust was one of the gutsiest, most feisty, courageous and generally unknown expressions of women's liberation that this country has seen. These were the women who challenged the Black Power over our attitudes to rape and who, at the end of the day, were responsible for a change in gang behaviour, nationally.'

There was a knock at the front door. Two policemen stood holding my Honda 50, covered in mud, the mirror buckled, a tear along the black vinyl seat.

'Evening!' said the tall one. 'We need to speak to—' He consulted the paper in his hand.

'It's mine,' I said. 'Where'd you find it?'

'Down a bank,' he said, pushing the mangled front wheel over the doorstep.

'Stop!' I said. 'I don't want it.'

'If it's yours, you have to have it.'

'But it got nicked. And now look at it, it's stuffed.'

'Inside or out?' he said in a bored voice.

'Oh, just leave it there,' I said crossly. I should have known this had nothing to do with the cops being helpful; they just wanted to palm off a piece of junk. What a pity they hadn't been as vigilant when it came to saving Abel Smith Street.

Another night, another knock.

'Can I come in?' said Pat.

'Sure!' I said shyly. Usually he gave me warning when he was in town and we met on neutral ground.

He was on his way back to university in Christchurch. I hurried him up to my room and swept a tangle of dirty clothes off the bed. Then we fell onto the lumpy mattress and remembered how to love each other. Later, he told me that if I'd been out, or offhand, or going with someone else, he'd have given up. It was my last chance. That's what he said.

By morning, we'd agreed that being apart was too hard, too lonely, too stupid. We'd set each other free like the old proverb said, flown as far as we could in opposite directions and now, like homing pigeons, found our way back. It was time to stop fighting this thing. Pat wanted to live in Wellington again and be a trade union organiser. I was still committed to Aroha Trust, but I wanted to be with him too. Somehow we'd make it work.

Around midnight, a few weeks before Christmas, two Molotov cocktails were thrown through the front window of Peter Womble's house in Epuni Street, and the van outside was torched. Most people blamed the Mongrel Mob. Mahina, who lived there, was burgling a house with Evelyn and some other girls on the hill opposite when she saw the flames. 'We got all this stuff and we were looking down, and we said, "We know that place,"' she recalled with typical understatement.

'Evelyn gave me a flash camera from that burglary, one of those ones that takes instant pictures,' Junior said. 'I gave it to Mum for Christmas.'

Che, the dog who'd survived the Nomad's boot, was badly burnt and nearly had to be put down. Everyone else managed to get out, but the old wooden house was gutted. A newspaper report said residents had no complaints about the gang members as neighbours, but an unnamed 'girlfriend' predicted the fire-bombing could spark a gang war.

'If it does, it'll be like the Third World War, with everyone in, including girls,' she said.

Not long after, the three top Wellington Blacks — president, vice-president and treasurer — were among four or five members charged with gang-raping a woman. Word went round that she was 'just' a hooker but they were found guilty and did prison time for it. How brave she must have been to press charges. For me, it was final proof — should I need it — that the whole gang took part in atrocities against women, not just the prospects or an out-of-control few as was sometimes suggested.

With the Black Power leadership inside, the usual skirmishes with the Mongrel Mob erupted into full-scale gang war. The 'girlfriend' had been right.

I discovered that one of the Nomads had stayed at our Thorndon house overnight. I told him he had to leave, was shocked when he obeyed, then fretted he'd gone to get reinforcements.

'You've got fuckin' short memories,' I shouted at the girls who'd let him. 'Do you want to end up on the streets again?'

None of our boys were home so I phoned Brougham Street for help. Mike Hancock arrived. 'Sorry, there's only me,' he said, standing on the doorstep with a sheepish smile, his skinny arms flung wide.

If there was one person less equipped to deal with a Nomad attack than me, it was Mike. I took a quick look up and down the street, and pulled him inside. Everyone retreated to my room and barricaded the door. We lay on the bed, limbs overlapping, strangely high-spirited. In the camaraderie of shared danger, all was forgiven: the girls' short memories, my shouting. There was no way we were going to abandon another house to the Nomads, though I'm vague about how we intended defending it. The only options if they found us were hand-to-hand combat down the narrow staircase or a two-storey jump out the window to the backyard.

They never arrived.

'Great timing!' said my younger sister, opening the door to her flat. 'You can save me from my packing.' She'd just finished her degree and was off to Tonga to teach for two years. She stared at my streaked face. 'Hey, what's up?'

'Nothing!' I said, bursting into tears again. We'd grown up sharing bedrooms and secrets — there was only a 14-month age gap between us — but I hadn't seen much of her since I'd joined Aroha Trust.

'Come inside!' she said.

I looked anxiously over her shoulder.

'It's okay, I'm the only one home.'

She took me down to her bedroom and handed me a hanky.

I honked into it. 'I've had a gutsful,' I wailed, sitting cross-legged on her bed and covering my face with my hands. I'd just walked out of a trust meeting, taken off in the van and bawled all the way to her flat. 'The girls complain I'm the boss, but they won't take responsibility themselves. They throw sickies and still expect to be paid. They moan about having to finish the catseyes on their days off, but that's how we get the money to go on trips and stuff. When I bring up the things we've all agreed on, they look at me like I'm a nark. Sometimes I think they hate me.'

The possibility that this was true made me cry harder.

'Did anyone stick up for you?' she asked.

'Ha! Annie didn't even come to the meeting. Georgie was sick. No one would hand over their 10 bucks for the kitty. They all had excuses: "I have to buy new jeans," "I've got fines," "*I'm* not going to if she doesn't." They expect the trust to be there for them, but when I said it has to work both ways, they called me a control freak. So I told them to go fuck themselves and walked out.'

'Way to go!' said my sister. 'I wonder what they did after you left.'

'Cheered, probably!' I managed a wan smile. There was something liberating about being the one to behave badly for a change. But I was getting tired. Maybe I *was* a control freak. If so, it wasn't working. No matter how hard I tried, things didn't always turn out for the best. People got hurt. Dreams were shattered. The truth was, I didn't know what to do with all the pain and confusion around me; I hardly knew what to do with my own.

Jane picked up on my new mood almost before I was aware of it myself. 'People like Pip really piss me off,' she wrote in her diary. 'All her life she's had love from her family, and for the past three or four years from Pat. And now when all seems really cool between them, she gives up on everything else. She can't be bothered anymore. She tries not to show it but I can feel it.'

The entry finished with, 'Gee, Pip should be really thankful for what she's got. I'd give anything to have someone to love and to love me back. It seems like an impossible dream. I must be greedy to want a home, money and love as well.'

I went away over Christmas and came back to find the Thorndon house a pigsty. This time, I didn't have the energy or motivation to clean up and start again. And in the back of my mind I had an escape clause: Pat.

Georgie and her partner wanted a fresh start too. It seemed perfect: two reunited couples, still connected to Aroha Trust but with our own space. I liked the idea of living with Georgie. She was fun, reliable and able to look after herself; I wouldn't have to be house mother. I was sure Pat would like her too, and I hoped he'd get on with her partner, who was off to a good start because he wasn't a gang member.

The four of us found a flat in the Aro Valley with a light, airy lounge and a bush view. I didn't notice the dank, dark bedrooms downstairs, hard up against the hill, until mould slowly crept over our shoes and clothes.

The hardest thing was telling Jane. I was still her anchor, but I didn't ask her to join us. I was burnt out. I needed to be free. And it was time to put Pat first. From my point of view, it made perfect sense. But from hers, I was just one more person who'd abandoned her.

'Everything that can go wrong has gone wrong,' she wrote in her diary. 'It's one of the worst times I've had in years but I'll pull through, I hope.'

Jane decided to go flatting with strangers. I went along when she answered the first ad, but she clammed up and I did all the talking. The next time, I left her to it and she came back smiling.

'Things have improved,' she wrote after she moved into her new room. 'We had a really good party. The [Black Power] boys came, but it was all cool.'

There was one other hitch. Dad, a devout Catholic, disapproved of Pat and me 'living in sin'. He forbade Mum to give us anything for the flat and banned my two younger sisters from visiting — though we were still welcome at my parents' house.

Mum, as usual, was more pragmatic. 'I'm not going to go on about it,' she said. 'There's only one thing I ask. Don't get pregnant!'

We sat under a pohutukawa tree on a grassy slope in front of the museum and opened two parcels of fish and chips, enough for the 10 of us. It was unusual to meet up during the day, but the Education Board girls were between jobs, and the city council team had just picked up their pay. Bells chimed from the carillon that towered over us like a giant chimney: layer upon layer of haunting, discordant sound that drowned out even the clicking, trilling cicadas.

I laid some chips side by side like corpses on a piece of white bread, smothered them with tomato sauce and folded it in half. The greasy newspaper wrapping showed Rod Stewart swinging off a microphone at Athletic Park under a caption, 'D'ya think I'm sexy?' Beside it, a story announced a weekend ban on petrol sales. There was even talk of carless days if the oil crisis got worse, but we'd be okay: we could juggle our vans.

When the bells died away, the conversation turned to babies. Agnes, fresh from the Hawke's Bay leadership course, was pregnant. Evelyn was due any day. Georgie, Junior and Tess had toddlers, Nayda a newborn. Bubbles was expecting her second child. Aroha Trust was drowning in children. No one seemed to be taking precautions.

'Why not?' asked Annie.

'My boyfriend didn't want me to use anything,' Evelyn said.

A number of heads nodded.

'And I suppose he's promised to get up in the night and feed the baby,' Annie said, softening her reply with a sympathetic smile. 'C'mon, you guys. Who's on the pill?'

Silence.

'I couldn't remember to take a teeny-weeny pill every day,' Junior said.

'That's cos you're always wasted,' said Tasi.

'Stop talking about your-fuckin'-self!' Junior replied. They traded thumps, then fell back in the grass laughing.

'IUD then,' Annie said. 'Once it's in, you can forget about it.'

'Mine got stuck in my tubes, it was fuckin' horrible,' Gini said. 'Then I tried the injection, but it made me too fat.'

'Me too!' said Junior, puffing out her cheeks and giggling.

I was appalled at how many doctors prescribed Depo Provera for the girls. A three-monthly injection might seem like the antidote to their chaotic young lives, but I'd heard it was banned in the States and the side effects meant most of them never went back after the first jab. No doctor ever suggested *I* take it.

Gini took a bite out of the last piece of fish.

'Give us a bit, Gin,' said Tasi.

'What d'ya think this is, gift week?' Gini grinned and shovelled the rest into her mouth.

Tasi glared at her, then searched the newspaper folds for hidden chips.

'What about making the boys wear a condom?' Annie said.

There were hoots of laughter.

'In your fuckin' dreams, Annie!'

'First they'd have to give a shit.'

'What's a condom?' asked a new girl.

'Think sausage skin!' Georgie suggested.

The girl's hands flew up to cover her red cheeks. 'No fuckin' way!'

I lay on the grass, staring at the sky through a canopy of leaves, happy to let Annie do the talking. She was great at this sort of thing: frank and matter-of-fact, never condescending. She opened the window onto a brave, new world, one where people had access to knowledge and made informed decisions, where they didn't just let life happen to them.

'Okay, how about a diaphragm?' Annie said, persisting. 'You don't have to rely on anyone else. There's no side effects. It won't get lost inside you. But you have to use cream.'

'Gross!'

'Where do you put it?' said the new girl, looking nervous. Everyone cracked up.

'I'll show you later if you want,' Annie said seriously.

In some ways, I sympathised with the girls. In my experience there wasn't a reliable contraceptive out there that didn't leave women fat or depressed or bleeding or in pain. No wonder they got fed up and took risks.

And so the babies kept on coming. We'd often talked about providing childcare, just as we'd talked about pooling all our wages and paying women with children more. But that's as far as we'd got. Annie and I didn't have a personal stake in motherhood, and no one else had the experience to make it happen. As it was, when girls had babies, they left the trust, or gave them to their parents to look after, or muddled through, bringing them to work and leaving them with their mates.

Or they had abortions, skirting the new law that had closed the Auckland Abortion Clinic. When she was 18, Junior got pregnant again. Mike Hancock and his partner were already looking after her young son at Brougham Street. Having a second child was out of the question.

'It was the saddest time of my life, actually,' Junior said. 'I was just over four months. I didn't know what was happening. They weren't meant to be doing abortions in clinics so they done it in the hospital and they took two days because I was so far gone. They just hosed it out and the nurse goes, "Do you want to see your daughter?" and then three or four hours later, they rang up, and Tasi and them came and picked me up and took me to the Trades Fair. I ended up freaking out actually; they had to rip me off the rollercoaster. I was just screaming, I was terrified.'

At her check-up, the doctor told Junior the abortion had made her sterile. 'It didn't affect me until about a year later when everyone else was having children and I couldn't. It blew my self-esteem down even more. I had hardly any left anyway, but then I gave up caring. I thought, all the shit was meant to come to me. So that's what I took on. If I could survive it, good.'

'And if you couldn't?' I asked quietly.

'Tough!' There was a pause, followed by the wheezy laugh that seemed to be her only defence against the world. 'I survived it.'

When Gini was 20, she got pregnant to JB and had an abortion while he was in jail. 'I remember being at Brougham Street and saying to someone, "Oh, I have to go up to the hospital." I didn't tell them why, I just said I had to go. I think Annie and somebody else came to see me after I'd had it. Tasi maybe. And I'd had the abortion, and even all through when the doctors were talking to me about what was happening, I didn't understand any of it. All I knew was that I needed to get this thing out of me. It was like a disease, I felt that bad about it. I wasn't ready to be a mother. I wasn't ready for the responsibility. I could barely look after myself, I thought. I regret it. But I've confessed it to the Lord and believe he's forgiven me. I've had a hard time forgiving myself. It was like I'd murdered my baby because I didn't know it was a baby, I didn't realise it was a human: breathing, living, kicking. When I realised, I went through a grieving stage of mourning for this baby. But I could understand how young girls come to those doctors and don't know what they're going through in their body and just want to get rid of it.'

Even after the abortion, Gini didn't use contraception. 'I wasn't really into sex at the time because of the abuse I got in my childhood. I was quite reserved and I thought that men had to mean more to me than just a one-night stand. I didn't feel I needed these contraceptives because I wasn't playing around. Then my partner got out of jail and we got back together, and it was like, oh well, if I get pregnant I do, but if I don't, I don't.'

Most of the girls adopted the same Russian-roulette approach. They had no careers, no future mapped out that a child might interfere with. But there were even more disturbing reasons behind their fatalism. For all their street-smart ways, they knew little about their bodies. Most had been abused as children and grew up without mothers or strong female role models through their critical teenage years. As young adults, they lived under a cloud of rape and cruelty, much of it brought upon them by their gender. Blocking out their sexuality — and its repercussions — was one way of coping with a world where danger lurked in every corner.

When I recorded the women's stories, I wanted to know if it was possible to break the tragic association of sex with violence, shame and powerlessness. 'Yes,' said several of them. They enjoyed sex now. But healing took a long time. One said her first positive sexual experience was in her thirties when she already had four children. 'That was sex without alcohol and drugs, when I really felt like a woman and it was a really sexual experience and it was really magical,' she said, her voice a mixture of pride and sadness.

Not long after we moved in together, Georgie had an abortion too. When I picked her up from the hospital, she swore me to secrecy; she didn't want her partner to find out. After that, she was sad and distracted, and they fought a lot.

Pat and I were struggling as well. He went back to the freezing works, an hour away by bus and train, to earn some money. After a hard day stripping sheep guts, he wanted peace and privacy, not a house bustling with girls and the latest trust dramas. He was never rude to them, but he saw it as my place, not somewhere he could relax and bring his own friends. Underlying his unease was a deep antipathy to gangs, something I was ashamed to admit to anyone else.

Georgie's partner shared Pat's misgivings, although I didn't realise that at the time. I wish I had: we might have all felt less lonely. I think I assumed that because he was Māori, he didn't mind her mixing in gang circles even though he didn't wear a patch himself.

The public mood made things worse. It was election year and gangs became a law-and-order scapegoat. Commentators later dubbed 1979 the 'year of the gangs', not because of the threat gangs posed — which was small, if brutal — but because of the hysteria whipped up by police, politicians and the media.

Two new laws were passed, giving cops the power to search vehicles if they suspected offensive weapons, and publicans the right to refuse entry to anyone who wore a patch or had gang associations. Aroha Trust was affected too. The rakes and sickles and scythes in the back of our vans gave the police more excuse than ever to harass us. And if the girls wanted to go out on the town, more often than not we went on our own.

UNITED WE STAND

Gini took small, noisy tokes on a joint, then waved it in my direction. I shook my head and glanced in the rear-vision mirror. Through the haze in the back of the rental van, I could see other girls smoking and swigging fizz. Tasi was bent over her guitar, crooning softly. Beside her one of the girls, a 17-year-old, was scoffing a chocolate bar. I caught her eye and she gave me the thumbs-up.

'Okay, just one puff,' I said to Gini. 'I don't see why it should be party time for everyone else.'

Outside the air was crisp and fragrant, tinged with autumn chill. It was nine o'clock in the morning, but this was no ordinary workday. It was Easter 1979 and Aroha Trust was off on its first-ever road trip.

Marilyn Waring had talked us into going to the United Women's Convention in Hamilton, the third such gathering of New Zealand women in six years. As one of the organisers, she promised to hire us a van to get around petrol rationing and find us somewhere to stay. Feminism wasn't just for the middle classes, she said. Our voice was important.

Reassured by the convention poster — a Polynesian woman holding a baby with nappies flapping on a line behind her — the girls chose the women's convention over the Black Power one being held at the same time. Though how any woman would contemplate spending three days with 200 pissed, stoned, lawless gang members was beyond me.

Nine of us set off for Hamilton, wishing we didn't have to leave behind Georgie, who was trying to sort things out with her man, and a couple of other girls whose boyfriends wouldn't let them go at the last minute.

Gini held out a bag of chippies. I felt her studying my face.

'What?' I said, wiping my sleeve across my mouth.

'Where did you get those spoony specs?'

Instead of my usual contact lenses, I was wearing small, round John Lennon glasses, a relic from my student days that were easier on my eyes for the long drive.

'What's wrong with them?' I said, pretending to sound hurt.

She giggled. 'They look like granny glasses.'

'These glasses were very cool when I bought them.'

'What? A hundred years ago?' She shook her head sadly. 'It's not very good for our image, Pip. We're meant to be tough, you know. It's lucky we're heading out of town.'

'Maybe people will think you've hijacked me,' I suggested.

She perked up at the idea. 'Hey look, there's grampa!'

A balding hitch-hiker waited hopefully on the side of the road. Beside him, a stand of toitoi flicked in the breeze like feather dusters.

'Room for one more?' I called to the girls in the back.

'Only if they're spunky!'

I eyed the guy's bushy beard and bandy white legs sticking out of khaki shorts two sizes too big, grinned at Gini, and pulled over. He swung a pack almost as large as himself through the side door and clambered up after it.

'I think he wanted to run,' Jane recalled. 'Everybody pulled out their dope — we all took up an ounce each, which was incredible — and started rolling joints. And he was like, "Where the fuck am I?" There was this look of horror on his face. But everyone was really nice to him, so he survived.'

Gini classed the trip as a highlight of her life. 'I was buzzing because it was all the women going,' she said. 'We'd always had these men about who more or less dictated what we did and how we did it. The Nomad gang travelled around the country, but it was all against the law, whereas this was legal. We bought the petrol, we paid our way, which added to the freedom of the enjoyment because you knew you weren't running or hiding from anything. And the country was so beautiful. We only rushed through it from one pub to the next with the gang, but with the girls it was like having a look at the countryside. Being free to travel up and down with no other commitments like children or even a partner, because he was in jail.'

In Hamilton, we dropped our bags at the school hall Marilyn had organised, and went to register at Waikato University. 'In my mind, I thought, yee-ha, we're going to meet women just like us,' Charmaine said. 'Our women were really strongly bonded and we fought a lot of oppression in our own rights.'

But, contrary to the convention poster, only a handful of the 2000 participants were Māori and Pacific women, and even they weren't necessarily allies. At a wine and cheese function on the first night, one of them hassled Gini about having 'honkies' in the trust and tried to get her to desert Annie and join a group of exclusively Māori women.

'I can remember Gini making a choice that we all stayed together because we were all together,' Annie said, still savouring Gini's loyalty.

Everything about the convention was alien to the girls. 'There were a few hui I wanted to go to,' Charmaine said. 'It took me half my time to try and find the place. It was so big I always got lost, and by the time I found where it was, it was over. So that was really frustrating. Then when I did get to the hui I wanted, there was a big *don't come in here* wall. I wasn't sure whether that wall was about being a Māori woman, about them being really scared, or what. They were quite intimidated by our presence. Not that we were giving them any reason to be.'

Charmaine felt patronised by the organisers, who tried to give the girls things for free. 'Everyone else had to pay, and we had our money. And they'd go, "Oh no, no, no, you have it, you have it, take it, take it, take it." Well, for me what it means is paranoia; I saw an extreme case of white man's paranoia that weekend. It freaked me out. I would have had more fun at a Black Power convention. In all honesty, I would have had more fun.'

She remembered battling with one woman. 'Saying to her, "I've had enough of this shit. You talk about fighting for the rights of women, you talk about being empowered. This is all about rich women having a wild weekend. It's not your reality; you don't have to live with it. We live with it every day.'"

Jane agreed. 'My biggest memory was feeling like there were all these bullshit, academic women who were spouting all this stuff about sexual abuse and rape and all these other feminist issues. And we thought, what the fuck would they know?'

Charmaine was also turned off by the anti-men message. 'Because I came from a whānau concept and that's what the trust was about. So that included our men as well. Okay, we demanded changes from our men, but it didn't mean they were to be isolated, ousted or cut off like they didn't matter.'

On the second day of the convention, the girls pulled out their dope in the cafeteria and started rolling joints. 'It was the start of the *fuck you*,' Jane said. Most of them retreated to the van. When Marilyn Waring came out to say hello, someone offered her a joint and she accepted. 'I remember thinking, fuckin' hell, an MP having a joint with us,' Jane said. 'I also felt quite cynical, that she was just keeping us happy.'

Torn between two worlds, I slipped away to a workshop by myself. I wanted to give some space to the young woman who'd enrolled in the first-ever women's studies course at Victoria University, who'd spent three happy years in an academic environment just like this. But I couldn't get past the impersonal lecture theatre, the sea of white faces, intimidating experts, exclusive language. I didn't need the girls sitting next to me to feel their alienation as acutely as if it were my own.

It was a relief when Charmaine asked me to drive her to visit

Shorty at Waikeria Prison, 45 minutes away. They'd met at The Sunset Strip nightclub when she was 12 and he 13. Since then they'd been best mates, the two babies of the scene. On the way back, she was uncharacteristically quiet. I let her be. I knew how hard it was to see your mates inside; I couldn't imagine what memories it might trigger if you'd been locked up yourself.

Back at the convention, the other girls were on a high. They'd gone to an open forum on the lawn. It had been crazy, they said: lesbians screaming at one another, a woman performing a bizarre ritual with a knife, a nun reading from the Bible.

Then Tasi persuaded them to get up and speak. 'I did it because I wanted to voice my opinion about what I believed, what I wanted,' she said. 'Because a lot of the time, us younger generation really didn't have much say.'

Jane stood up too. 'It was so powerful because it was the first time any of us had spoken in public, and the first time we'd ever spoken about our own experiences. I remember so many women being there and they were listening to us. They were actually listening to what we had to say.'

For reasons known only to themselves, they chose 'Jeremiah Was a Bullfrog' as their waiata. I wondered if the lesbian separatists, with their purple armbands, had joined in the chorus about all the boys and girls.

'It was awesome,' Gini said. 'Being in this huge crowd of women and feeling so strong, dressed rough as, singing this song with all my heart. And I always remember being so shy, and so low self-esteem that I dare not be in front of a crowd seen to be singing, let alone giving it my full bore. I totally enjoyed it. I felt proud to be called a working woman, to be part of a group that had started up fresh, first one in New Zealand.'

There was a mixed response from the audience, she said. 'Some thought, who do they think they are? And others thought, good on ya, getting up and saying it.'

I was gutted that I'd missed their star turn. But I consoled myself that if I (or Annie, who'd sloped off somewhere) had been there, it probably wouldn't have happened. We'd got out of their way and they'd demonstrated all the things the trust stood for: self-belief, courage, solidarity. I felt proud of them, yet strangely bereft, like a mother watching her five-year-old walk across the school playground without a backward glance.

That night there was a disco. At last we were on familiar ground: a smoky, crowded hall full of women, loud music, everyone up dancing and getting drunk. Rangi put on a purple armband, not realising what it represented. 'She couldn't understand why all these women were hitting on her,' Charmaine said. 'We cracked up laughing when we finally figured out why. It took about five heads to work it out because she came back freaked.'

By the third day, the euphoria of speaking at the forum had worn off and the strain started to show. 'None of us coped well,' Charmaine said. 'We all started getting shitty and turning on each other. In the end we said, "Fuck, let's get out of here, this is freaky."'

Leaving early, we missed the closing session where organisers called in extra policewomen to keep the radical lesbians and Māori separatists in line. We also missed the last two keynote speakers: an American who gave half her time to Māori activist Rebecca Evans to talk about white racism, and a French feminist who criticised the absence of Māori and Pacific women and said feminism had to include everyone.

It wasn't until I came across a copy of the convention report years later that I discovered we hadn't been the only disgruntled group. Women had been at loggerheads about everything: sexuality, abortion, marriage, the church, childcare, paid work, body image, leadership. Mainstream women felt threatened by hardliners. Everyone was cross about the queues, overcrowding and programme changes. The cracks in the women's movement had become chasms. Women, it turned out, were not united after all.

The anguish of the committee, who'd spent two years organising the convention, leapt out of the closely typed, badly photocopied pages of the report. They seemed shocked by the divisions, unreliability of their sisters and lack of thanks for their efforts. 'We all experienced tremendous fatigue and anxiety during the weekend as we struggled to keep the whole thing together,' they wrote. 'We did not have a hot meal from Thursday to Sunday night.'

The committee documented their efforts to attract 'non-Pākehā' women to the convention. They'd contacted Pacifica, the Māori Women's Welfare League and ethnic women's groups, but the response came back that they had some sorting out of their own to do first. 'Not satisfied, committee members personally sought out, encouraged and sponsored non-European women of diverse ages.' Marilyn Waring's interest in us had obviously been part of this drive. 'It was not enough,' they admitted.

The report contained another surprise: three grainy black-and-white photos I'd never seen before. Two showed the Aroha Trust girls singing at the open forum, their presentation described as 'an emotional and illuminating experience for many of us'. In the third photo, a line of seven young women stood arm in arm. At one end was Jane, wearing a jersey emblazoned with the words 'WOMEN POWER'. At the other end were three more Aroha Trust girls, Rangi wearing jackboots and a 'Black Power Wellington' t-shirt, flanked by Sis and Waynnie.

Jane was astonished when I showed her. 'I didn't know that photo existed before today and I had no memory whatsoever of what I was wearing. For the first time in my life, I'd knitted a jersey. It was blue in the trust colours and the lettering was white; it was probably all the wool I had. I was so proud of that jersey, eh. That embodied how I felt about being part of the trust and the one-finger salute to the world. Women, I guess, were my whānau, and the trust embodied that. It was like my tūrangawaewae at that time, my place where I could stand tall.'

She held the photo for a long time, visibly moved by the memory of the passionate young woman who'd worn her beliefs on her chest as proudly as a war medal. 'It's interesting looking at that because I guess I've been focusing on the downside. I think there was a real strength there for people who were in a really vulnerable position. I wonder where the hell I would have been if I hadn't come into the trust. I certainly don't think I would have survived the way I did.'

In 2005, Jane made a special trip from Ngāruawāhia to another women's convention in Wellington. It was the first attempt since Hamilton to get New Zealand women together, although the word 'united' had been discreetly dropped.

She was disappointed. 'Nothing drove it, there was no passion. It was a nice, clean non-event.'

Again she left early and missed the closing session. She may have been heartened to see a group of young feminists receive a standing ovation when they lamented the absence of Māori, Pacific, refugee and migrant, young and low-income women, called for an end to the large numbers of women and children living in poverty, and identified the ongoing abuse of women as still one of the most significant concerns for their generation. Or she may have just wondered if any progress had been made in 26 years.

From the Hamilton convention, we headed for Auckland to see Bob Marley perform at Western Springs Stadium on Easter Monday. 'Which was much more of a buzz,' Annie said. 'And probably appropriate as well. We left the United Women's Convention because they were not talking about things that we were into or experiencing or feeling, and Bob Marley was all around us. We can't have had tickets but we got there somehow. Oh God, I don't even know. Where did we all stay?'

I couldn't remember either. All that mattered was the concert. Bob Marley sang about our world — about poverty, dispossession, racism, police harassment — and made sense of it. He wore dreadlocks and treated marijuana as sacred. Even better, his solution was peace and love, not violence.

We didn't know then that he'd be dead in two years from cancer, or that our benefactor, Marilyn Waring, would be the government's representative at his state funeral in Jamaica. Nor did we know that he was born on 6 February, Waitangi Day, and that his music would become entwined with this country's ongoing search for unity and identity.

Although Pat was somewhere in the stoned, swaying throng at Western Springs, I stuck with the girls. We met up with the Black Power and followed them into the stadium. 'It was like Moses parting the water on the Red Sea,' Jane said. 'We had the big Black Power flags on poles. The crowd parted as we slowly walked up to the front; today kids would call it the mosh pit. I felt a huge sense of whānau, pride, a sense of power and control. People had to make way for us.'

But when Marley came on stage, he urged the boys to lower their banners. 'We are one!' he reminded them, to the roar of the crowd.

And they did.

Three months after we moved into the Aro Valley flat together, Pat announced he was moving out. He was tired of living in my world, he said. He wanted us to get a place by ourselves, but it was over to me. Either way, he was going.

Jane gave a low whistle when I told her. We stopped work and lit a cigarette, keeping an eye out for our builder boss. We were renovating a house in Newtown, a flagship for the council's Housing Renovation Advice Service, and he'd been moaning about how long it was taking us to burn off the old paint.

'Mr and Mrs Martin, eh!' she said.

'Doubt it! I don't know what to do. I'll feel cut off living on our own, but if I don't go, I'll never know if we're right for each other.'

'I can't imagine settling down,' she said.

'Yeah, but you're just a baby!' She still looked like a waif, her slight body swallowed up in shapeless overalls, blonde fringe straggling into her eyes. But she was happier these days, more self-assured. Perhaps pushing her out of the nest had been the right thing to do after all. I felt a stab of jealousy. I couldn't imagine settling down either. Settling down was for grown-ups.

'Oops!' she said. 'Here comes old eagle-eyes.'

We scrambled to our feet and directed our heat guns at the peeling paint a little nervously. A few days earlier, sparks had got under the weatherboards and started a fire after we left for the day and the whole house nearly went up.

⊕

The lead story in *The Evening Post* slammed 14 Māori activists for beating up a group of Pākehā engineering students in Auckland who were practising a mock haka for their graduation ceremony. Ignoring the pleas of Māori students, they performed it every year, complete with grass skirts and lipstick tattoos, but now it had been cancelled.

'Good fuckin' job!' Charmaine said, nestling into Paddy's side on the couch. 'Look at them bleating about their rights. What a fuckin' cheek. Since when did they care about our rights?'

I crouched on the floor, the newspaper spread in front of me.

'Wankers!' I agreed, although I found it depressing that five minutes of violence had achieved what a decade of polite protest had failed to do.

I turned to the 'To Let' section. 'This one sounds good. One bedroom, up behind the hospital, fifty bucks a week.'

Pat looked dubious. 'I dunno about Newtown.'

Paddy leaned forward, his arm still draped around Charmaine. 'I wouldn't live there, bro,' he said. 'You could be walking home at night and get bashed over the head by a Coconut.'

'I like Newtown,' I protested. 'There's always people around. It makes me feel safe. Anyway, it's the only one. Let's go and have a look.'

The flat was cosy, half a house with a picket fence and a veranda that never saw the sun. The landlady offered it to us on the spot. To my surprise, Pat agreed. It was my fifth move in two years, one I wasn't sure I wanted to make. With Abel Smith Street demolished and Epuni Street firebombed, most of the girls had opted for smaller places, less likely to attract trouble. Even so, living by ourselves felt like a sell-out, a move away from the edge, putting the personal before the political. But I'd come to a crossroads. I'd tried to combine the two and it hadn't worked. Now I was being forced to choose.

The city council girls were sent to a draughty barn in Lyall Bay to dismantle old buses. The job was tedious, and our foreman — an officious young Pākehā — bored us at smoko with unlikely stories of his weekend exploits. One of the our best workers kept disappearing; I'd discover her asleep on a bus seat and wake her up, only to find her gone again 10 minutes later. Nothing I said or did could snap her out of it. It didn't occur to either of us that she might be pregnant.

For the first time, the trust had something to offer girls like her. Te Waka e Manaaki, the Black Power trust, had invited us to set up an inner-city base with them. We agreed on condition that we were equal partners. The large building the city council offered us had room for a crèche. We applied to the Labour Department to renovate it under the relief work scheme and make a child-safe area. Georgie and Mahina started working in the office and volunteered to look after the kids when the crèche opened. The last of our five aims, 'to help young mothers participate in the trust', was about to come true. Aroha Trust had done it again.

The Black Power sergeant-at-arms invited everyone to his sister's wedding in Whakatāne. A whole crowd of us went: 'Two vans loaded, a carload of Nomads, another of Wellington Blacks and a little putt-putt Morris with Denis O'Reilly,' Jane recorded in her diary. 'And untold dope. We spent just about the whole time out of our trees — which isn't unusual. At nite [*sic*], we slept in the marae meeting house which was cool. Neither Mike Womble or Ricki could try anything,' she said of two ex-boyfriends. 'Then at the reception (which wasn't very good — they kept closing the bar), we took off for a drive — to have another blow. That was pretty cool. We sat down by the water's edge and got smashed. That's all we seem to do these days. Smoke dope and more dope and more dope etc.'

Jane's diary entry brought up memories of my own. The strongest — apart from the prolific dope, or perhaps because of it — was feeling like an intruder. None of us even knew the bride or her family. I wondered how welcome our stoned, dishevelled group really was. The reason they kept closing the bar was because we drank so much.

Jane saw it differently. 'It was awesome,' she said. 'The bride was a tomboy; she wore a white dress and gumboots.' But it wasn't just about having a good time. 'That really epitomised for me that we were an urban whānau. He [the sergeant-at-arms] wasn't ashamed of us. We might have come from ngā hau e whā, the four winds, but we were all his family. He didn't just acknowledge his whānau, which was unusual enough in those days, he invited us into it. He took that risk.'

On the way home, our convoy raced along the back roads. I was last in line, trying not to lose sight of the two red smudges in the darkness, all I could see of the vehicle in front. As we drove through the Kaingaroa Forest, row after row of tall, thin tree trunks flickered at the edge of my vision, the only witnesses to our passing through. All my passengers were asleep, except for Jane, loyal as always. The burden of their safety sat like a stone on my chest.

It was midnight by the time I dropped everyone off. I plonked my bag in the hall and peeped into the bedroom at Pat, a humped shape under the blankets. He was working as a barman at the Cambridge, chalking up experience to become a union organiser. I wanted to wake him up, tell him about my weekend, bring my two worlds together somehow. Instead, I made a cup of tea and lay on the couch, too wired to sleep, my legs shaking with fatigue. In eight hours, it'd be time to pick the girls up again for work.

A friend of Mum's asked her if I would speak to the National Council of Women about Aroha Trust. I arrived at St John's Church on a chilly September evening, nervously clutching my typed notes and wishing I'd refused.

Sitting up the front, I scanned the packed hall as Mum's friend introduced a stranger: doctor's daughter, head prefect, university graduate, now working with welfare kids. There was no sign of Mum in the audience. She wasn't a member of NCW and might have thought she wasn't welcome, or that I wouldn't want her there. Or perhaps she was scared of what I might say. I felt a pang of disappointment.

Suddenly, I was back at the United Women's Convention, trying to straddle the abyss between these middle-class Pākehā women with their sensible skirts and well-meaning smiles, and the outlaw girls I hung around with. I hadn't asked any of them to come. The convention had shown me these two groups were like oil and water: they didn't mix, no matter how hard you shook them up together.

I still have the speech I gave that night, my only written record of the Aroha Trust days. I ran through our achievements: work, houses, vans, training courses, common bank account, sports teams, trips away. 'In other words, we are a group of so-called unemployable, criminal no-hopers living and working together, supporting ourselves and each other,' I said.

I described wringing our first job out of the Labour Department. How work had led to new skills, personal development, independence. How our all-women house at Abel Smith Street had been destroyed by the cops and the gangs.

I talked about the strong emphasis we placed on democracy, rotating roles so that one person wasn't always swinging decisions their way. I also acknowledged our power struggles and the painful process of growth. 'Everyone has had to change and it has only happened after a lot of hard words, criticism, tears and arguments.'

I learnt about feminism at university, I said, but it was the trust that taught me about sisterhood. 'The women I know waste little time on the trappings of womanhood such as fancy clothes and make-up. They are themselves, they know how to look after themselves and they don't need the masks that so many other women seem to need.'

I didn't go into our efforts to stop rape — it was a world too far removed from my audience — except to say that 'the boys have often felt threatened by our outspokenness and what they call our crazy ideas, but we have a respect which is very rare for a group of women in a gang scene, because we have stood strong together and refused to be trampled on'.

I issued a challenge: 'The girls I know have so much to offer the women's movement and it is a great shame that they, and all the women like them, feel so out of place in established women's organisations.' Then I told them about our experience at the United Women's Convention.

I concluded by saying, 'I hope you can understand that we are not a voluntary branch of Social Welfare looking after wayward girls and trying to turn juvenile delinquents into good, solid citizens. It is true that none of the girls who have joined the trust have been back inside since, but that is simply a side effect. For when people get the chance to work and make the decisions about that work, when they get the chance to live decently, when they know they have friends they can always turn to and something they can call their own, then they don't throw that chance away lightly.'

When I finished, the hall was silent. They don't get it, I thought; they're pissed off that I've criticised them. But slowly they began to clap. The clapping went on for a long time. There were questions from the floor, women lining up to shake my hand. I felt relieved and a bit overwhelmed. Mostly, though, I felt guilty. There was one thing I hadn't told them — or anyone. I was not the heroine they imagined. I couldn't do it any more. I'd decided to leave Aroha Trust.

But first there was Gini's twenty-first birthday. We planned a surprise party at the Aro Street Hall, to be financed from our communal funds. It was a year since the trust's first birthday and we wanted to recapture the magic of that night, put aside our failures and disappointments, and celebrate a second year's survival. For me at least, though, there was one major drawback. The hall would be crawling with Nomads, not just from Wellington but from the Wairarapa. JB had invited them, as Gini would have wanted: they were her whānau as much as we were.

In the week before the party, Gini got more and more suspicious. 'Everybody was going missing,' she said. 'I couldn't find people to go out to the pub with. They were all scheming because they were doing this thing secretly. I'd had enough by the third day and I made my partner tell me what was going on.'

On the night itself, she filled herself up with pills and dope. 'I remember getting as wasted as I could, but always trying to be in control. I wanted to go out there and know who I was, and be grateful for everything that they had put on, but having to have all this stuff to motivate me to even get there. It was like fighting with two people inside me — one wanting to go and one having no courage at all. I'd rather just call the whole thing off.'

Gini got through the speeches with JB's arm around her in a rare public display of affection. Candleman presented her with a silver key. Us girls produced the fur coat we'd bought her from the Salvation Army. It cost $40, half a week's wages. She stammered a thank-you, blew out the candles on her cake and vanished.

Forgetting her promise not to drink and drive after her mother was run over, Gini took the trust van, talked Sis, who was always on for an adventure, and Evelyn into going too, whistled her Doberman into the back and headed for her flat in Newtown. As she raced the lights into Riddiford Street, she hit a car double-parked outside a takeaway bar where we often tamed the late-night munchies. The van landed on its roof. Gini and Sis flew through the front windscreen, Evelyn through a side window.

'I remember lying on the concrete covered in blood and all these people were around,' Gini said. 'I wasn't sure if my other friends had died or if they were alive or where they were. But I knew that I didn't want to get picked up by the police and taken to hospital or to the police station. I wanted to go back to my birthday.'

Gini dragged herself off the road and grabbed Sis. 'We could see Evelyn moving, so we knew she wasn't dead. We carried ourselves around the side of this building and by this time we could hear the sirens coming and the ambulance. We stood there and waited for them to take Evelyn to know she was all right. Then we just left the van there and all the glass and all the screeching noises and people and caught a taxi, covered in blood, and went home and washed it all off and changed our clothes.'

When they'd cleaned themselves up, Gini and Sis caught another taxi back to the party. 'My face was out there,' Gini said, cupping her hand away from her cheek. 'People automatically assumed that my partner had given me the bash. They were ready to hang him, and he didn't even know what had happened, let alone that I'd gone anywhere. So I had to stop that. It was probably the worst car accident I'd had.'

Evelyn had a broken collarbone, Sis a broken ankle. Gini partied so hard she didn't notice her own injuries till the next night. 'My teeth were way up in my gums and I couldn't eat, and I was in pain,' she said. 'I went along to the hospital and by the time they took the little bits of glass out of my cheek, it was too much of a time lapse so they couldn't sew it up. That's why there's a scar there.' She ran her finger over a jagged line under her right eye, criss-crossed by a smaller one. 'They pulled my teeth out, so I had two false teeth. That was painful. I remember the needle going in and thinking, is this the pain that I have to pay for telling lies about what had happened?'

All she would say was that she'd had an accident. 'My answers in those days were one-word answers. As much as people would try and get things out of me, I'd just say, "yep", "no". It came with the attitude thing and the resentment at prying. What do you want to know for? What's it got to do with you? Who do you think you are for me to tell you? And then that authority thing come, and then the white and the brown and the colour thing would come, and before I knew it, I had closed myself off that I wasn't going to disclose anything. The best they could do is wash their hands of me and send me on my way.'

Gini was horrified when she saw the van through the fence at Kearneys tow-away service the next day. 'It was all squashed up and every window was broken. It was rammed like one of those musical things, *eerh-eerh-eerh-eerh*.' She pumped her arms as if squeezing an accordion. 'It was like that time I was in my cell at the girls home, that loneliness and that thinking about God thing. I thought about it standing outside that fence, thinking it's a miracle that we're out of that alive, walking and talking and not at least paralysed, because the state of the van was shocking. You would never think that people would survive such a crash. That was the second time that God came into my mind. But it was only a split second.'

When the police questioned Evelyn at the hospital, she told them she couldn't remember who the driver was. They traced the van back to the trust and contacted the city council. Years later, I found a letter in the council archives.

'I have previously had a conversation with the Senior Traffic Officer regarding this accident and advised him that I was unable to assist in identifying the driver of the vehicle,' assistant town clerk Colin Knox wrote to the claims supervisor at State Insurance. 'I suggested that he contact one of the trustees, Mrs Sonja Davies, who may have some influence in the matter. I am afraid I do not have a current address for the organiser of the Aroha Trust as this has recently changed. I am sorry I am not able to be of greater assistance.'

'Wow!' said Jane when I showed her the letter. 'I was in charge of the council team then. Colin Knox knew where I lived. He must have been covering up for us.'

Gini was never prosecuted.

I have a confession to make. I'd forgotten all about Gini's accident on her twenty-first until she reminded me. My abiding image was of the fur coat we'd given her, so soft and sleek and heavy. I desperately wanted one myself.

I find this disturbing. From a night when three girls nearly died, all I remembered was an item of clothing I desired. Had I seen so many young women with lumpy faces by then that I'd become immune to their pain? Did the smashed-up van slip my mind because I was leaving the trust and it wasn't going to be my problem? These don't seem like good enough reasons but they're the best I can come up with.

When I started reconstructing the story of Aroha Trust, I imagined that I would arrive at the end waving the truth proudly above my head, like a child retrieving a stone from the bottom of a swimming pool. I see now that all I've brought to the surface are fragments: isolated pictures lit up for an instant like a night scene in a camera flash, vague feelings nagging at me till I name them. And when I try to assemble these small trophies, wondering how much to trust them, they fade into the fog of what is missing or contested or remembered by each of the women through her own eyes and heart and herstory.

Like the blind men who argue about the nature of an elephant depending on whether they touch its tail or trunk or tusk, our view of the world is one-eyed and incomplete. My job has been to put together as many pieces of the picture as I can find — more patchwork quilt than jigsaw puzzle — hoping that the whole will end up being greater than the sum of the parts. And indeed that was Aroha Trust: unknown, imperfect, yet somehow containing the power of all our lives.

TWENTY

MOVING ON

On a Friday afternoon in October 1979, I took off my blue overalls, collected my final pay, handed over the keys to the vans and slipped quietly away from Aroha Trust. My plan was to have a few weeks off, then learn to drive the Big Reds, as the city buses were called. I felt like I was leaving the trust in reasonable heart: the city council team would be fine in Jane's capable hands, and Annie and Georgie would look after the Education Board girls.

Almost immediately, Annie packed up and moved to the Wairarapa, a spur-of-the moment decision that was a double blow for those left behind. I was gutted when she told me she was going, but I was in no position to point the finger.

'I was probably at the end of a road,' she recalled. 'Maybe just burnt out. I felt I was getting into a lot of bad habits, a lot of pills, just a bad space for me to be in. And I'd say things had got fairly much out of control around us, like some of the gang things.'

I ran into Peter Womble in Cuba Mall. He seemed exhausted and edgy, and confided in me in a way that was rare. The conviction of the three top Wellington Blacks and others for gang rape had been one betrayal too many. With the leadership inside, he felt he had to stick around to help manage the war that erupted with the Mongrel Mob, but he hated some of the tactics. Young Black Power prospects were being rostered on roofs of gang houses all night long with loaded, high-powered rifles, ordered to shoot Mongies on sight, he said.

Assistant town clerk Colin Knox got involved, brokering several meetings between the Blacks and the Mob that eventually secured a kind of peace. Soon after that, Peter disappeared up north, his faith in the possibility of change from within the gang shattered.

I continued to see the other girls round town. They'd jump on and off my bus, filling me in on the latest gossip and never thinking to pay.

Tasi rang one day when I was between shifts. She and Mahina were moving to Taumarunui, to what became known as 'the bush', where a local Māori family had offered the use of their land to people from the work co-ops. Mike Womble, Mike Hancock and Tam were going too. And, by the way, Tasi said, could they drop off two of the girls' babies for a couple of hours while they got organised?

'It's good practice for you,' she said, propping the babies side by side in the middle of my lounge and handing me a bag of nappies.

I stared at the double set of welling eyes and quivering chins, and wondered what on earth I was meant to do with them.

I could hear Mahina giggling as they headed out the door.

'Why would I need practice?' I called after them.

Tasi and Mahina had a shout at the Cambridge before they left. I walked into the pub and waved to Pat, pulling beers behind the bar. Tasi hurried over and put her arm round my shoulder.

'Excited about going?' I said, relieved to discover that others could and would leave Aroha Trust when an opportunity arose.

'Fuck, yeah! Get away from the rush. I'll never forget the trust, though. And you, Pip! You've always been my role model.'

The compliment was unexpected and thrilling. I hugged her hard.

When I recorded her story, Tasi was equally generous. 'I've never met any group of people that were so close. I think a lot of it was you too, Pip. Because you were like the head of everything. We'd be going all over the place, but you had everyone under control. It was really good. You done a lot of thinking for everybody and everyone trusted you, and it was like you knew what you were doing, and everyone was supportive towards you.'

'I think you got mad with me sometimes,' I felt compelled to say.

'Oh yeah, but that was just teenage tantrums. I can still feel that aroha there between the people. If I go and see one of them, it's still there. I've never come across anything like that in my whole life. That close.'

I scurried across the dark playground to the safety of the Aro Valley Hall where the Black Power were holding their Christmas party. I hadn't been there since Gini's twenty-first, three months earlier, and I suddenly felt shy.

To my delight, Mike Hancock was on the door.

'Back already?' I said.

'Only to see you! Got those Big Reds under control?'

I looked at him suspiciously, wondering if he'd heard how Charmaine, Tam and Mike Womble had pulled up beside me at the lights just after I wedged my bus halfway round a tight corner at peak hour, causing a major traffic jam. Judging from their glee, I knew it'd be all around town by now.

'No sweat!' I said. 'How's the bush?'

'Cool, if you like mud and rain, cooking on a wood stove and washing in the river. You should come and stay.'

'And you should be a salesman!'

'We eats lots of wild goat too. Have to shoot them first.'

'As I said—'

A handsome Black Power boy with tight curls and a cute smile interrupted us. 'Gidday, stranger, give us a kiss for Christmas!' he said, bending down and offering me his cheek.

I was more than happy to oblige.

'She kissed me, she kissed me,' he crowed, crossing his hands over his heart and staggering off into the crowd.

Mortified, I turned to Mike. 'Do they really think I'm such a snob?'

'They've got you on a bit of a pedestal, that's all. Not a bad place to be.'

'Hmmm. I need to think about that.' I pushed my way to the bar, remembering with affection all the drunken nights I'd spent in this place. Already I was glad I'd come, even if Pat had gone quiet when I told him where I was off to.

Georgie stood with her back to me. When I tapped her on the shoulder, she swung round. 'Hey, girlfriend! I was hoping to see you before I left.'

'Why? Where are you going?'

'Home, mate. Hastings. To my baby. I've had enough of the big smoke.'

My heart sank, not just at the prospect of never seeing her again, but because Aroha Trust was about to lose another leader. Who'd run the crèche now?

'Are you taking your man?' I asked.

'Nah! He's gone up "the bush" with the others. It's over.' She clapped me on the back. 'What's with the sad face? It's Christmas!' Then she called out to the Black Power boy behind the trestle table. 'Barman, get your arse over here!'

Charmaine and Paddy came to stay for a few days. Pat didn't mind. Of all the gang guys, Paddy was his favourite.

'That was our reconciliation,' Charmaine said. 'We decided no more love dancing, we were going to live together, because we'd been seeing each other for a long time on and off. He was just as scared of commitment as I was, but we'd both tired of the dance, and the conflict that came with me being with the Black Power and him with the Highways. We had both come to a point of saying, "Fuck everyone, we'll do it." He gave me the money and said, "Go find us a flat." We went from your house.'

But if love was going well for Charmaine, work wasn't.

'The trust just dwindled,' she said. 'No one actually said this is the end. No one. They says, "I'm leaving now, I'm going to this," so obviously it was time for them to move on. But no one considered talking to me about it, and I was left behind with the new ones coming through. I was passionate about the kaupapa of Aroha Women's Trust. We'd gone through so much in terms of questioning the boys, getting things acknowledged, our growth and unity together, the pains, the struggles. It had become more than a passion, it was life. I would have liked to have seen it develop. A whole lot of younger women were starting to come on board, but they weren't given the kaupapa, they were just given a job. That was the difference. That's when trouble came.'

Gini and Junior, living amidst the chaos that was the Nomads, were little help.

'We weren't producing the work the Education Board expected,' Gini said. 'The van always needed work on it. We were always losing tools, and always complaining. At the end, everybody was driving the van. Everybody was getting dropped off in the pubs and left there, and the people that left for work weren't the number coming back. It got worse, and I don't blame them if they sacked us, but I can't really remember if they did.'

When the girls started using the van for burglaries during work hours, Charmaine resigned. 'I knew once I moved that it would close within weeks because there was no one the Education Board would trust,' she said. 'I knew it had to close cos Aroha Trust was gonna die in a blazing heap and there was no way I was going to allow that to happen.'

She remembered arguing with the new girls. 'I says, "The trust was given for people that absolutely had nowhere. I was one of those people. You came in, and now you're licking the ice-cream on the cake, but you don't care about the people that are coming in behind you. All you're going to do is screw it up because you don't care. Well, fuck you too." And they said, "Oh, you're just a power-tripper." I says, "Call it what you fuckin' like." I went home and I can remember talking to Paddy about it and my heart was really sad, cos I knew it no longer had the meaning it was established for.'

Without the trust, Wellington lost its pull for Charmaine. 'I woke up one morning and said, "That's it, I'm going to the bush. What do you think of that?" And Paddy says, "If I stop you, you'll hate me. I don't ever want you to hate me. You go. I'll find you." I left him with the flat and everything, and walked out. I just took a bag of clothes. Not realising how devastating that would have been for him and how strong he was.'

For a few months, they travelled back and forth to see each other. Then Candleman arranged for Charmaine to stay at The Big House in Allenby Terrace. Paddy moved in too. 'It was good,' she said. 'We had that time together.'

Left to fend for themselves, the city council girls kept the flame of Aroha Trust alive. 'It was a growing up,' Jane said. 'All the older girls had gone. We had to take on responsibility. We learned from what had happened. We were up and down from the bush, kept in touch with those who'd left, and even paid for a couple of girls to go to a Māori women's hui in Auckland.'

At work, they became increasingly politicised. 'We started having huge battles with the council about our conditions — we'd have one paintbrush between us, that sort of thing — to the extent that they withheld our pay. So we went on strike.'

A few months later, the government announced radical changes to its relief work programme. Only individuals could be employed — not trusts or groups — and no one under 18 was allowed to work outside. Jane helped organise opposition to the changes, rallying relief workers on other sites and speaking at a public meeting on the same platform as the president of the Federation of Labour.

'That was a biggie for me, the first time I'd done political organising,' she said. 'I was operating on a lot of anger, I think, but it had a positive channel.'

Jane remembered one picket outside the FoL when Jim Bolger was Minister of Labour. 'We got all the remaining trust members and Black Power to come. It was amazing, it got national TV coverage, and was in the newspapers and stuff. And it was really hilarious because there were about 60 or 70 of us standing outside the FoL buildings, and the boys got hungry so they went off up the alleyway to get something to eat, just as Bolger's car drove down the alleyway. So there were all these big Black Power guys running after this Crown car, and Bolger didn't know what he'd hit. Everyone just surrounded him. There was no violence or anything but it was very satisfying seeing the fear on his face.'

In spite of their efforts, the council sacked all its relief workers in August 1980. Jane became the first coordinator of the Wellington Unemployed Workers' Union that emerged out of the protests. The few remaining girls drifted away. Three years after it had begun, Aroha Trust was over.

TWENTY-ONE

WEDDING BELLS

Pat landed a job as an organiser for the Hotel Workers' Union. With two reliable incomes and only ourselves to think about, we began saving for our OE. But I hadn't been feeling well and my breasts were sore. I did the sums, then called into Family Planning on my way to a bus drivers' stopwork meeting.

The pregnancy test was positive.

'That's fantastic,' Pat said, squeezing me so tight I nearly threw up.

I buried my face in his chest. I was glad someone was excited. I didn't know what to think. Other people got pregnant, not me. I knew nothing about children. And how was I going to tell my mother?

The phone rang as I walked in the door after a 12-hour split shift. I lay on the hall floor in my grey bus driver's uniform and held the receiver to my ear. Whoever had coined the term 'morning sickness' should be shot.

'It's Paddy,' Jane said. 'He came off his bike. On the motorway. There's a service tomorrow night before they take his body home.'

Pat came too. We stood in a pew, staring numbly at the closed-up coffin with the black and gold Highway 61 patch spread out on top, a skull between two ape-hangers.

From behind us came a cry so heart-rending that my eyes instinctively filled with tears. I turned to see Charmaine walking slowly down the aisle, her arms out from her sides, her hands fluttering like small, wounded birds. Her wailing came from a place I'd never been: bottomless, ageless, universal. As if she'd reached into the depths of her soul and was pouring out the sorrow of the world. I stood transfixed. She was 18 years old.

When I recorded Charmaine's story 20 years later, she was still in mourning. 'Him and me had planned to be married, had talked about our children,' she said. 'It was like people that I loved or things I held dear were taken away so fast without warning. It was almost like I had lost the zest for life. It left me dispossessed in every way possible.'

Charmaine used everything she could to blunt the pain: alcohol, pills, dope, pethidine, speed, acid. 'I didn't cope. There was no grieving school. When my nanny died, there was no grieving school and when Paddy died, there was no grieving school. When the trust finished, there was no grieving school.' She gave a hollow laugh.

Several times she attempted suicide. 'I didn't want to be here, I wanted to be with him. I saw that everything I loved got taken away. When he met me, I had become really hardened by life and its knocks, hardened by the system. And he forever saw the star. The thing that I love about him the most is that he never ever wanted to change me or rearrange me. He loved me wild, he loved me gentle, he loved me exactly the way I was. I was his queen. And he made no qualms about telling the world. He never swore at me and I was never ever under threat of violence with him. Never. And I could say whatever I wanted to say, I could be whatever I wanted to be, I could go wherever I wanted to go.

'At the funeral I realised how deep in my heart he'd reached. He had started to take all the blocks away that were in front of my heart without me even knowing. I was really angry at him for dying. And angry with the heavens because, as far as I was concerned, they just shat on every fuckin' party that came my way. That doubled the blow to everything else that had happened in my life. Just as something good was happening for me, and life was going along okay, it disappeared in the middle of one night. All gone.'

She was weeping now, her face wet with tears. I asked her if she wanted a tissue, but she shook her head. There was no shame in sorrow, no need to tidy it up.

At Paddy's unveiling, a year after his tangi, Charmaine got a chance to farewell her beloved in the only way she could.

'I sang "Hey, That's No Way to Say Goodbye". It was amazing. From that day forward, I ended up gaining a lot of respect from the Highways when they saw just how strong the love was between myself and Paddy. The whole of Ruatōria was there cos he was so loved. And all the Highways were there. It was drizzling when we went up to the urupā,[1] and then as I started to sing, the sun come pounding down on my face and it was like for that moment Paddy and I were there alone. No one else in the world existed. Everyone disappeared. We were granted that time for that moment. And I run with it. After I had finished singing, I turned around and hundreds of patch members had tears in their eyes. It was there that they witnessed the strength of our love, in his whole whānau. His father never cried when his son was killed, then when I sung at the unveiling, the father broke. They realised how wrong and how robbed we had been. That was the word. Robbed. Of a lifetime. I still cry about it.'

For years, Charmaine refused to get professional help. 'If someone had suggested I go to a counsellor, I would have throttled them: "You think I'm fucked in the head, you arsehole."' She laughed. 'People tried, eh. I'm not saying they didn't try. But they were getting really hōhā.[2] They think you can turn it off after a year. "You must forget, Charmaine. You got to carry on." I was like, "No!" I couldn't forget and I couldn't carry on. I stayed stuck for a long time.'

---

1 graveyard
2 fed up

With a baby on the way, family pressure mounted on Pat and me to get married. We didn't need a wedding to prove we loved each other, but if it made our parents happy, we decided, we could handle one.

Six days before Christmas 1980, we exchanged our vows in the lovely little Catholic church with wooden pews and stained-glass windows a minute's walk from Mum and Dad's house in Wadestown. The ceremony was family only, about 30 people. Pat bought a suit. I tucked a fresh flower behind my ear and put on a strappy pink dress with a loose jacket that Mum had persuaded me to buy to hide my tiny bulge.

The priest was an old friend who let us write the service without mentioning the word 'God'. I quoted Kahlil Gibran: 'Your children are not your children . . . You may give them your love but not your thoughts . . . You may house their bodies but not their souls.' It was a message to both our parents and ourselves, I said, openly acknowledging my pregnancy. No baby of mine was going to think I'd ever been ashamed of them.

Mum organised dinner at their house. We were anxious about putting the freezing worker and doctor clans together, and looked forward to the celebration we'd planned for our friends the following night.

After the meal, I perched on the arm of Pat's chair. Next to us, his dad and my mum, both keen gardeners, were discussing the finer points of compost. Beside the piano, his gruff, unemployed older brother was deep in conversation with my aunt, a Mercy nun.

'We should have had more faith in them,' Pat said.

'And the champagne cocktails!' I leaned my head on his shoulder.

'Did I tell you what my uncle said to Dad about the salad?' Pat spoke out of the side of his mouth in a crusty, drainlayer's drawl: '"Don't touch it, Jock! They've forgotten to cook the mushrooms."'

I laughed.

He put his arm around my waist. 'You two okay?'

I nodded and bent to kiss him. Beneath his hand, I felt a flutter as delicate as an eyelash brushing bare skin.

Next morning, Pat's workmate, a chef, took over our tiny kitchen to transform five kilos of beef into his special curry. A cousin went diving for crayfish. Mum made her famous pavlovas. Friends cooked chickens, folded tinfoil around loaves of garlic bread, and helped string Christmas lights and balloons around the hall.

As evening fell, Pat and I stood at the door greeting people. I'd issued an open invitation to the Aroha Trust girls and others like Mike Hancock and the Wombles, though so many had left town I wasn't sure who'd turn up.

Jane, Charmaine and Tasi arrived early. They settled themselves next to the DJ, a weedy Pākehā looking flustered as he wrestled with miles of extension cord. Then Gini appeared with JB and two other Nomads. If I'd known one of them would later be dubbed the Parnell Panther after a string of rapes in Auckland, I might have felt differently. But at the time, it seemed easier to let them stay than question their presence. At least they were wearing mufti.

Gini looked lovely, her hair a circle of tiny plaits that tickled my cheeks when she kissed me.

'The others are over there.' I pointed to the group spilling into the DJ's space, ignoring his dirty looks. 'Free drinks at the bar,' I added, conscious that pros like them could demolish the top-shelf in minutes.

Peter Womble was behind them. He shook Pat's hand, then passed me a pile of thin books. 'Sorry I didn't have any wrapping paper,' he said.

'Thanks!' I was oddly moved until I saw the Baha'i covers on all of them. He'd become a convert since I'd last seen him; he was pushing his new beliefs in the same way he'd once proclaimed the revolution.

The party was warming up, but the music wasn't. I went over to the DJ. 'You promised to play all our favourites,' I said.

'If I didn't have to cope with them—' He glared at his unruly neighbours whose high spirits were increasing with each new arrival.

'They're harmless,' I said, hoping it was true. 'I'm sure you're used to dealing with worse than that. And can you turn the sound up?'

'It is up!' he snapped.

I retreated to a table of bus drivers. A motherly woman with a swag of kids leaned over and patted my stomach. 'The things some people will do to get off the number five route!' she said.

I was amazed at the liberties people felt they could take with my body now that I was pregnant, but there was something reassuring about her friendly pat too.

'Actually, I miss the troll—' I began. But all eyes had moved to the back of the hall. I turned to see five leathered, studded, patched-up Black Power members standing in the doorway. For a moment, I thought they'd come looking for trouble. Then I saw a senior member at the front. Of all the boys, he was the kindest and most respectful. I couldn't imagine him deliberately sabotaging my wedding.

I hurried over, feeling everyone watching me.

'Congratulations!' he said, clasping my hand in the Black Power handshake, then kissing me on both cheeks.

I welcomed each of the others in turn, then pulled him off to the side. My voice quavered. 'Can you please tell the boys to take their patches off? They're going to freak everyone out.'

'Sorry, Pip,' he said, digging his hands into his jean pockets. 'We're proud of our patches. We don't take them off for nobody.'

I tried again. 'You're welcome here as yourselves, not as gang members.'

He shook his head and a silver earring, the shape of a teardrop, caught the light. 'We're not ashamed of who we are. You shouldn't be either.'

'It's not about that. It's my wedding. You'd take them off if you really wanted to.' Without waiting for an answer, I walked away, blinking back the tears.

I felt worst for Pat, knowing how embarrassed he'd be in front of his hard-working, conservative relatives. What sort of a wife would invite the Black Power to their wedding? That's what they'd be thinking.

As I looked around, the DJ bailed me up. He jabbed his finger at the circle expanding further to make room for the Black Power. 'They're slopping beer on the speakers and bumping the turntable.'

'Sort it out yourself!' I said.

'If they don't stop, I'm packing up,' he threatened.

On the dance floor, Charmaine and Jane were showing two of my sisters some tricky footwork, clutching one another's arms and laughing. The music wasn't great, but it might be the only thing that held the night together.

'Okay, I'll have a word,' I said. 'As long as you start playing the songs we asked for.'

I grabbed Pat and found my brother, who was MC for the night. We agreed to keep the speeches short, highlight the merit of bringing people together from so many walks of life, then get on with the dancing.

Mum had begun setting up supper in the middle of the hall. At least the food would be superb. Suddenly, I saw her stride, stony-faced, towards the kitchen. My brother took off after her. I gave Pat a what's-all-that-about look. He shrugged. We were way past words.

My brother returned. Apparently, the Black Power boys had whisked two platters of freshly caught crayfish off the table and down to their corner. Mum had stormed after them, taken one back and given them a lecture about manners. She seemed rather pleased with herself, he said, though she was still shaking. He looked at our long faces. 'Cheer up, you two! This is fun!'

After the speeches, Pat grabbed the carving knife and brandished it above the two-tiered wedding cake. Everyone laughed. I tugged at his arm, pulled it down and laid my hands on top of his. Together, we made the first cut.

I was just starting to relax when my two youngest sisters, 18 and 20, sidled up to me, pulling on their coats.

'Leaving already?' I said.

'Sorry, Pip,' said the older one. 'There's been a bit of a scuffle in the men's.' She worked at the police station and her boyfriend was a detective; the younger one was dating a mate of his, another cop.

'Shit! Is anyone hurt?'

'Nah, only a few egos.'

Two guys with short hair and broad shoulders nodded curtly as they walked past. My sisters hurried after them. The Blacks and Nomads had already gathered in the carpark, invigorated by the prospect of a scrap. Insults were hurled and for a moment I thought it might be all on. But my sisters hustled the cops into the back of their Mini, their heads brushing the roof of the small car, and sped away.

'Fuck off, demons!' one of the boys shouted. Others joined in, punching the air with their fists, savouring the rare victory.

For the rest of the night I circled the room like a plane unable to land, just wanting it to be over. Then I fell into bed and stayed there for 48 hours.

Afterwards, Mum and I focused our frustrations on the DJ. By mutual unspoken agreement, we never mentioned the boys who'd nicked the crayfish and wouldn't take off their patches. Pat and I didn't talk about them either. We'd fallen out over the Black Power hundreds of times before, although never quite so publicly. I felt as if I'd failed both sides. I'd hoped I could pick out the good bits of Aroha Trust and combine them with the rest of my life. But the trust came as a package, gang patches and all. If I wanted one part, I had to be prepared to deal with the other and, even harder, with people's reactions to the whole thing.

A few days later, Pat arrived home from work shaking his head. Two Black Power boys who hadn't been at the wedding had stopped and congratulated him in the street.

'Heard it was a great do,' they said. 'Sorry we couldn't make it.'

TWENTY-TWO

AFTERMATH

When our daughter, Megan, was 10 months old, Pat and I moved to Sydney for a year. We lived in a big house with lots of people again. Pat got a job as a storeman; at night I worked in a bar. To my surprise, I loved it. Things had happened too fast. One minute I'd been living in the underworld, the next I was a married woman, defined mostly as someone's mother. Getting away gave me time out, a chance to take stock and reinvent myself in a strange city.

Back in Wellington, I had two more beautiful babies, both boys. Annie arrived at the hospital when each was born, just as she had with Megan. Somehow she always seemed to know. But gradually we lost touch. I was elbow-deep in nappies; she was a single woman, travelling New Zealand and the world working in shearing gangs and training to be a wool classer.

She loved the lifestyle. 'We were always roaming, moving,' she said. 'I never had a proper house or an accumulation of furniture or anything like that. I was very transient for a long period of time.' When she met the father of her two girls, a shearer, they continued travelling until her father died suddenly in his mid-fifties. Then they returned to her home town, Kaitangata, to be near her mum.

And what of the other women?

Charmaine, grieving for Paddy, was contemplating suicide when she found out she was pregnant at 20. The baby's father denied responsibility, something she didn't hold against him. 'I'm not saying that's okay, but coming from the life he came from and where I'd come from, it was like two different time bombs got together.' Her son changed her focus. 'I decided I had to live for him. That was one of the best things that happened to me.' She went home to Rotorua and joined her whānau on a march to Waitangi. 'We lived on the road for nearly five weeks. That was really powerful. Everyone took my baby, loved him. We had a wonderful time.'

Finally, Charmaine was fighting for her deepest beliefs. 'Empowerment and healing for Māori nation and Māori peoples. That for me was the waka, that took me back to everything I originally knew growing up with my grandmother. There was a homecoming.'

But the transition was rocky. 'There was a part of me that still felt really non-belonging. Because I'd been through the justice system, I'd been to war and back again, then I come home and there was no one I could actually talk all this stuff with.' Eight years later, she ended up in the Taha Māori drug and alcohol programme at Hanmer Springs, where she finally began to understand and heal her pain.

At the age of 23, Gini had two boys, 11 months apart, to JB. Still with the Nomads, she was embroiled in gang warfare, especially with the Mongrel Mob. 'We're talking guns now and not just the punch in the nose. It's gone up from that to knives to weapons to guns and Molotovs.' Rules about not attacking houses with children were ignored. 'I remember fleeing in the middle of the night to places, wrapping them up in a blanket. And a broken window inside the bassinet of the second one. If he'd been in that bassinet, he would have shattered glass all over him — and that would have given him the fright of his life.'

Gini moved from house to house trying to protect her children but never breaking free of the scene. When she was three months pregnant with her third baby, JB left her. 'Neither of us knew I was hapū,'[1] she said. 'I'd had enough. I thought, if this is life, it sucks and I'm out of here. I was into pills and dope in a big way. Could easily have overdosed, ended it all.' After beating one of her young sons, she turned to God. 'I said, look, if you're out there, you'd better help me. Because this is it for me. I've had it. I knew that I didn't want to live doing this to my children. That I'd rather die. So I cried out to the Lord, not believing or knowing if he was there or not.'

Gini started going to church, sitting down the back wearing dark glasses, always stoned. 'At the beginning I felt like it was another gang, but this time these people were doing good things. They cared about me genuinely, they wanted to help.'

On 9 August 1987, she became a Christian. She wrote this on the bottom of a printout of her criminal convictions — more than 30 in the previous decade — which stop abruptly on that date. At the same time, she gave up drugs and alcohol and cut her gang ties. 'I felt like I'd stepped out of *Once Were Warriors* and into the light.' A few years later, she married a man from her church.

Junior ran with the Nomads for a long time too. When her mother could no longer look after her son, Junior begged Mike Hancock's partner to take him at Brougham Street and eventually signed over guardianship to her. 'She would always be scared someone would ring up and say, "Junior's dead", cos of the lifestyle and the guys I was going with. I'd come back and I'd be baseball-batted and ODing, or doing something stupid, that drunk I'd be falling off trains, and she'd have to come and get me out of the hospital. I didn't see my son often because I was never straight. I was always getting into trouble, I was always going in and out of jail. My life never changed for years.'

Out in the Hutt Valley with three small children, Bubbles kept her ties with the Wellington Nomads although her partner was vice-president

---

1   pregnant

of the local Black Power chapter. When the police found a Black Power gun stash underneath her house in 1981, they gave her 24 hours to get out of town. She left her partner and joined Annie in the Wairarapa, another Nomad stronghold.

Seven years later, Gini and Tasi's brother, a member of the Nomads and one of Bubbles' best friends, was killed in a car accident. 'A lot of things went on during the funeral which really made me sit back and think, do I want to be here?' Bubbles said. 'Do I still want to be tied to all these people?'

Before the service had even taken place, she and Charmaine were arrested when they took a young boy who'd been stabbed to hospital. 'The hospital wouldn't let us go, and rang the police because, if he died, we were the only witnesses to a murder. It was a really good friend who'd stabbed this boy and it was for a t-shirt that was worth jack shit. Charmaine was locked in the police room with her baby and I was locked upstairs in another room. We had to sit in the police station till this young boy was out of theatre and had woken up and recovered sufficiently so there wasn't a murder inquiry. They tried to charge me with a stolen vehicle, but I was lent the vehicle to take the boy to the hospital. All we were worried about was helping this young fulla. I felt really, really sorry for him. Things like that, before I didn't give a shit, didn't worry me one little bit. But must have got a conscience by then.'

Bubbles sold her house and everything she owned. 'I didn't want nothing to do with it. No memories, no nothing. It was probably the best decision I ever made in my life. Just get the hell out of here and try and start all over again, and be normal.' Again, she went to Annie, now living down south. At first, she kept in touch with her old gang friends. 'But over the years everyone had changed so much, and a lot of them had families and quietened down, and good times basically weren't good times any more. I gradually weaned myself off hopping on a plane and pissing off to the North Island regularly. Cut all ties, and hard-out went to work, and hard-out brought the kids up.'

Up in 'the bush' at Taumarunui, Tasi met a young possum-trapper. After a year, they joined another work co-op and, at 22, she had her first baby. Soon after, her younger sister's seven-year-old daughter was killed. It was a turning point for Tasi. 'It's like you're on this big cruise and then all of a sudden, death strikes your family. It's like you stop, but everyone's still going. On this cruise. And you think, wow. It really hits you in the face, eh, death. It really makes you wake up and say, this could have happened to your children, this could have happened to you. You could have killed somebody. You could have killed your own baby. That's what I started thinking.'

Tasi's siblings, including Gini, were scattered all over New Zealand, none of them in any state to offer support. She and her partner borrowed a van and took her niece's body back to Porirua for the tangi. 'I thought, wow, start taking some responsibility for your family. Be the one to stand up for them! And so not long after that, we gave our lives to the Lord.'

When everyone else left 'the bush', Mahina and Tam stayed on. They raised their son there for nine years without electricity before moving to another house in the valley. From there, Mahina got a job as a part-time store assistant, had another son, developed her passion for gardening and lived with Tam until the fateful morning his bike slipped on black ice.

Georgie met the father of her next five children, a Pākehā, not long after she moved home to Hastings. 'We had a really massive relationship for the first year that we were together,' she said. 'It wasn't till after our baby was born, she was about three months old, that things started to change. He was very jealous, very obsessive, very domineering. Yep, but I loved him. So our relationship from there on was good, was bad, was sad, but we hung on, eh. Sixteen years. Put up with a lot. Went through a lot. Yep. My previous partner had never ever hit me in the whole time we were together. I didn't know what a hiding was until I met him.'

Nayda also got stuck in a violent relationship, with a Mongrel Mob member. 'My strongest bad memory of him is for eight Christmases in a row, I had black eyes,' she said. He was very controlling, isolating her from family and friends and wearing down her self-confidence. 'He'd punch me up and degrade me. Make me feel like nothing. Call me a slut. And this is a woman who goes out maybe once every four or five months.'

After a serious car accident — 'all because his jeans weren't dry' — Nayda went home from hospital in a wheelchair. 'I was all broken and my heart was broken too.'

When he drove their car off the same road after another argument and it plunged 15 metres into the Whanganui River, Nayda realised he would have watched her drown without trying to free her. She began standing up to him. 'Inner strength: you don't even know where it comes from.' On the night she left, he got out his .22 rifle and put it behind the kitchen door. But she was past being frightened. 'I said, "Go on, use it then. Put me out of my misery. No, you won't, will you? Because you'd go to jail and you don't want to go to jail."' Soon after, she began a relationship with another gang guy, the president of the Whanganui Mighty Mongrel Mob.

I asked Nayda why women stayed so long with abusive partners. 'You don't want to break the family unit,' she said.

Annie agreed. 'You put up with it because you want your children to have a father. You want to be a family. And it's not all bad. It's a slow slide. You're not in full-blown ugly all the time.'

Amelia took the opportunity to escape from her violent partner when he went to jail. 'I was sure I'd never end up in the hospital like my mum, cos she got smacked around and I was too,' Amelia said. 'I used to say to Mum years later, "Why didn't you fight back?" She said she couldn't, she was afraid. Then I found myself in the same situation.'

Amelia moved to Kaitaia, where her eldest brother ran the local Black Power chapter. There she met the father of her three youngest children, also a gang member, and moved into a house in Black Power Lane.

In 1988, the death of her 19-year-old brother after a bouncer threw him down the stairs of a Wellington nightclub shattered her large whānau. 'It broke us up, destroyed all our family togetherness. It changed members of my family, especially my brothers. They were all on hatred trails to get even.'

Over the years, Jane was the only woman I regularly kept in touch with. Her political activity escalated. During the 1981 Springbok tour, as part of a small, fearless unit that confronted the Red Squad and stormed the Rugby Union headquarters, she was arrested several times and beaten by police. I asked if she'd been concerned about her safety.

'I wasn't used to feeling safe,' she said. 'I guess the difference was that I was putting myself into danger for a good cause rather than just a fact of life. There's a certain element of thinking that you're bulletproof too. Now with a family, I think I'd have quite a different attitude.'

The anti-tour protests reinforced Jane's belief in the power of collective action. 'I didn't have the experience to know that it was pretty extraordinary for the people of this country to get out on the streets. I thought it was normal. I guess that was good because it didn't put limits on what I felt that people could achieve if they got organised.'

Jane also continued her work with the unemployed workers' movement. In 1984, as national spokesperson, she became the media darling of an economic summit called by the new Labour government, her face beamed around the nation as she spoke up for the poor and dispossessed.

Two years later, she and her partner, a veteran protester she met during the Springbok tour, moved to the Wairarapa. There she helped set up a community worker certificate at the polytech, gave birth to the first of two sons, and began a lifelong journey to reclaim her Kāi Tahu roots.

EPILOGUE

I don't remember the exact moment I decided to write about Aroha Trust. It was as if I was always going to. One day. When the time was right. For a long time, I shared this dream with almost no one. Pat was relieved that I'd moved on. I'd kept my family and old friends at bay during those years, and they rarely asked about them. New friends looked sceptical if I mentioned gang women or assumed I'd been a social worker.

Then Mike Hancock died and I went to his tangi to say goodbye, hoping some of the trust women would be there. I knew they were still part of me but was I — and the trust — still part of them? And had it made any difference to their lives?

'Yes,' said Jane. For her, Aroha Trust was the springboard to leading the unemployed workers' movement and a life of political action. 'Over those three years, I think I built up the confidence and the political awareness to see that I could actually do something and I think, without Aroha Trust, I would never have got to that space.'

For other women, it was less clear-cut. When the trust folded, a few of its members settled down and never offended again. But many spiralled into lives of crime, violence, abuse, alcohol and drugs. By the time I recorded their stories, they were in their thirties and early forties. All had children, ranging in age from babies to adults. Many had gone through enormous personal growth, extricated themselves from abusive relationships, were studying and working. Those with a strong belief system — taha Māori, religion, politics — seemed to be doing best.

Nine years later, things have changed again. Some women are in a better space; others seem to have lost their way a little. I realise that pinning down progress is like chasing mercury across a table. Any line I choose to draw is arbitrary; any conclusions have to take into account life's inevitable ups and downs, the fact that none of us can ever say, 'I've made it, I'm there.'

I realise, too, that this is a story with no end. It is not only about the women of Aroha Trust, it has helped shape them. Dredging up the past, and offering it up for public scrutiny, has come at a personal cost. Their lives are no longer just their lives, they are stories in a book with a life of its own.

It is important to note that some things cannot be said. The women are not fictional characters for whom there will be no repercussions. Some pain goes too deep. Some activities are illegal. People must be protected: children, whānau, the women themselves.

When I began writing their stories, I wanted them to tell me everything. As their friend and fellow traveller, I have learned there are things they keep close to their hearts and that is how it should be. They have shared far more than can be reasonably expected; what matters most to me now is that their offering is received with respect, and becomes a force for good.

The most noticeable shift in the last nine years seems to be in the women's sense of identity. Being Māori was always their foundation stone. But now, for most, it's their search, their journey, their passion and their healing. There's a great sadness at what they missed out on as children. 'I feel really ripped off,' says Georgie, a qualified nurse working in Māori mental health. 'I wish I could speak my own language. Fluently, like my grandparents. But I don't want to go to a school and learn it. And it's hard to find a nanny these days where I can live and she can teach me.'

Many of the women are taking steps to regain their birthright: working for Māori-based social service and health organisations, learning te reo, searching for relatives and whakapapa they never knew. Charmaine has turned the weaving skills she learned from her nanny into a successful business: her harakeke work won gold at Ellerslie in 2008 and stimulated international interest.

There are some exceptions. For Junior, being adopted has complicated her search for identity. Devastated by the death of her mother last year, the past is still too painful. 'I hated it because I was brought up white. Māori families looked so good cos they had big whanaus, and there was just me. I was jealous. I still am jealous. So yeah, there's a lot of hurt and rejection and things that I'm still dealing with. I still won't get into the depths of Māoridom. Even though I've tried, there's something there that I need to deal with and, I don't know, one day I most probably will.'

All the women are still coping with the fallout from their childhoods — as are the rest of us. After the Kāwhia reunion, Gini, who has a social work degree and works with tamariki[1] dealing with abuse, finally sought counselling over her father's incest. Until then, she'd relied on religion to get her through, and had rejected ACC help or compensation.

The decision to use her own name in this book was a huge catalyst, Gini says. 'I've done a lot of healing in church, but there's still a bit I can't get out. I still get angry and uptight. I decided to get professional help to look at the triggers.' It's hard, slow, painful work, even with a supportive husband and self-belief. 'My life's been like a lake, frozen over, and I've been skating on the ice for all these years. Now I've gone through into the freezing, horrible water underneath. But it has to be brought out into the light. Once it's

---

1   children

out there, it's been identified, it doesn't have so much power, you can see what you're dealing with, and deal with it. I don't want to be known as a survivor. It's all very well to survive. I want to be known as more than a conqueror.'

Drawing on their life experiences, many of the women have ended up helping other people through their work. 'I've looked after people all my life,' Amelia says. 'My children, my mother, the family, being a barmaid.' When being around booze took too much of a personal toll, she switched to home help instead. 'I still look after people that I used to look after when they drank, but I'm not serving alcohol.' Amelia's still tied up with the Black Power. 'Now that I'm getting older, it's like, gosh, I'm a bit long in the tooth to be kicking around with gang members.' But there's no blocking in her chapter, and the boys are expected to treat their partners and children well, at least in public, she says.

Charmaine has a new partner and is working in alcohol and drug counselling for young Maori. She has signed up to a combined lawsuit over alleged historical abuse in state-run children's homes.

Annie has a social work degree and diploma, and a postgraduate psychology qualification, and works in a hospital mental health team. She and her partner have separated and, like everyone except Jane, she will soon be a grandmother.

Jane's passion is still social justice. When she first became involved in the trade union movement, she was shocked by the way people romanticised the working class. 'They saw me as a real working-class girl and that was considered wonderful. And yet my experiences of those who have come from a background of poverty or violence or whatever, you don't want to stay there, no matter how romantic people might make it out to be. It isn't.'

At the same time, Jane acknowledges her past has been a powerful driving force. 'It gave me a strong passion, a strong fire in my belly to do something that could make changes happen for people.' Today she manages a regional community advisory service, is on the board of the New Zealand Council of Social Services and is spearheading a national project to overhaul employment conditions in the community sector.

She's proud of her postgraduate diploma in not-for-profit management from Waikato University — a far cry from the 14-year-old who left school with nothing. Now she's considering completing her Masters, something that would have once been unthinkable.

Jane often wonders what she could have accomplished, given the right opportunities. 'It blew my mind to discover that it was quite predictable where I would end up, that psychologists can identify the factors at an early age that will just about ensure someone goes off the rails.'

Mahina agrees. 'I'm quite pleased with the way I have turned out, but I wish I was back in my twenties, trying to achieve it again. Because I know I would have got further than I have got to now.' Last year she gave up her job as a manager in a large retail store to finish her windmill thesis and look after her young, newly adopted daughter in the colonial-style homestead she and her partner have created. For the last three years she's also had scholarship funding for an annual trip to London's Kew Gardens to lecture on New Zealand native plants.

Most of the Aroha Trust women still rank within New Zealand's poor. No surprises there, given their backgrounds, ethnicity and family sizes. For some, child-bearing has spanned more than two decades: Nayda tops the list with a combined family of 10 children and nine mokopuna.

Most of the women have brought up most of their own children. Only a few have gone into state care, a source of pride after their own experiences, as well as a sign of changing social practices. Even within the same family, children can have had vastly different experiences. Older ones have often borne the brunt of their mother's unstable lifestyles; younger ones, if they're lucky, may have been more protected.

'Our three eldest children saw a lot of abuse,' says Georgie. 'The two babies, I managed to shield them from a lot of it. As far as I was concerned, they weren't going to see that side.'

She's back with her partner again, but on different terms. 'I was always staunch, but doing my nursing training and securing a good job made me stronger and more confident. My partner works hard too; we've both had to change.'

Some of the women's children are still at school. Others are in steady jobs and training. Some have children of their own. A minority are gang members, unemployed, in borstal, jail or psychiatric care. There are notable successes: Nayda's oldest daughter is a business analyst. Annie's and Jane's oldest children have achieved high grades at university. One of Georgie's boys has a bright rugby future.

Mahina is ambitious for her children. 'I'd like them to better their education more than I have done. And I want them to get into a job more or less straight away rather than lout about.' Her older son left school with School Certificate but not in subjects she approved of. 'He got history and Māori, but Māori doesn't get you anywhere, does it?'

Tasi's a more relaxed Christian these days, wears trousers and cuts her hair. Nine years ago, she questioned if education was for everyone. 'I just want my children to marry young and have a Christian marriage. I always wanted to marry young and all my burdens gone away.' Life hasn't been that easy but for the last two years Tasi's been doing community courses, including te reo Māori. 'Education's good,' she now says.

Charmaine agrees, but warns against using it as a measure of her children's success. 'For me, the battle was to grow them away from the swamp I grew up in. I am there for them. They have not been abused and dispossessed all their lives. They have not been sent to foster homes. Academic progress can come later.'

All the women want better lives for their children than they had. They want them to know their roots, be financially secure and stay away from gangs.

'To be quite honest, I can't see my kids getting into any gang, cos I've brought them up too well,' Georgie says. 'If one of them did, I'd have to question where I or the father went wrong. Isn't that the thing that all parents ask themselves, "Where the fuck did we go wrong?"'

Gangs are different now, she says. 'What I fear most is a lot of the young Mongies coming up, whose ideas are a lot more radical than the old ones. They're a lot more angry. And they're not scared. They'd quite happily walk up to a bloody Highway and blow their brains out. But they don't worry me. They're just kids that are out of control.'

Bubbles agrees. When her partner died in a car accident, she disappeared into the nomadic shearing world, losing contact even with Annie. Now she's helping her 25-year-old daughter bring up her six children.

'Gangs and violence are totally out of control,' she says. 'Even I wouldn't like to be associated with what goes on now. The younger ones got no respect. I don't know what it is. The youth out there is not the youth that we were.' At the same time, she's resigned to the fact that two of her boys have been involved with the Mongrel Mob. Cutting gangs completely out of their lives for women such as her would mean cutting off their own children.

Georgie's and Bubbles' lament about modern gangs may partly be the universal tut-tutting of the old about the young, but it also signals the growth of a more hardened underclass, trapped in second- and third-generation gang membership.

Last year, Nayda finally made the break with gang life. Methamphetamine was behind her decision to leave her Mongrel Mob partner. 'I stayed for the last six years because I always thought our love would endure,' she says. 'When one of my daughters was involved in a raid by the Armed Offenders Squad, I realised that wasn't going to happen. My children and I have experienced what comes with P use: the paranoia, distrust, deceit and lies, my partner's loss of empathy.'

P addiction destroys people, Nayda says. 'My partner used to be well respected in the community. People outside the gang and even the cops would ask him to help sort out local problems. He encouraged his members into paid work. He knocked down all the walls inside the pad so there'd be no rape there, and it would be safe for women. Our chapter was very tight. Most of the boys are related by blood; they know tikanga Māori; most whakapapa to the awa.[1] If there was a tangi, they'd go up the river and get some meat, always two mutton, and give a koha. They played rugby on Saturday mornings; we'd take our families and our kai. There was always a Christmas party for our kids.'

Recently, Nayda moved town with three of her children. 'To let them be children. No more dramas!' She's also had a nasal reconstruction: her nose had been broken eight times by previous partners. The surgeon removed her facial tattoos at the same time. 'I feel great,' she says. 'I've survived — rape, sexual abuse and years of physical violence.' But walking away from the gang has come at a price. 'I didn't just lose my partner, I lost my rōpū.[2] The Mongrel Mob were my family for 30 years.'

Today, Nayda works as an Auahi Kore[3] health promoter and is studying towards a BA in Health Sciences, after studying te reo Māori last year. Her older son is a Mob member with another chapter, but for him, whānau comes first, she says. Her focus is now on her younger son. 'Boys need boundaries and rules, especially when it comes to the way they treat women.'

Nayda's personal experience has prompted her, along with a number of other Aroha Trust women, to lodge an historical claim with the Waitangi Tribunal on behalf of all Māori women affected by gangs. The claim, 'Ko te Whakatipuranga o te Whānau Māori i te Āhuatanga Whakarōpū Tāngata', has yet to be accepted. It alleges that 'failures of the Crown have led to the cultural alienation, economic despair, impoverishment and violent abuse of Māori women and their whānau in gang environments'. She hears Dame Whina Cooper urging her on: 'If you're going to go against the Crown, do it as a rōpū.' And again, 'Do it once, do it right!'

Nayda believes there's a reason for her life journey. 'Aroha Trust has been a learning curve for me as 'he wahine Māori'.[4] I want to

---

1 trace their genealogy to the river
2 group
3 smoke-free
4 a Māori woman

give all gang women a voice. We've all endured hardship from our men. Now is the time for them and the Crown to acknowledge us for who we are. This is far greater than the patch. We will make life better for our mokopuna.'

The adversity faced by the Aroha Trust women would bring most of us to our knees. In spite of it, they somehow retain their zest for life and the ability, time and time again, to find a way through their troubles. Personal experience has given them a profound understanding of the human condition that could not be learned from books. I struggle with the contradiction that the past has also deeply wounded them and often their children. Despite their best efforts, it continues to permeate their lives and those of future generations. It's not something I'd wish on anyone, certainly not something I'd want my own children to go through.

Having said that, the years I spent in Aroha Trust enriched my own life beyond measure. The unfamiliar world I ventured into — and the girls themselves — acted as a mirror in which I could better see myself, my culture, my country.

In those years, I learnt to jump the barricades that, in our fear and ignorance, make us define difference as other, enemy, inferior. I learnt that fundamentally we all want to belong: the trouble begins when some of us don't. I learnt that life is wonderful and dreadful, sometimes in the same breath. That it isn't fair, and that the odds stacked against people in childhood multiply throughout their lives. I learnt that underneath the toughest exterior is a person just as vulnerable and uncertain as me. That my heart sings when I'm with strong women. That I can't mend the world, only be in it. And I learnt that there are two societies in this country, two realities. That doors open automatically because I'm Pākehā and middle-class and have the right networks and family ties, and they slam in my face as soon as I adopt the outward trappings of the excluded.

Annie agrees: 'I feel privileged that I got to see things that are usually denied a white person like myself,' she says. 'You have a different understanding of why people get to be at certain places, a whole different understanding of the society you live in, from other people's point of view. Gang life, Māori people, everything. It changed my whole perception.'

And what of the other women? What legacy did Aroha Trust leave them? All I can say with certainty is that it gave around 30 young women a short-term buffer and a glimmer of hope. Doing, not just being done to. Power, not just powerlessness. Together, not alone.

It didn't transform their lives: the forces against them were huge and came from all quarters. But it kindled their spirits. None of them have ever forgotten the years they spent living and working for the trust, building solidarity and sisterhood in a harsh and hostile world. For most, there was no other time when they stood side by side with other women so strong and so proud.

In that, we are the same.

ACKNOWLEDGEMENTS

This book is what is known as 'creative non-fiction', combining elements of memoir, biography and social history. It spans more than 30 years: from the story of Aroha Trust itself, 1977–1980; the first reunion of the women in 1998, where they supported my proposal to write about the trust and their lives; the recording of the women's stories in 2000; the second reunion in 2007, where they gave me permission to go ahead; and, finally, publication in 2009. I think there is a reason it has taken so long to write — that only now do the women within its pages have the personal and collective resources to cope with such public scrutiny of their lives.

All the women have chosen to use their real names, or the name they are known by — an act of great courage. It was impossible for me to verify the facts of each of their childhoods. However, I constantly searched for evidence that their accounts were authentic. In every case, they stacked up. If anything, I believe they have downplayed the violence inflicted on them as children and young women and adults. What you have read here is but the tip of the iceberg.

All the events in the story of Aroha Trust happened. As I have re-created them, with the help of memory and imagination, I have tried to capture their essence. Other people would have come up with other stories and other interpretations. In a few cases, I have been unable to determine the exact timing of events. In those cases, I have constructed the most credible sequence I can muster from the facts in front of me. While I have talked to many people about what happened in those years, any errors, omissions or wrong attributions are mine.

Many people must be thanked for helping along the way. First and foremost, I want to thank the women of Aroha Trust who opened their lives to me in the late 1970s and later agreed to let me tell their stories. In particular, I want to acknowledge the 11 key women in the book — Amelia, Annie, Bubbles, Charmaine, Junior, Georgie, Gini, Jane, Mahina, Nayda and Tasi — and their whānau. Over the last decade, they have welcomed me into their homes, shared intimate details of their lives with honesty, courage and humour, and kept faith in me as the years rolled by. Special thanks also to Rangi, Sis and Waynnie for agreeing to the powerful image on the front cover, and to Dorothy and Evelyn whose stories were recorded but are not specifically included. They — and all the women of Aroha Trust — form the heart of this book and are its reason for being. Wahine mā, e kore e mutu ngā mihi, tēnā koutou, tēnā koutou, tēnā koutou katoa.

In recording the women's stories, I am indebted to Judith Fyfe for passing on her passion and expertise in oral history, and for being my mentor. Funding from the Australian Sesquicentennial Oral History Awards enabled me to travel around New Zealand in 2000, visiting 13 of the Aroha Trust women and capturing their lives on tape. Linda Evans and Joce Chalmers from the Alexander Turnbull Library gave me invaluable help and encouragement to collect, transcribe and store the women's stories in the national oral history archives, while Lynette Shum was a welcome companion as she completed her own project on the Chinese in Haining Street.

Al Morrison encouraged and developed my journalistic skills and kindly recommended me to Ruth Dyson, who kept a job as her parliamentary press secretary open while I completed the oral history project. Ruth continued to support me even when, six years later, I deserted the corridors of power in favour of a writer's loft.

Harry Ricketts' Creative Non-Fiction undergraduate course at Victoria University's International Institute of Modern Letters gave me the confidence to apply for the 2006 MA creative writing programme. There, my tutor Damien Wilkins and supervisor Chris Price skilfully coaxed the first draft of *Trust* out of me, with invaluable feedback (and great morning teas) from my classmates Rebecca Lancashire, Amanda Samuel, Sarah Barnett, Nick Stanley, Michalia Arathimos, Rob Egan, Rachael Schmidt, Amy Brown and Therese Lloyd. A $5000 scholarship at the end of the year spurred me on, as has the ongoing writers' group that emerged out of the class.

A number of family members and friends — Liz Mason, Matt Desmond, Rose Desmond, Mike Fitzsimons, Kevin Kane and Denis Wright — read further drafts and gave me timely advice at critical stages. My two other sisters, Ginny Pang and Kate Gard, provided practical and moral support, and shared their memories of our family during the Aroha Trust period.

For the last three years, Mum told everyone that Pip's book was going to solve all her Christmas presents, but she died in February before I could honour her wish. Dad is not alive either and, while he would surely have disapproved of some of what I got up to, it is he who instilled in me the strong sense of social justice that led me to Aroha Trust. Thank you both for making me who I am.

George and Jenny Packard, and Garry Cockburn, nurtured my spirit and soul in their professional capacities while I grappled with the ghosts of the past. Friends, especially Pru Dryburgh, Bernice McMahon, Louise Peters, Brent Williams, Sue Ryall, Petra van den Munckhof, Stephanie McIntyre, and Jack and Joanne Doherty, spent hours discussing every aspect of the book with me, steadying my nerves and stepping up with practical assistance whenever I faltered.

Denis O'Reilly and Peter Vaughan shed light on the Black Power and the work cooperative movement of the 1970s, as did the excellent document, *Nga Rongo Korero: Ten Years of Work Cooperatives and*

Trusts, published by the Cooperative Workers' Trust in 1985.

The photos have come mainly from my own and the women's collections, apart from Marti Friedlander's image on the front cover, Hillary Watson's stunning black-and-white photos of us at work in the seventies, and two photos from the *Dominion-Post* collection at the Alexander Turnbull Library.

Special thanks must go to my agent Michael Gifkins and Random House publishing director Nicola Legat for backing this book in uncertain economic times. As my editor, Nicola has shown endless patience, wisdom, flexibility and good humour, while Michael's know-how and care have made the experience of publishing my first book much less fraught than it would otherwise have been. I'm also grateful to Natasha Hay, Rebecca Lal and Sarah Thornton at Random House for their efforts, and to Ana Tapiata, Lucy Te Moana and John Whaanga for checking the Māori spelling and translations.

Marilyn Waring and Colin Knox, who knew and supported Aroha Trust in the 1970s, continued to back various funding applications over the years. Heather Henare and Debbie Mickell gave us preliminary media training and advice.

I am especially grateful to Harry Tam, Julia Carr and other staff at Te Puni Kōkiri for understanding the importance of giving the Aroha Trust women a voice and ensuring they were well supported at the time of publication. So too Kōkiri Marae Keriana Olsen Trust, the National Collective of Independent Women's Refuges and Wellington City Council.

I want to thank my three children, Megan, Liam and Jackson, who have been endlessly interested and encouraging — and occasionally apprehensive — about what might lie between these pages.

My final words are for my husband Pat, who has been there from the beginning. Thank you for knowing I had to write this book, for paying the bills and putting up with me as I relived my youth. Our love is forever.

Pip Desmond
Wellington, May 2009

Pip Desmond comes from Irish stock, with a dash of German and Scottish. She was born in Dunedin, the third of six children, and grew up in Wellington. A freelance writer and journalist, she has spent most of her adult life working in the community sector. From 2000 to 2005, she was a parliamentary press secretary and political adviser. In 2006 she did the MA in Creative Writing at Victoria University, where she wrote the first draft of *Trust*. Pip is married with three children and two beautiful grandchildren. This is her first book.